Managing Risk of Supply C Disruptions

This book discusses important issues related to managing supply chain disruption risks from various perspectives. It explores the essence and principles relating to managing these risks and provides the framework and multi-goal model groups for managing such risks.

The book also discusses research developments in managing supply chain disruptive risks, supply chain risk conduction, and loss assessment methods of supply chain disruptive events. It includes the consideration of supply chain coordinating models in cases of demand and supply disruption risks. It also deals with the subject of managing models of supply chain disruption risks by looking at manufacturers and their responding methods relating to demand in disruption and coordination. It also summarizes the relevant findings and provides future research questions and orientations.

The book will contribute significantly to the growing body of knowledge concerning the theory of managing supply chains.

Tong Shu is an associate professor at the Business School of Hunan University.

Shou Chen is a professor at the Business School of Hunan University, and a member of the Discipline Assessment Group in the Academic Degrees Committee of China's State Council.

Kin Keung Lai is currently the chair professor of management science at the City University of Hong Kong.

Xizheng Zhang is a professor at the Business School of Hunan University, and one of the major members of Project Management Centre, Hunan University.

Shouyang Wang is currently a Bairen distinguished professor of management science at the Academy of Mathematics and Systems Science of Chinese Academy of Sciences and the Lotus distinguished professor of management science of Hunan University at Changsha. He is also adjunct professor at over 30 universities around the world.

Routledge advances in risk management

Edited by Kin Keung Lai and Shouyang Wang

Managing Risk of Supply Chain Disruptions

Tong Shu, Shou Chen, Kin Keung Lai, Xizheng Zhang, and Shouyang Wang

Routledge
Taylor & Francis Group

LONDON AND NEW YORK

First published 2014
by Routledge
2 Park Square, Milton Park, Abingdon, Oxfordshire OX14 4RN

and by Routledge
711 Third Avenue, New York, NY 10017

First issued in paperback 2017

*Routledge is an imprint of the Taylor & Francis Group, an informa
business*

British Library Cataloguing in Publication Data
A catalogue record for this book is available from the British Library

Library of Congress Cataloging-in-Publication Data
Shu,Tong (Business writer)
Managing risk of supply chain disruptions / Tong Shu, Shou Chen,
Shouyang Wang, Kin Keung Lai and Xizheng Zhang
pages cm. – (Routledge advances in risk management ; 3)
Includes bibliographical references and index.
1. Business logistics. 2. Risk management. I. Title.
HD38.5.S558 2015
658.7–dc23
2013043452

ISBN 13: 978-1-138-06798-1 (pbk)
ISBN 13: 978-0-415-84195-5 (hbk)

Typeset in Times New Roman
by Cenveo Publisher Services

The authors

Tong Shu received his Ph.D. in management sciences and engineering from Hunan University in 2008. He is an associate professor at the Business School of Hunan University. He has published over 20 papers in academic journals, including several international ones. His research interests include supply chain management and business intelligence.

Shou Chen received his Ph.D. in management sciences and engineering from Hunan University in 1998, and he is a professor at the Business School of Hunan University. He is member of the Discipline Assessment Group in the Academic Degrees Committee of China's State Council, serves as the editor-in-chief of many influential academic journals, and has published over 100 research papers in academic journals. His research interests include risk management and strategic management.

Kin Keung Lai received his Ph.D. from Michigan State University in the United States. He is currently the chair professor of management science at the City University of Hong Kong. Prior to his current post, he was a senior operational research analyst for Cathay Pacific Airways and an area manager on marketing information systems for Union Carbide Eastern.

His main areas of research interests are operations and supply chain management, financial and business risk analysis, and modeling using computational intelligence. He has extensively published in international refereed journals in these areas. He is the editor-in-chief of the *International Journal of Computational Science, International Journal of Optimization: Theory, Methods and Applications*, and *International Journal of Operations Research*. He is also on the editorial board for the *International Abstracts in Operations Research, Journal of Operational Research and Management Science of China, Journal of Management of China, Journal of System Engineering of China, International Journal of Operations and Quantitative Management, International Journal of Manufacturing Technology and Management, International Journal of Industrial Engineering and Management*, and *International Journal of Simulation Modelling*.

He is the member of the International Advisory Committee of the *Journal of Operational Research Society* in the United Kingdom, Council of International

Federation of Operational Research Societies, Council of Association of Asian Pacific Operations Research Societies, Council of the Asia Pacific Industrial Engineering and Management Society, Council of Chinese Society of System Engineering, and Council of Chinese Society of Decision Sciences. Currently, he is the president of the Asia Association on Risk and Crises Management. He also received the Joon S. Moon Distinguished International Alumni Award from the Michigan State University in the United States.

Xizheng Zhang received his Ph.D. in management science and engineering from Central South University in 2003. He is a professor at the Business School of Hunan University, and one of the major members of Project Management Centre, Hunan University. He has hosted and participated in more than 10 research projects at national and ministry levels, and published over 50 papers in academic journals. His research interests include supply chain management, knowledge management, project management, and collaborative business.

Shouyang Wang received his Ph.D. in operations research from Institute of Systems Science, Chinese Academy of Sciences, in 1986. He is currently a Bairen distinguished professor of management science at Academy of Mathematics and Systems Science of Chinese Academy of Sciences and the Lotus distinguished professor of management science of Hunan University at Changsha. He is also adjunct professor at over 30 universities around the world. He is/was the editor-in-chief, an area editor, or a co-editor of 16 journals, including *Information and Management* and *Energy Economics*. He was a guest editor for special issues/volumes of over 10 journals, including *European Journal of Operational Research, Annals of Operations Research*, and *IIE Transactions*. He has published over 20 monographs, including nine by Springer, and over 200 papers in leading journals. His current research interests include risk management, economic forecasting, and supply chain management.

Contents

Figures

Tables

Acknowledgments

We would like to extend our sincere thanks to the many people and organizations who provided so much of support and understanding, which helped us compete this book. We also appreciate all the researchers and organizations who provided us with references during the process of writing up this book and thus made great contributions to the content of the book.

1 Introduction

In the past decade, a multitude of events related to supply chain disruptions have occurred in succession, causing great losses to enterprises. As a result of the earthquake in Central Japan in 2007, Toyota, Nissan, and other major automobile-manufacturing enterprises had to shut down their production lines either completely or partially for 1–4 days. The main reason was that companies that produced auto parts and components, such as sealing rings for automatic transmission and piston rings, were affected by the earthquake and had to shut down, and thus the supply was interrupted.

Supply chains face disruption risks caused by natural disasters, events, and catastrophes; social unrest and related events; and other factors or events related to the logistics process, market demand fluctuations, information gap, and human errors, or a combination of several such factors (Sheffi, 2001). It follows that diverse factors of significantly varying forms might induce supply chain disruptions. Consequently, supply chain disruption risks refer to events that might emerge in supply chains and influence flows of materials and components (Svensson, 2000).

According to theories such as the lean, just-in-time, and centralized manufacturing, enterprises have entered an era of super-strong connections. The risks induced by supply chain disruptions often get transferred to the entire system of enterprises, and the cascading effects can destroy safe operations of supply chains. Entire supply chains can become interrupted and invalid, and the value chain system related to supply chains can get disturbed and then collapse.

Currently, global economy is maintaining a rapid growth rate, and the living standards of common people are improving significantly. The processes of marketization and liberalization have accelerated in several countries, where various risks will emerge in their development. Many enterprises in each country across the world are gradually getting integrated, and, therefore, risks of supply chain disruptions are inevitably transmitted to the markets and the real economy in each nation.

Recent research has focused on functions and strategies related to intra-enterprise and inter-enterprise transactions in supply chains, laying particular stress on the reduction of enterprise operating cost, optimized resource allocation, cutting manufacturing and logistics expenditure, and coalition strategies, among others, for the sake of improving the long-term performance of supply chains and their associated enterprises. The management and minimization of supply chain risks constitute not only a major component of supply chain management but also management of enterprise risks. In both theory and practice, the importance of managing supply chain risks has been acknowledged. However, the behavior of supply chain disruptions varies dramatically, making its standardization difficult.

The status quo

Origin, categorization, influence, and conduction of supply chain disruptions risk

Supply chain risks have attracted growing attention from enterprises and scholars; the Center for Transportation and Logistics at MIT has studied this phenomenon and defined its origin (Sheffi, 2001). Chapman *et al.* (2002) analyzed the vulnerability of supply chains to disruptions and proposed the 3P management approach for managing supply chain disruption risks. Zsidisin (2003) defined supply chain risks and noted that buyers encounter supply risks emanating from impact factors, market characteristics, and supply chain risk events related to suppliers. Cavinato (2004) analyzed the sources of supply chain risks from five aspects, namely, logistics, capital flow, information flow, relationship network, and innovation network. Chopra *et al.* (2004) discussed nine risks, including supply chain risks, and examined potential sources and preventive measures related to risks. They pointed out that different risks might interact, and that it is important to strike a balance between risk and profits when risk management measures are implemented. At the same time, Lei and Xu (2004) introduced the issue of managing events-related supply chain disruptions, defined and categorized events, and analyzed emergency management of disruptive events. Built on causes and forms of supply chain events, Ding (2006) explicated forecasting methods and preventive mechanisms for supply chain events. Zhu and Li (2006) also discussed the methods of studying supply chain events by typology, classification, and staging.

Kleindorfer and Saad (2005) further categorized supply chain disruptions as a whole and evaluated their influence, introduced 10 corresponding risk management methods, and summarized experiences of American chemical enterprises in managing supply chain events and risks. Elkins *et al.* (2005) also introduced 18 suggestions proposed by the Supply Chain Resource Association to deal with supply chain disruptions. Zhou *et al.* (2006) analyzed supply chain disruptions and discussed their findings from the perspective of risk management. They state that inventory reduction decreases the possibility of supply chain disruptions for enterprises, and that the variations of supply chain forms reduce the loss. Kull and Closs (2008) investigated supply chain disruptions in the second tier on the basis of theories related to inventory and resource dependency. The results indicated that a rise in inventory increases risks rather than decreasing them in the hierarchical supply chain, requires requests enterprises to treat supply chain disruptions more systematically.

Supply chain risk induction consists of basic elements such as risk initiators, propellants, conduction carriers and recipients, forward and reversal conduction in risk chains related to supply chains, and network-centralized and interactive conduction patterns in the course of conduction (Cheng and Qiu, 2009). Cranfield (2002) suggested that supply chain risks emanate from a variety of factors; as supply chain enterprises are interdependent, problems emerging from any enterprise spread to and affect the whole supply chain, which amplifies the risk. Chen and Xu (2007) introduced the coefficient of resilience and discussed the effects of supply chain risk conduction on enterprises. Their results showed that the price risk of the supply chain gradually declines as products move downstream and manufacturers' and retailers' profits transmit risks to enterprises in the next node gradually, through risk propellants, and eventually achieve risk adjustment. Zhai (2008) constructed risk conduction models and provided mathematical analysis related to collaboration and innovation among enterprises on the basis of the definition of risk conduction, knowledge transfer and collaboration, and innovation. Also, he proposed that the management of risk conduction can be enhanced through prevention and process controls.

As discussed in the preceding text, extant literature has shown that research on the origin, classification, and effects of supply chain disruption risks are grounded on public events or macro-level dimensions, while, in reality, it is the micro-level mistakes or errors in the supply chain that lead to supply chain disruptions. Different supply chain enterprises cause different types of disruptions, which are not consistent in the macro or micro dimensions. Even though the supply chain risk conduction has already been expounded, it is necessary to further investigate the specific supply chain risk conduction mechanism.

Early warning and control of supply chain disruption risk

The identification of supply chain disruption risk is an important step in managing the frequency and impact of supply chain disruptions. Thus, Trkman and McCormack (2009) demonstrated new methods to identify and predict supply chain risks and discussed supplier assessment and classification methods based on supplier characteristics, performance, and supply chain properties. As the transformation has been made from storage to progressive perspective in the supply chain among modern enterprises, a number of advantages as well as new risk sources are generated for enterprises, which reduces the vulnerability of supply chains. Neiger *et al.* (2009) noted that value-centered projects could help identify supply chain disruption risks and improve performance of the supply chain and its members. Ellis *et al.* (2010) studied the importance, possibility, and risk of supply chain disruptions from the perspective of the behavior risk theory and constructed a product and market factor model. They verified their model by analyzing data related to 223 purchasing managers and buyers, which indicated that the possibility and importance of supply disruptions play a pivotal role in identifying supply chain risk.

In terms of the assessment of supply chain disruption risks, Harland *et al.* (2003) decomposed the management of supply chain risks into a number of cyclic processes such as risk identification, risk assessment, formulation of risk control plans, and implementation plans. Grounded on case studies in the electronics department, they suggested that a framework of warning, assessment, and management of early supply chain disruptions should be constructed. Kleindoffer and Saad (2005) claimed that natural disasters, strikes, economic crises, and terrorists' actions might result in disruption risks, and as such a conceptual framework is constructed to assess and reduce supply chain disruption risks. He studied the issue of supply chain risk management system by using data related to American chemical industry events. Wu *et al.* (2006) proposed a comprehensive approach to classify and assess supply disruption risks, found supply risk factors, and constructed a model for the classification of supply risk factors in the form of stages. Schoenherra *et al.* (2008) assessed supply chain disruption risks in relation to American manufacturing enterprises purchasing decisions, found 17 risk factors, and classified them by integrating action research and analytic hierarchy process. They came up with an assessment model grounded on supply chain disruption risk factors in an empirical study. With respect to the assessment of supply chain disruption risks, it is common to use chance constrained programming (CCP), data envelopment analysis (DEA), and multiple objective programming (MOP) models. Wu and Olson (2008) simulated supply chain risk at the third stage and its probability distribution features with the risk assessment models. The new model constructed enabled the enterprise decision-makers to strike a balance between the anticipated cost, quality levels, and delivery time.

Smelzer and Siferd (1998) discussed supply chain disruption risks from the perspective of purchasing managers, analyzed supply disruption risks by applying the transaction cost theory and the resource dependency model, and pointed out that active purchasing management meant managing the supply disruption risk. Zsidisin (2003) analyzed suppliers' operational risks, suppliers' productivity constrained risk, product quality risk, technology change risk, and various disaster risks, and maintained that a huge number of strategies and techniques could be applied to minimize supply disruption risks and their effects. Hallikas *et al.* (2004) came up with the general structure of supply network risk control, examined supplier network risk control in complicated network environments, and showed that risk exposure increases as the interdependency among enterprises grows.

For the sake of cost advantages and market shares, many enterprises change their organizations and production. Sheffi (2005) showed that the construction of flexible supply chains could deal with disruption risks. Tang (2006) reviewed a number of quantitative models related to supply chain disruption risks and proposed a framework of supply chain risk control in relation to the issue of vulnerability of supply chain systems induced by outsourcing of manufacturing and product diversification. As supply chains become active, it is vital to respond to real-time emerging events. Goh *et al.* (2007) applied the Moreau-YosidaLiu method and proposed a random model concerning the issue of hierarchical global supply chain network for the purpose of achieving maximum profits and minimum risks. Liu *et al.* (2007a) showed that the Timing Petri Network Model could be applied for coping with supply chain disruption risks. They designed models to simulate supply chain disruption risks, and studied enterprise performance by using sensitivity analysis in relation to parameter values. Yoo *et al.* (2010) came up with the optimized budget allocation method to reduce the simulated value related to supply chain disruptions by applying the nested partition method, aiming to simulate discrete events to improve supply chain optimization efficiency.

For example, Hendricks and Singhal (2003, 2005) examined the effect of supply chain disruption risks and uncertain factors on enterprise performance by drawing on data from listed companies.

As discussed earlier, extant literature has shown that identification of supply chain disruption risk constitutes a significant link in managing supply chain risks. Although there are some findings concerning supply chain progress, enterprise value, and behavior risk theory, research on disruptions risk is still at the preliminary stage. Conceptual and mathematical models have been proposed to assess supply chain disruption risks, but the majority of them are empirical, and, therefore, the models need to be verified by extensive application. In order to manage supply chain disruption risks, many feed-forward control methods have been proposed, such as active purchasing management, supplier network risk control method, enhancement of flexibility in supply chain, and sensitivity analysis through simulation.

Optimization of supply chain disruptions

It is essential for enterprises to assess both internal and external environment and conditions, and initiate the corresponding measures to reduce the potential consequences and optimize the performance of various resource allocations to cope with risks. As mentioned earlier, what follows will be concerned with management strategies of inventory or manufacturing in the supply destabilization caused by supply chain disruptions, coordinating measures to manage supply chain disruption risks, and to recover from supply chain disruptions.

Inventory or production management strategies in supply disturbance caused by supply chain disruption

To improve supply reliability, enterprises can adopt either duplex or multiplex patterns. That is to say, enterprises should order from more than one supplier. For this, researchers have considered enterprises that divide their orders between two suppliers and the effects of this strategy on inventory management, and have constructed and analyzed supply models accordingly (Anupindi and Akella, 1993). Moinzadeh and Aggarwal (1997) applied the production strategy (s, S) to examine the optimal decision related to unreliable production storage system in response to supply chain disruptions. Meanwhile, Parlar (1997) investigated the issue of inventory management with assumed random demand and lead time, when such events as machine faults and strikes by workers occur. The supply disturbance is considered a Markov process. When events lead to supply chain disruptions, the optimal inventory is achieved by target function of average cost in the constructed time frame.

Abboud (2001) constructed a production storage system model based on Markov chain and analyzed suppliers' cost function, and treated machine faults and repair time as random parameters. He also compared the results when time was treated as the continuous parameter. Li *et al.* (2004) showed that unpredictable events such as machine fault, order cancellation, maintenance errors, and strikes can lead to supply disruptions and affect the production storage system; the construction of inventory checking system within one period can help cope with random demand and uncertain supply, and hence supply certainty can be described as an alternative renewal process. Xiao and Yu (2006) discussed the gaming conditions related to maximal strategies of income and profits when supply chain environment was normal and analyzed the optimal selection with the strategy of stable plans. As events result in demand changes and materials supply discontinuity, the optimal strategy of retailers in supply chains is provided. Taskin and Lodree Jr. (2010) discussed the purchase and production decision in hurricane seasons and constructed a random model of inventory control at different stages on the basis of hurricane forecast.

In conclusion, the literature has shown that enterprises can adopt duplex and multiplex patterns to deal with supply chain disruption risks. Although the ordering quantity and inventory strategies are determined, the previous studies were based on homogeneous time spans. A random model of inventory control at different stages has been constructed with hurricane forecast as the premise in some research works but it failed to extend to normal or accidental supply chain disruption risks.

Coordinating methods in supply chain disruption risk management

When logistics, information flow, and capital flow lag behind relatively in supply chains, it is essential that the supply chain be established on the basis of disruption risk management to improve their capacity and performance levels (Li and Zhang, 2003). Disruption risk is a significant factor that affects supply chain efficiency, and the supply chain risk management system and flow can be constructed to discover disruption risk rapidly (Zhang *et al.*, 2004). Enterprises, suppliers, and retailers can collaborate (Wang and Chen, 2004), such that the supply chain is able to respond swiftly, and competitiveness is enhanced. Liu *et al.* (2007b) established a model of fuzzy search through the fuzzy mathematical method, and the relative managerial information can be found by integrating database technology to facilitate enterprise managers to make correct decisions concerning supply chain disruption risks.

As the demand function is fixed, sudden changes in demand can affect a supply chain consisting of suppliers and retailers in the second stage. For this, Xu *et al.* (2003) considered the optimal response in the context of power centralization and separation under a quantity discount contract. Wang and Hu (2006) studied the optimal strategy to deal with emergency events in supply chain related to power centralization and decentralization in the third stage of supply chains, when the market demand alters suddenly and the extra cost is non-linear. Xiao *et al.* (2005) showed that manufacturers can change unit wholesale price and discount rate to modify supply chain when demand changes. They also showed that manufacturers alter their production if investment sensitivity coefficient changes beyond a fixed range. Zeng and Wang (2007) discussed the issue of demand distribution disturbance faced by retailers and discontinuity of supply chain coordination because of events and came up with the quantity discount contract relating to random demand and suggested measures to cope with events.

Yu *et al.* (2005a and 2006) and Yu and Chen (2007) contributed to the coordination method in managing supply chain events. To address events-related changes in demand distribution faced by retailers, supply chain coordination can be achieved by counter-purchasing contracts. If demand function is linear, to address changes of price-sensitive coefficients caused by event-related changes, consider the extra cost generated by emergency events in the case of non-linear duplex function; power centralization and decentralization of supply chains are optimally achieved by quantity discount contract. Regarding the response of supply chains to events in case of wholesale contract, the optimal coping strategy is based on the premise that event-related changes in supply chain are random. To address the issue of coordinating supply chains with profit-sharing contract, consider the effects of events on supply chains and the optimal emergency price for retailers and suppliers in timing sequence, and a two-stage profit-sharing contract is proposed to cope with events.

Li (2006) studied events and their characteristics in supply chains, how to select the optimal path after events emerged, and achieved the optimal solution by modeling and using the hereditary algorithm. Tapiero (2007) investigated coordinating methods related to supply chain strategies and applied the Neyman-Pearson framework for dealing with events and controlling quality. He claimed that the extent of assuming consequences of events related to supply chain enterprises depended on the relationships among organizational members and their motivation and power. Scheller-Wolf and Tayur (2009) examined the model of unbalanced Markov production and inventory by summarizing and expanding the model of production and inventory, and found a valid supply chain coordinating mechanism that facilitates matching of supply and demand and helps improve the overall performance. Tuncel and Alpan (2010) demonstrated a method of applying the timing Petri Network model to simulate and analyze supply chain disruption risks, integrated cases of enterprises, and the assessment process of supply chain performance, and showed that supply chain coordinating actions can improve their performance and cut the costs in the system.

As discussed in the preceding text, the literature has shown that information technology is conducive to coping with supply chain disruption risks collaboratively. As the supply chain disruption risks result in changes in demand, the manufacturers can coordinate supply chains by changing prices and discount rates, and new investment can be used to increase production. The degree of assuming disruption risks by enterprises in supply chains rests on the specific circumstances of their members.

recovery of supply chain disruptions

(et al. (2004) studied the optimal coping strategies of power centralization and (centralization of supply chains by adjusting quantity discount contract when .nand is linear in supply chains, and they found that disruptions or changes in arket demand could cause linear cost deviation. Xia *et al.* (2004) investigated ne wholesale model of classic optimal production in two-level production system when demand variables were fixed, and they discussed the solutions when the production initiation cost, storage cost, productivity, and demand ratio parameters alter due to supply chain disruption risks.

Higher control and coordinating mechanisms are required to deal with supply chain flow disruption risks. Kumara and Wainer (2005) studied the model related to supply chain flow process changing because of events and conditions, which can be managed by different actions and applied to the recovery and treatment of special circumstances in the event of supply chain disruptions. Adhitya *et al.* (2007) proposed a recombined model in the case of supply chain disruptions, which helped find the cause–effect relationship in supply chain variables, identify the consequence of supply chain disruptions, and achieve the completeness of supply chain recovery program and functional flexibility.

Knemeyer *et al.* (2009) proposed a process of coping with supply chain disruption risks based on risk analysis models by applying innovative methods of insurance to quantify these risks. Oloruntoba (2010) pointed out that the event of Cyclone Larry in Australia was considered the most effectively managed in all cyclones that occurred suddenly in Australian history. He analyzed the chain of event treatments and some factors contributing to the event treatments, and came up with humane measures to recover from supply chain disruptions.

In conclusion, the literature has shown that the recovery of supply chain disruptions concerns a vast number of factors relative to achieving the status before disruptions. It is also necessary to provide a higher level of control over the coordination of different activities. The recovery programs are supposed to be complete and flexible in their functions.

Management procedures and principles of supply chain disruption risk

Procedures of managing supply chain disruption risks

The Olton Risk Center studied disruption risks and proposed a management method relating to disruption risk in different stages, including the following four steps.

1. Achieve an understanding of and approval for better management of the enterprise and formulate organizational functions responsible for managing disruption risks. This is usually associated with risk management in all enterprises.

2. Clearly describe the key flow affected by disruption and find the characteristics of the affected equipment, capital, and human resources. The typical flow includes research and development of new products, supply chain operation, and production. The key capital includes the tangible (property and inventory) and the intangible (brand images and public opinions) resources.

3. Adopt risk management methods in the key flow, identify uncertain factors and their triggers and occurrence frequency, and take remittance measures and risk transfer strategies, which is the core of managing disruption risks. The corresponding results are achieved. First, disruption risks involving key capital in enterprises are categorized. Second, the corresponding methods are implemented in the system of risk management in enterprises, and the system is supposed to ensure integration of risk management activities with other management systems in enterprises (quality, production, maintenance, environment, health, and safety).

4. Report, audit periodically, manage and implement programs, and check and complete disruption risk management flow. In terms of auditing procedures, it is necessary to manage equipment performance among supply chain members, and also the implementation of supply chain standards.

Principles of managing supply chain disruption risks

Tang (2006) proposed managing supply chain disruption risks on the basis of industrial risk management and supply chain management in the framework of managing supply chain disruption risk.

- *Above all, it is important for enterprises to manage themselves well, and then it is possible to expect or require other members to manage their enterprises in supply chains.* This principle derives from the fact that a supply chain network consists of three subsystems: supplier relationship management (SRM), internal supply chain management (ISCM), and client relationship management (CRM). ISCM is the core. On the one hand, manufacturers are connected with suppliers. On the other hand, manufacturers are associated with client/retailer networks. Therefore, internal supply chain management is prior to intra-enterprise management. Also, the core is the network stations and equipment management system related to the description and remission of supply chain disruption risks. This principle indicates that senior management is obliged to supervise supply chain disruption risk management flow.

- *Apply or expand investment combination theory though reducing risks in diverse ways.* This principle is the expansion of capital combination theory in the financial field, and the result is risk reduction through diverse combinations. In managing supply chain disruption risks, the theory can be expanded to equipment location, products and service production, selection of purchasing sources, operating patterns, and flows. Such diversification can maximally achieve risk minimization.

- *Robustness is determined by the weakest link in supply chains.* The principle shows that the management of supply chain disruption risk is supposed to provide risk aversion among supply chain members and reduce motivated collaboration. Grounded on the properties of products and supply chain, robustness and profitability are influenced by the weakest links in supply chains to a great degree. The principle requires that uncertainty be defined within the overall range in supply chains, integrating the management of early warning systems. The potential internal and external disruption risks in supply chains can be handled by checking and modulating periodic events.

- *Prevention is better than cure and loss aversion, and prevention is prior to remission after loss in general.* This principle shows that risk aversion measures are primary, and that risk assessment is to define the key uncertainty and the potential worst situations, which is a vital step in managing supply chain disruption risks. The emergency program coping with risks is prior to remission strategies.

- *Extreme accuracy and efficiency might increase uncertainty, whether individual enterprises or the overall supply chain.* The principle shows that it is important to note the robustness of disruption risks treated by supply chains and the overall efficiency in order to minimize disruptions and the potential ultimate loss. Although the accuracy of internal and external operations in enterprises is emphasized, little research has addressed accuracy and systemic stability, and the result is the huge increase in supply chain disruption risks and cost.

- *Construct supporting systems and emergency programs, and maintain rational relaxation to improve the level of managing risks.* The principle means that the supply chain is supposed to follow the reliable theory and have methods to improve flows, including some redundant and rational supporting systems in tangible or virtual forms (such as the agile alliance).

- *Sharing information among supply chain members helps define risk sources and taking measures to manage risks.* The principle shows that different departments in inter-enterprises and supply chain members are supposed to coordinate and collaborate. Without collaboration, the weak links are difficult to define and management measures related to risks are hard to determine. Collaboration among supply chain members in different stages can be a win-win proposition, which is the core for the supply chain association to propose the supply chain operation reference (SCOR) model.

- *It is not sufficient to have emergency management of risks, and it is important to integrate risk assessment and quantify technology. The potential damage induced by supply chain disruption risks relating to enterprises need to be evaluated and the necessary remission measures need to be taken.* The principle illustrates the result of developing risk management practices, following Drucker's concept: you cannot manage the stuff that cannot be measured. Without the measures to quantify risks, warnings can be issued in enterprises and supply chains only in a general sense, and the risk remission measures that are cost-efficient cannot be produced, unless risk assessment and risk probability calculation are applied to managing supply chain risks and a variety of rational measures have already been checked and passed. The use of warning triggers, such as fault prevention programs in systems and quality management, enables identification of the weak link(s) and facility operation to be embedded in flow management.

- *Appropriate supply chain flow and agility can cut supply chain disruption risk in raw materials and components in particular.* The principle emphasizes that quicker supply chain response implies agility to obtain resources and improve the flexibility of the supply chain, and the response speed can be incorporated in the design of supply chain structure.
- *Adopt total quality management (TQM) theory, and a higher supply chain security level can be accomplished, which reduces disruption risks in process of operation.* The principle shows that the application of T such as the Six Sigma can reduce supply chain disruption risks. This me can enhance supply chain security, and also cut operational costs, suc in international sea transportation service. Application of recent information coding system and radio frequency identification device (RFID) will increase supply chain security level to some extent.

Organization of the book

This book consists of eight chapters, and it considers the issue of supply chain disruption risk from diverse dimensions. It explores the nature and principles of managing supply chain disruption risks for the purpose of providing a framework and multi-target models of managing supply chain disruption risks. It is expected to enrich the understanding of the theoretical system of supply chain management.

Chapter 1 deals with extant research on supply chain disruption management in terms of origin, classification, influence, and conduction of supply chain disruption risks; monitoring warnings and risk control; optimization of risk management; and procedures and principles of supply chain disruption risk management. This chapter contributes to the understanding of the status of research on supply chain disruption risk management and the related fundamental issues.

Chapter 2 discusses supply chain disruption risk conduction, including the mechanism of conduction, changes of path of conduction, and assessment of intensity of risk conduction. The chapter divides supply chain disruption risks into intrinsic and extrinsic risks, including environmental risk, supply risk, demand risk, process risk, and control risk. It introduces properties of carriers and forms of disruption risk conduction; the three stages of the key path, which changes dynamically with time; and the path model related to supply chain disruption risk conduction. It studies the fundamental elements and the general energy vector models relating to supply chain disruption risk transmission.

Chapter 3 explicates the method of assessment of loss caused by disruptive events and introduces the basic models of loss assessment, with focus on the additive method. The process of assessment of loss caused by disruptive events is composed of five steps: partition stage, short-term assessment, rolling updating, loss analysis, and summary. The loss process induced by disruptive events can also be divided into five event stages. The information-updating steps in the loss evaluation of supply chain disruptive events can regulate the function expression of predictable performance trends, providing more accurate function expressions of operational status trajectory for enterprises.

Chapter 4 explores the supply chain coordinating model related to demand disruption risks. It mainly introduces a two-stage supply chain model of demand disruptions by describing the relevant supply chain models, and provides supply chain coordinating models with and without central decision-makers in the context of demand disruption risks. Through quantitative analysis, suppliers and retailers can achieve maximal profits in supply chains by modulating their own strategies in relation to demand disruptions. The numerical experiments show that this model can achieve maximum profits compared with the previous supply chain models.

Chapter 5 focuses on supply chain coordinating models in the case of supply chain disruption risks. It discusses the coordinating issues related to preventive measures and then the recovery process of three supply chains. In the two-stage coordinating model of supply chains, which consists of one supplier and one retailer, two circumstances of risk neutralization and aversion related to suppliers in disruptive events are considered. In supply chains consisting of one supplier and many retailers, centralized and separate supply chains are considered; supply chain coordinating methods are discussed in terms of assistance and penalty; and the satisfying conditions, which the coordinating methods are supposed to meet, are provided in relation to preventive measures and recovery processes in supply chains.

Chapter 6 considers management models in relation to supply chain disruption risks, with manufacturers as the core. It analyzes the emergency coordinating issues related to demand and supply disruptions on the basis of a three-stage supply chain system: suppliers–manufacturers–retailers. In the case of demand disruption risks, apart from adding deviated cost to target function, the target function includes the cost related to dealing with demand disruption risk, and the fixed cost relating to manufacturers and retailers is also taken into account. In the case of supply disruption risks, the penalty contract can be applied for coordinating manufacturers and suppliers, given that the risk is neutral for suppliers and manufacturers, and the relevant conclusions are achieved by applying the model of minimal expectation cost.

Chapter 7 centers on methods for making decisions to respond to disruptions, and introduces modulation rules preferred by decision-makers. It improves upon methods that need to satisfy certain constraints that apply to supply chain response decisions in the event of disruption of demand. To address one or a continuous consumption system, the supply of multiple-point coordination will be investigated during the demand disruption. At the same time, the distribution decision model of supply chains during production disruption is constructed and optimized to ensure a reasonable supply sequence and quantity after production disruption.

Chapter 8 summarizes the major findings and discusses future research orientations and limitations. The future research can further explore the origin, classification, influence, and conduction of supply chain disruption risks; monitoring and early warnings and risk control related to supply chain disruption risks; management strategies of inventory and production in the case of supply disturbance induced by supply chain disruptions; the coordinating methods in managing supply chain disruption risks; and the recovery of supply chain disruptions.

2 Risk conduction of supply chain disruptions

This chapter discusses supply chain disruption risk conduction, including the related mechanisms, changes of related path, and assessment of the levels of risk.

Introduction

At the moment, economic globalization has made competition among enterprises increasingly intense. Nonetheless, enterprises tend to collaborate, that is, they do not struggle individually, and they compete in the form of many alliances, which means there is competition and more collaboration among enterprises.

Michael Porter (1985) proposed the concept of value chain in *The Competitive Advantage*, which enables enterprises to understand that the value between the upstream and downstream enterprise in supply chains can be added, and collaboration in supply chains can reduce cost and increase profits. Therefore, collaboration among supply chain enterprises has become the most effective method to compete in the market.

Numerous uncertain factors might bring risks to supply chains for various reasons, internal and external. In the new economy, enterprises adopt accuracy in production, global purchasing, business outsourcing, and centralization to remain competitive in an increasingly external market environment, and for the sake of improving operations flow and resilience relating to enterprises. However, the application of advanced management methods, technology, and strategies makes supply chains more prone to risks than ever before. The main reason is that supply chains lack sufficient resilience.

As an intermediate organization gets formed between enterprises and the market, supply chains face many risks because of restraints imposed by internal and external environments. Supply chain risks conduct through many channels such as capital, technology, information, price, interest rates, confidence, policy, and events, among many others. Realization of the key risk factors is important to prevent crisis outbreaks; supply chain risks are extensive, and risk conduction is diverse and incubation of existing crisis and supervision can mutate. Supply chain disruption risk is one of the factors.

There is direct and indirect association among node enterprises in the supply chain system, and hence there is risk conduction. Supply chain disruption risk conduction refers to risk released from disruptions in external environment and system via a specific path or channel. It relies on tangible objective entities or has intangible effects and spreads or extends to the nodes and flow of each operational function in supply chains. It diffuses with time or amplifies gradually, which might endanger the overall supply chain network and make production and operational activities relating to supply chain enterprises to deviate from expected targets and suffer losses. The tangible or intangible effects related to carrying and conducting these uncertain disruption risk factors become the carriers of supply chain disruption risks.

Supply chain disruption risk conduction might accumulate, amplify, or mutate through specific risk conduction mechanisms and produce "contagious effects" and, therefore, ultimately endanger the overall supply chain. The fundamental circumstances related to supply chain disruption risk conduction, including conduction mechanism, conduction path changes, and conduction energy assessment of supply chain disruption risk, which have significant practical implications for supply chain disruption prevention, are discussed.

Risk conduction mechanism of supply chain disruption

Categorization of supply chain disruption risks

Christopher (1992) described supply chain risks as: supply chain risks = probability of damage occurring × influence. Risks cover two key concepts: emerging probability and degree of influence (Yates and Stone, 1992). The equation by Christopher had one defect—that is, it is impossible to differentiate the circumstances when the probability is huge with little influence and when the probability is tiny with huge influence, but their multiplication is the same. In the weakest location that can be easily attacked in a supply chain, the emerging probability is relatively small, but the influence might be devastating. Various factors that might cause damage to the supply chain constitute supply chain risks deriving from enterprise interior and exterior.

If supply chain node enterprises are taken as classification standards, disruption risks can be divided into six types: supply risk, demand risk, and environment risk from the enterprise exterior, and control risk, process risk, and event risk from the enterprise interior. From the perspective of the overall supply chain system, the risks can be classified into three types: first, extrinsic risks from the overall supply chain, namely, environment risks, such as terrorism and natural disasters; second, the risk can derive from within, that is, member enterprises, induced by incomplete collaboration among them. This incomplete collaboration might be indicative of a lack of visibility or inaccurate prediction, including supply risk and demand risk. Thirdly, the risk might originate from internal enterprises, including process risk and control risk.

Overall supply chain exterior: environment risk

Whether it is individual enterprises or supply chains, environmental risks are extrinsic. A number of factors contribute to environmental risks, such as changes in political environment, some economic events, and natural disasters (typhoon, earthquakes, and flood, among many others). Environmental risks might derive from disruptions in customs and harbors, paralysis of traffic system, or fire and terror attacks. From the perspectives of enterprises, the majority of these risks are uncontrollable and difficult to predict. Research at Cranfield University investigated the seriousness of the influence of different external environment risks on supply chain member enterprises and found that the protests and demonstrations against oil price rise in the United Kingdom in 2000 had an extensive influence. Of those interviewed, 82% thought they were affected, among whom 34% claimed that they were seriously affected. It is important to note that the influence on different node enterprises was not symmetrical. In other words, retailers and wholesalers were more seriously affected than suppliers and manufacturers. In addition, the 9/11 terror attack event in the United States caused many airports in North America to shut down temporarily and the speed of border passage reduced, which had a prominent influence on global supply chains.

Risks from enterprise exterior and interior: supply risk and demand risk

The supply risk originates from upstream member enterprises, including potential or actual disturbance in the flow of raw materials, components, and information in supply chains. Meulbroek (2002) stated that supply risk refers to any negative events that happen in supply flow. Zsidisin (2003) described supply risk as breakdown or dysfunction in the supply process related to individual suppliers or the supply market, and this supply dysfunction results in clients losing sales and can even endanger their life and safety. He also showed that supply risk might be generated by some suppliers or the overall market. Some suppliers might break down when they deal with demand fluctuation, or if quality problems occur in the manufacturing process, or they might fail to catch up with the development in science and technology, among others. Supply market is often associated with market capacity.

Demand risk is defined as potential disturbance in capital flow, information flow, and logistics in downstream enterprises in supply chains. Numerous factors contribute to demand risks. Errors in demand prediction, increased changeability in sequential arrangement, excessive response to orders, excessive cut in inventory, lack of communication and collaboration between upstream and downstream enterprises in supply chains, and delays in information flow and logistics might lead to substantial fluctuations in demand faced by upstream enterprises in supply chains. On some occasions, demand risk does not always derive from error factors. In terms of demand fluctuations, enterprises modulate their own safe inventory according to demand changes in the downstream parts of the supply chain. Considering supply shortage, enterprises are prone to making more orders than the actual needs. Nevertheless, as the circumstance in which demand exceeds supply is mitigated, enterprises that placed more orders than actual needs find their inventory levels very high. In order to save cost, enterprises prefer quantity orders. Since the market change cannot be reported promptly and each order quantity is relatively large, the demand risk grows. Member enterprises in supply chains generally hope that market demand prediction can alleviate demand risk. However, members in supply chain stages do not consider rationally, or add some factors such as damage and incomplete orders. Generally, they increase a certain proportion of order quantity from their upstream suppliers. As members in each stage increase their order quantity, it adds up in the supply chain upstream, and the total increase might be excessive.

Risks within enterprises: process risk and control risk

Process risk is defined as disturbances in production and management activities within enterprises. The process management within enterprises concerns many aspects, such as capital management, transportation management, and communication and collaboration among departments, among others. The processes of manufacture and management within enterprises might amplify and absorb supply chain risks, which rests on the process design and implementation status within enterprises (Jüttner, 2005). Many researchers have shown that enterprises should establish flexible supply chains to alleviate various risks in the manufacturing process. Resilient supply chains ensure that member enterprises are able to respond and manage when they fail to anticipate risks. Given that suppliers encounter some problems, the just-in-time (JIT) system adopted by enterprises brings them serious consequences. On the other hand, provided that during process management enterprises maintain a certain amount of material inventory, the supply risk might be completely or partially absorbed. In the management of the process risk, it is extremely crucial to find the bottleneck link in the process. The improvement of the bottleneck link increases the efficiency of enterprises.

The control risk covers many aspects, such as the uncertainty of order quantity, design of the batch sizes, and settings of safe inventory, among many others. "Control" here refers to the design, rule, system, and procedure related to enterprises, which guide and control the process of manufacturing and management. The control risk originates from the decision-makers and managers who formulate rules and regulations in enterprises; inappropriate policies and principles in the process of manufacturing and management exert a negative influence on supply chains.

Vulnerability of supply chains

The modern supply chain system is becoming increasingly sophisticated and has many horizontal and vertical relationships. In most cases, supply chains are more like a network. Owing to the complexity of supply chains, they are fragile and easy-to-go-wrong. Vulnerability of supply chains refers to one type of exposure related to serious disturbances induced by intrinsic and extrinsic risks in supply chains (Christopher *et al.*, 2002). From the earlier analysis relating to supply chain risk typology, there is a vast number of uncertain factors in the operational process of supply chains; risks are always accompanied by each node enterprise in supply chains, from which the vulnerability of supply chains originates. The disruption risk is one intrinsic nature of supply chains; it is impossible to completely avoid it. Nonetheless, resilience of supply chains can be enhanced and robustness can be achieved through studying and mastering various factors contributing to the vulnerability of supply chains. The factors contributing to such vulnerability can be summarized as follows.

Attach greater importance to efficiency but not efficacy. In order to satisfy the intense competition for demand, enterprises usually place more emphasis on efficiency, which makes the resilience of supply chains shrink. If enterprises in supply chains go wrong even slightly, the overall supply chain might be affected and disrupted.

Increase the trend of business outsourcing. Business brings many advantages to enterprises but business outsourcing also makes the number of node enterprises in supply chains and their connections increase, which renders supply chain relationships more complicated. Therefore, potential interference is more likely to happen than ever before.

Under the influence of globalization, the range and scale of supply chains have expanded. In order to pursue competitiveness in terms of manufacturing cost, modern enterprises extend purchasing activities from the domestic to the international market, resulting in an enormous expansion of logistics operations, requiring more from supply chain management. It is important to note that as the length of supply chains expands from the domestic to the international market, the supply period becomes longer and the uncertainty grows accordingly.

Centralize production and sales. In order to obtain economies and efficiency related to scale of manufacture, enterprises normally concentrate an enormous amount of production in one factory and then transport and sell the output to different places, which engenders more test and pressure on supply chains.

Cut the number of suppliers. At the moment, a number of enterprises are attempting to reduce the number of suppliers relating to raw materials and components. In the past, they used to purchase one type of raw material or component from one supplier. Currently, they are switching to the purchase of numerous types of raw materials and components from one supplier, which undoubtedly brings more advantages to enterprises. However, when something goes wrong with suppliers, the impact on affected enterprises is more than before and, therefore, this tendency also increases supply chain disruption risks.

In an environment of continuously changing demand, the market too changes swiftly; the rapid developments in science and technology are shortening product cycles, and intense competition is resulting in the emergence of promotion in a limitless number of forms. It is difficult for enterprises in supply chains to plan well in advance. The market chaos reduces the predictability of market demand, which has become an uncertain factor in supply chains.

The lack of visibility and confidence can be reflected in many aspects, such as order cycles, order status, demand prediction, transportation capacity, manufacturing capacity, and product quality, which have a negative effect on the performance of supply chain and lead to vulnerability. As there is a lack of confidence in predicting market demand, enterprises tend to store more inventory than normal to manage any potential demand that may arrive abruptly.

Supply chain disruption risk conducting carriers

Supply chain disruption risk conduction occurs when the effects of some disruptive events in some node enterprises are transmitted to other nodes and dimensions. The effects gradually amplify and spread as time passes, owing to internal and external influence and constraints. Those which contain and conduct these tangible objects and intangible effects related to uncertain factors of disruption risks are the supply chain disruption risk conducting carriers (as explained in the article 'On the Carriers of Conduction of SCR', Zhu, 2009).

Characteristics of supply chain disruption risk conducting carriers

- *Objective existence:* The objective existence of supply chain disruption risk conduction carrier refers to a form of representation closely associated with real-life activities, regardless of human thoughts. The constraint of internal resources and external environment in supply chain node enterprises and the direct or indirect correlations among supply chain node enterprises contribute to the uncertainty of supply chains and the objective existence of disruption risk conduction. Disruption risk conduction relies on carrier transmission, and the tangible objects and intangible effects themselves as carriers also have objective existence. The complexity of supply chain disruption risk conduction determines the diversity and sophistication of risk conduction carriers. In a general sense, supply chain disruption risk conduction has economic carriers and social carriers as well as passive carriers that prevent risk conduction and active carriers that accelerate risk conduction. In terms of the form of existence, supply chain disruption risk conduction can be differentiated by overt and covert carriers. These overt, covert, and diverse carriers constitute the network of risk carriers, which affect the process of risk conduction.
- *Random:* Risk itself is random, and risk analysis mainly follows the theory and method of probability and mathematical statistics in general, which suggests a hypothesis in relation to random variables. The random risk conduction exhibits that risk conduction cannot be precisely predicted as it happens randomly with risk events, implying that carriers too are random.
- *Carrying:* Carrying refers to various elements in the carriers related to supply chain disruption risks that can interact. The subjects, objects, and the

contents in risk conduction are risk factors that can exist independent of each other. As they exist independently and in unrelated conditions, there are no conduction activities, but they are fragmentary and exhibit only partial risk. If these elements are interconnected and interact, real activities of supply chain disruption risk conduction will be produced. Then, carriers bear these elements and act as "mediums" and "bridges."

- *Conduction:* Conduction means the carriers transmit the information and content of supply chain disruption risk. The carrying function of carriers is the premise and condition for conduction. In terms of supply chain system, node enterprises participate in the processes of supplying raw materials, manufacturing, and marketing. Hence, the risk factors can accumulate and spread to each node enterprise through the supply flow. As each element of risk carried by carriers interacts, conduction initiates. The disruption risk of node enterprises in supply chains follows certain conduction principles, and it affects and transmits by taking different routes in different environments, forming a complicated conduction chain and network related to supply chain disruption risks.

- *Path dependency:* Path dependency is a new term in the new constitutional economics, referring to a system with positive and negative feedback mechanisms. Once it is accepted as being under the influence of external events, it follows a certain route, evolves, and forms a certain inherent habit, which is difficult to replace by other potential routes and systems.

The initiating mechanism means the risk conduction system will initiate, as different conditions are set up. The formulation and operation of supply chain disruption risk conduction system are made up of many cause–effect chains, which consist of different risk sources, events, function nodes, and subsystems. The cause–effect chain is thus the logical relationships among these elements. Forming status means that some status or results might emerge in the process of risk conduction. In other words, the path of conduction relies on the initiating status and risk properties of the system. Path dependency is one of the characteristics of supply chain disruption risks, which reflects that disruption risk conduction depends on various conduction carriers, and their operational mechanism can be summarized as four processes: specific conditions, initiating mechanism, forming status, and signing out and locking. Specific conditions indicate that random events, namely, internal and external events, occur and can initiate and determine route selection, but events derive from changes in the external environment and internal system status in supply chains, such as natural disasters, economic crisis, and social turmoil, among others. Once formed, the disruption risk conduction path displays features that are coherent and interdependent. Signing out and locking indicates that although the risk of supply chain disruption risk conduction is path dependent, this dependency can be interfered with and replaced. Once the dependency pattern of supply chain disruption risk conduction routes has been found and understood, the corresponding control and management can be implemented, and supply chain disruption risk conduction can be signed out to form a conduction locking status.

Typology of supply chain disruption risk conduction carriers

In the light of the characteristics of risk carriers, they can be classified into two major types: macro-carriers and micro-carriers. Macro-carriers mainly refer to environmental, demand, and financial risks that cover events, market, and foreign exchange risks. Micro-carriers mainly concern internal risks such as capital, cost, quality, technology, and information, and can be divided into overt and covert carriers. Overt carriers cover capital, information, and logistics, whereas covert carriers contain the whip effect (Lee *et al.*, 1997), financial leverage effect, and domino effect, among many others.

The role of carriers in supply chain disruption risk conduction

The carrier and process of risk conduction cannot be separated. To have an in-depth understanding of carriers and to enhance the management of supply chain disruption risks, it is necessary to have a clear understanding of the role of carriers.

Completion of the process of supply chain disruption risk conduction should take advantage of some forms or methods, where carriers are the most important core form of expressions. Carriers are the media in the process of supply chain disruption risk conduction, and they are considered as the bridge that connects various elements. In the supply chain system, the process of disruption risk conduction is composed of many interconnected and interacting elements. Also, it is the process of interaction between risk source and risk spreading group under a certain principle. If the direction, intensity, and time are viewed as an overall integrated factor (carrier), the fundamental factors in the process of supply chain disruption risk conduction are risk source, recipient source, and risk carriers. That is to say, as various elements of supply chain disruption risk conduction enter the conduction chain, they are connected through a certain medium, and the risk source and conduction carriers produce coupling effects in the process of risk conduction. Different disruption risks accumulate and mutate in the conduction process, and the chain expands and amplifies. The core of managing supply chain disruption risk is to prevent risk conduction. Only when the characteristics and principles of conduction carriers are actually understood, and the conduction mechanism is mastered, can the conduction, transfer, and spread of disruption risk be effectively controlled.

Forms of supply chain disruption risk conduction

Disruption risk conduction in the form of bubble evaporation

Risk conduction through information and intangible elements as carriers has features of bubbles, for example, risk conduction related to real estate enterprises which can suffer loss of investor confidence. Risks, systemic and external, exist in each link and the overall process in the supply chain. Nonetheless, supply chain disruption risk conduction needs certain conditions; after the disruption risk accumulates and reaches a critical point, it transmits and spreads.

Under the condition of open capital market, as bubbles burst, investment confidence declines first and then international hot money runs away. Demand and capital supply fall, accelerating the burst, and the crisis spreads. Demand dips and the supply chain gets disrupted.

Characteristics of disruption risk conduction in the form of bubbles are as follows. First, it spreads externally through capital channels. Bursting of bubbles significantly reduces finance availability and investment appetite, and this curbs the growth of the macro economy. Second, it extends externally through wealth effects as the wealth of investors shrinks due to bursting of the bubble. This affects growth prospects of supply chain enterprises. Third, it transmits externally through the financial credit system. Leveraged investors lose the ability to repay debts, which results in disruption of capital chain, and, therefore, the risk (deficit) spreads to the commercial banking system. As such, the loss in the banking system by itself is sufficient to cause a credit crisis.

Disruption risk conduction in the form of element scarcity

Take the organism of the growth process as an illustration. Organisms cannot grow healthily without a variety of chemical elements. If they lack a certain element, they will suffer from mal-development and may even die. Likewise, in the manufacturing and operational process of supply chain enterprises, if the key elements in manufacturing and operation (such as inferior ability in technological development) are scarce and uncertain, supply chain enterprises are significantly affected, and disruption risks emerge.

Characteristics of disruption risk conduction in the form of element scarcity are as follows: (1) there is a lack of elements—that is, in other words, there is serious short-term behavior in supply chain enterprises; (2) the development space is constrained and restricted, and the future development is damaged; (3) the capacity to prevent risk is low, and there is a lack of further advancement; (4) risks have a long-term latency, and the short-term damage is not serious; and (5) risks have a relatively deep latency; once they are transformed into a crisis, the consequence is serious.

Disruption risk conduction in the form of structure collapse

Disruption risk conduction in the form of structural collapse is also called mechanical disruption risk conduction. This can be illustrated with the example of collapse of projects and buildings. External factors contributing to structure collapse might include destruction of hilly land, foundation settlement, and faults. Internal factors contributing to structure collapse might include vulnerability to destruction of building pillar tops, poor fixed supports of the top, improper structure system configuration, leftover damage, destruction of accessories, and non-structural elements.

Characteristics of disruption risk conduction in the form of structure collapse are as follows: (1) environment—the external environment in supply chains has a significant impact on disruption risk conduction; (2) backbone—the enterprises in supply chains are supposed to have stable backbones in need of joint mainte-nance; (3) dynamism—enterprises in supply chain are dynamic and changeable, and they encounter much uncertainty and dynamic change. As such, periodic self-check and inter-check mechanisms are necessary for enterprises in supply chains.

Disruption risk conduction in the form of tsunami and waves

Disruption risk conduction in the form of tsunami and waves has a fiercer start, and it is abrupt, difficult to predict and prevent. At the early stage, it has a strong penetra-tion and causes considerable damage. To illustrate, the financial crisis in Thailand had such obvious features of risk conduction, and it did spread to other Southeast Asian countries. The financial crisis first destroyed the economy in Southeast Asian countries, and then it penetrated the world financial system and affected the world economic growth. As a result of this, a number of enterprises closed down.

Disruption risk conduction in the form of tsunami and waves (see Figure 2.1) has the following characteristics: (1) sources—tsunami originates from a central point and spreads; (2) orientation—it takes the source as the center and the carrier as the medium, and spreads to other bordering areas and objects of resistance; (3) waves— the type of risk can release energy a number of times, which results in intense market fluctuation; and (4) weakening—disruption risk conduction in the form of tsunami and waves is extremely powerful and devastating, whose risk conduction follows the principle of approximating the strong but distancing the weak.

Disruption risk conduction in the form of chain reaction

Disruption risk conduction by way of a chain reaction is also called gradual strong risk conduction. This type of risk conduction causes a relatively minor damage at the beginning but the damage develops rapidly, and the destruction intensifies in the final stages. For instance, when coal prices in China go up, the

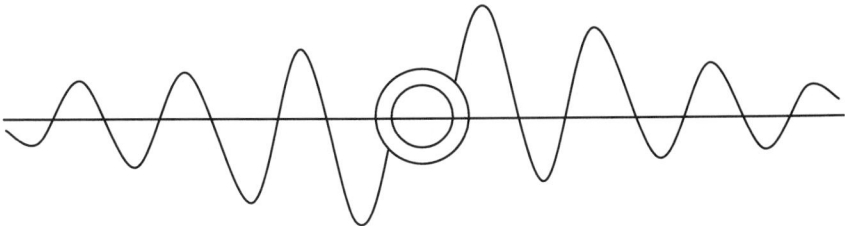

Figure 2.1 An illustration of disruption risk conduction in the form of tsunami and waves.

government may restrict electricity prices and hence the income of power generators may decline because of the higher expenditure on purchasing coal. Therefore, the power generators would rather generate less electricity and the gap between electricity available for enterprises and residents may result in some enterprises having to shut down.

Disruption risk conduction in the form of chain reaction has the following characteristics: (1) direction—if there is risk in supply chain links, it follows a certain direction and transmits along corresponding channels, affecting all economic entities in the specific direction; (2) fission—the supply chain system is enormous and sophisticated, and there are some active and influential factors contributing to a series of long-term effects on chain disruption risk conduction; for example, energy shortage or price rise is most likely to be the conduction factors in this type of risk; (3) complexity—the conduction processes and links related to this type of disruption risk tend to be more complex and mostly penetrate specific industries and areas; (4) strengthening—this type of disruption risk has a minor effect at the start, and the power increases in the final stages, following the conduction features of approximating the weak and distancing the strong.

Disruption risk conduction in the form of paths

Disruption risk conduction in the form of paths can be divided into single-path and multiple-path conduction and simple-path and complex-path conduction. From the perspective of risk prevention, disruption risk conduction can be further divided into series-connected and parallel-connected disruption risk conduction.

Some disruption risk conduction displays the feature of series connection, as illustrated in Figure 2.2. For instance, the price of raw material in the supply chain upstream rises swiftly, which brings risks to the manufacturing and operations in downstream enterprises. Series-connected disruption risk conduction has the following features: the conduction path is specific; the conduction process is time-dependent; and the risk control is uncertain.

Some disruption risk conductions display the feature of parallel connection, as illustrated in Figure 2.3. For example, supply chains encounter environmental risks such as earthquake, flood, great strikes induced by labor-and-capital conflicts, local conflicts, and wars. These factors not only contribute to disruption risk conduction in an industry and some departments, but also all industries, departments, and enterprises in the area. Parallel-connected disruption risk conduction is abrupt, with high risk and strong penetration, enormous damage, and an extensive conduction route.

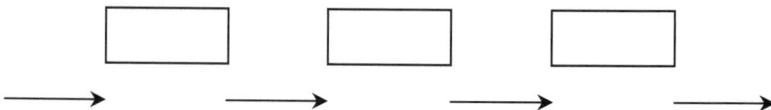

Figure 2.2 Disruption risk conductions in the form of series connection.

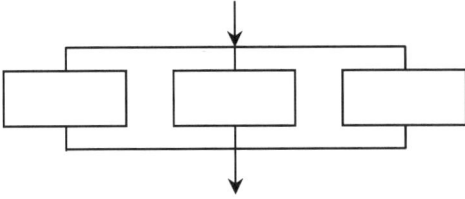

Figure 2.3 Disruption risk conductions in the form of parallel connection.

In addition, there is a mixed-risk conduction, which has the features of both series-connected and parallel-connected disruption risk conduction forms.

Risk conduction route variation of supply chain disruption

Supply chain disruption risk conduction paths are composed of a series of processes such as raw material supply chain, product manufacturing, and product distribution. Node enterprises closely connected in supply chains participate, and disruption risk of node enterprises transmits to other enterprises in supply chains. As the uncertainty of node enterprises in supply chains accumulates to a certain degree, the potential disruption risk depends on various risk carriers, and the original risk form along the supply chain or the new risk form after coupling mutation will transmit in supply chains, which destroy supply chain operation. As a result, disruption risk conduction routes are directions of risk conduction.

Supply chain disruption risk transmits through enterprises with minor resistance and forms coupling effects, which also affect enterprises with great initial resistance. After the coupling effects, new conduction routes emerge, whose range might be more extensive than the original paths. For this, in their article, 'To Study on Changing for Transmitting Path of the Supply Chain Risk', Cheng and Liu (2009) analyzed the launch and conduction of risk current and found the key paths of risk current conduction according to the dynamic changes of risk current in the conduction process. They also analyzed the new conduction paths caused by coupling effects.

Mechanisms of supply chain disruption risk route conduction

Accumulation and release of disruption risk flow

Supply chain disruption risk accumulation covers internal as well as external disruption risk. The release of supply chain disruption risks means that the risk within the system emits to the outside or transfers some risks, and the risk that does not emit remains within the system and accumulates and ultimately spreads to risk recipients. The release of disruption risk occurs when the quantity of risk accumulation or the speed of risk change exceeds the risk carrying limitation in supply chain systems or enterprises.

Selection mechanism of disruption risk conduction route

Owing to the complexity and correlation of conduction network, supply chain disruption risk conduction generally transmits in several directions. At first, it usually transmits and spreads to enterprises that are closely related, weak in risk resistance, and low in risk carrying capacity. This is called the minimum obstacle principle in enterprise risk conduction. The direction of disruption risk conduction follows business flow chain, profit chain, and value chain. The selection mechanism of disruption risk conduction paths is shown in Figure 2.4.

Route direction of supply chain disruption risk conduction

The supply chain disruption risk conduction is not random. It depends on a certain path with an obvious direction, as illustrated in Figure 2.5. Supply chain disruption risk conduction paths start from the risk source and reach the recipient enterprises. In the light of different disruption risk conduction routes, the conduction paths can be divided into the following types: forward conduction path, reverse conduction path, and radiating conduction path.

The forward conduction path demonstrates that the risk starts from suppliers and transmits to manufacturers and retailers, the downstream member enterprises. The path $A_2 \rightarrow B_2 \rightarrow C_4 \rightarrow D_5$ can be found in Figure 2.5. The reverse conduction path shows that the supply chain disruption risk starts from retailers, downstream member enterprises, and transmits to upstream enterprises, and the path $D_1 \rightarrow C_1 \rightarrow B_1 \rightarrow A_1$ can be found in Figure 2.5. Radiating conduction path illustrates that supply chain disruption risk starts from the core enterprises and transmits to the neighboring enterprises along supply chains, and the path $A_1 \rightarrow B_1 \rightarrow C_1$ can be found in Figure 2.5.

Coupling mechanism of disruption risk conduction

Supply chain disruption risk conduction is the "collaboration" of various subsystems in space and time in the conduction process. Every risk subsystem interacts and influences others, till the risk current integrates, strengthens, and weakens, or the risk mutates. The conditions for disruption risks to couple depend on the status of each risk subsystem, business connection of each function node enterprise, and the match among risk properties.

Analysis of supply chain disruption risk conduction routes

Supply chain supply chain disruption risk conduction routes' model

Assuming a supply chain network has N member enterprises, according to the selection model of disruption risk conduction routes, the preliminary conduction path selects the closely connected enterprises with minor risk resistant capacity, namely, $A_i (i = 1, 2, \ldots, n)$, as illustrated in Figure 2.5. According to

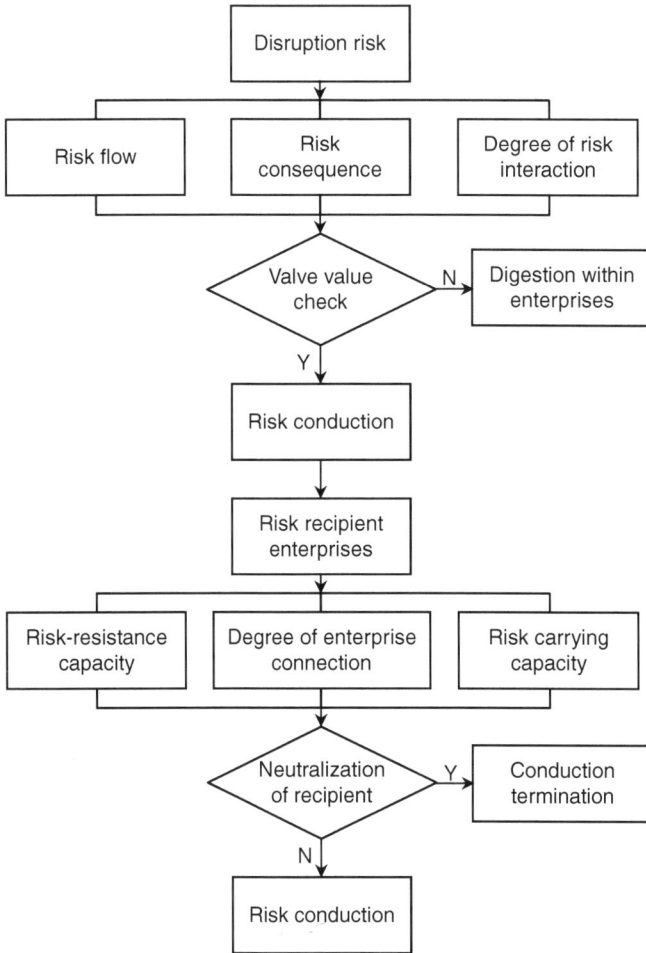

Figure 2.4 Selection mechanisms of disruption risk conduction paths.

disruption risk conduction system mechanism, assuming the category of risk subsystem is k, the k th risk subsystem value in Enterprise A_i is R_{Aik}. As each risk subsystem in Enterprise A_i couples and coupling effects occur in Enterprises A_i and A_j, disruption risk intensifies and exceeds the carrying limit θ_B of Enterprise $B_i(i = 1, 2, \ldots, m)$, which has stronger risk resistance, and hence the conduction routes expand further. Given that coupling effects continuously intensify, the conduction routes continue to extend to Enterprise C_i with much stronger risk resistance capacity, before N enterprises become the nodes in conduction routes, as illustrated in Figure 2.6. The model of supply chain disruption risk conduction paths can be found in Figure 2.6.

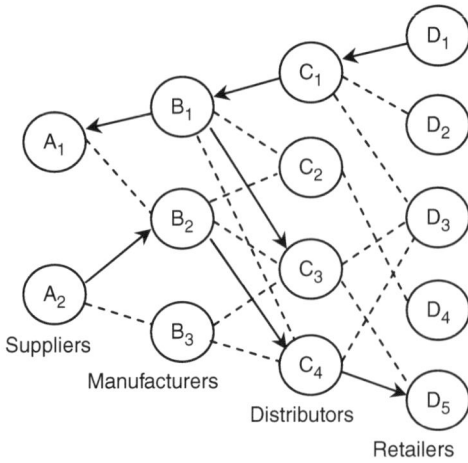

Figure 2.5 Disruption risk transmission paths.

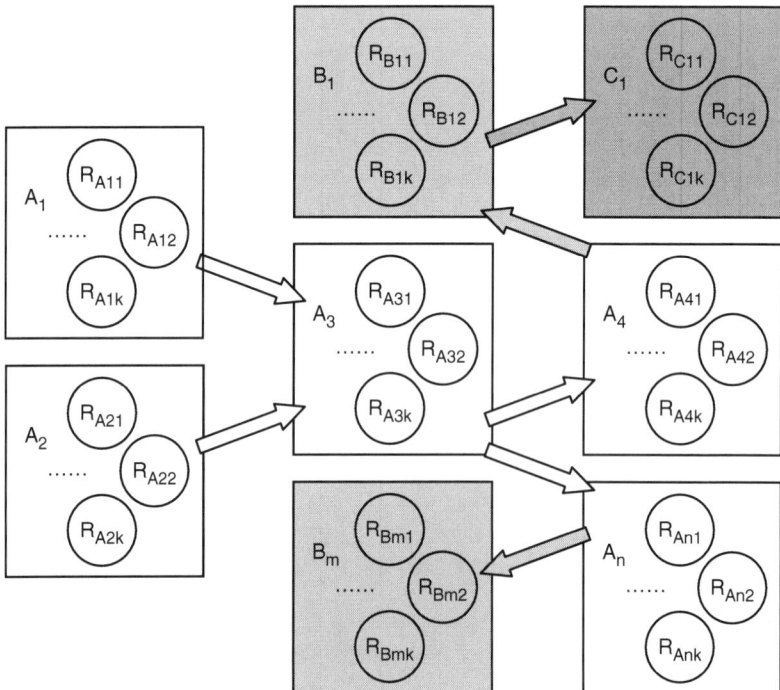

Figure 2.6 A model of supply chain disruption risk conduction routes.

Preliminary conduction route

The preliminary conduction route is the white block node A_i in Figure 2.6, which indicates that the capacity to resist disruption risk is low and risk value of type k is calculated by the nerve network.

In Figure 2.7, x_1, x_2, ..., x_n is input information value; Node k in the hidden stage is Type k sub-risk; and the output value in the hidden stage is risk value Y_k of Type k. The correlation weight between input and hidden stages is W_{ij}, and the correlation weight between hidden and output stages is V_{ij}. θ_j and Φ_i indicate the value of each node in the hidden and output stages, respectively. The input information value is entered from the input stage, and after it is transformed by the node function in the input and hidden stages, it is changed to output signal O_i.

The Sigmoid curve is applied into the node function:

$$f = \frac{1}{1 - e^x}$$

The disruption risk value without coupling effects is calculated, and the node output in the hidden stage is:

$$Y_i = f\left(\sum_{i=1}^{n} W_{ij} x_i - \theta_j\right) \tag{2-1}$$

Where W_{ij} is correlation weight and W_{ij} is node valve. As Type k disruption risk exceeds the carrying limit, the output value related to many risk subsystems is

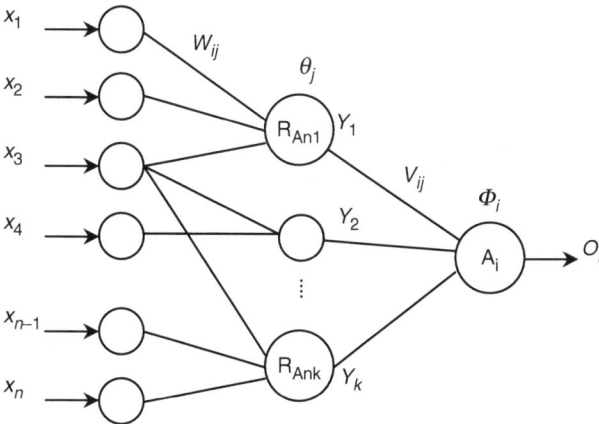

Figure 2.7 An illustration of supply chain disruption risk node nerve network.

exported and the overall disruption risk in enterprises is formed. Once the overall disruption risk exceeds the carrying limit of enterprises, risk conduction is exported and released from output nodes till it reaches the next node. The output node is:

$$O_i = f\left(\sum_{i=1}^{n} V_{ij} Y_i - \Phi_i\right) \tag{2-2}$$

The input information in each node comes from disruption risk information within node enterprises and the output information in the preceding node enterprise. The output information O_i in each Node A_i transmits to the next Node A_{i+1}.

Strong coupling effects in the conduction process

Coupling is an important property of disruption risk conduction change, including the inter-influence and interaction between the risk subsystem within enterprises and external enterprises, in the conduction process. The risk current contained in each risk transforms to some extent and the strong coupling effects expand conduction paths. The overall disruption risk of enterprises after coupling exceeds that before coupling. Disruption risk coupling in the conduction process accelerates the conduction and spread of risks. Here, risk coupling in the process of disruption risk conduction is further analyzed from the mathematical perspective.

If, at time t, there are two types of risk currents with different properties $R_{i(t)}$ and $R_{j(t)}$ within a supply chain disruption risk conduction system and strong coupling occurs in the conduction process, part of the risk current $R_{i(t)}$ is transformed into Current $R_{j(t)}$, and part of the risk current $R_{j(t)}$ is transformed into Current $R_{i(t)}$. Then the following is achieved:

$$\begin{cases} Y'_{i(t)} = Y_{i(t)} + \Delta E(i) \\ Y'_{j(t)} = Y_{j(t)} + \Delta E(j) \end{cases} \tag{2-3}$$

If the source energy is E_1, $R_{i(t)}$ is transformed into $R_{j(t)}$ and the target energy is βE_1; if the source energy is E_2, $R_{j(t)}$ is transformed into $R_{i(t)}$ and the target energy is γE_2; then the following is achieved:

$$\begin{cases} Y'_{i(t)} = Y_{i(t)} - E_1 + \gamma E_2 \\ Y'_{j(t)} = Y_{j(t)} - E_2 + \beta E_1 \end{cases} \tag{2-4}$$

As $Y_{i(t)} \neq 0$ and $Y_{j(t)} \neq 0$, make $\gamma_1 = \dfrac{E_1}{Y_{i(t)}}$, $\beta_1 = \dfrac{E_2}{Y_{j(t)}}$, then the following is achieved:

$$\begin{cases} Y'_{i(t)} = Y_{i(t)} - \gamma_1 Y_{i(t)} + \gamma \beta_1 Y_{j(t)} \\ Y'_{j(t)} = Y_{j(t)} - \beta_1 Y_{j(t)} + \beta \gamma_1 Y_{i(t)} \end{cases} \tag{2-5}$$

where β and γ_1 are risk correlation coefficients and their values depend on the business correlation of each function node attached by risks; and β_1 and γ_1 are risk exchange rates determined by their properties and risk match related to the risk current.

Risk coupling each time induces change of the risk current, which is uncertain and unpredictable. However, in each case, the coupling of risk current follows a certain principle. If two different risk currents $Y_{i(t)}$ and $Y_{j(t)}$ with different properties $R_{i(t)}$ and $R_{j(t)}$ increase, namely, $Y'_{i(t)} > Y_{i(t)}$ and $Y'_{j(t)} > Y_{j(t)}$, the following must be satisfied:

$$\Delta E(i) > 0 \text{ and } \Delta E(j) > 0$$

As $\Delta E(i) > 0$, $\Delta E(i) = -E_1 + \gamma E_2 = -\gamma_1 Y_{i(t)} + \beta_1 \gamma Y_{j(t)} > 0$, namely:

$$\frac{Y_{i(t)}}{Y_{j(t)}} < \frac{\beta_1 \gamma}{\gamma_1} \tag{2-6}$$

As $\Delta E(j) > 0$, $\Delta E(j) = -E_2 + \beta E_1 = -\beta_1 Y_{j(t)} + \beta \gamma_1 Y_{i(t)} > 0$, namely

$$\frac{Y_{i(t)}}{Y_{j(t)}} > \frac{\beta_1}{\beta \gamma_1} \tag{2-7}$$

Therefore, as $\dfrac{\beta_1}{\beta \gamma_1} < \dfrac{Y_{i(t)}}{Y_{j(t)}} < \dfrac{\beta_1 \gamma}{\gamma_1}$ is satisfied, strong coupling occurs in these two risk currents, and each risk current increases, and thus the total risk current grows.

New conduction route after strong coupling effects

After strong coupling effects, risk current increases. Output O'_i in Node A_i after strong coupling effects transmits to Enterprise B_i with strong risk resistance capacity. The new input from the external environment increases and changes the critical value, which originally has stable balance in Node B_i, and the original equilibrium is disrupted. As a result, Enterprise B_i, which had no risk release conduction originally, integrates the new risk and the previously accumulated risk R_{Bik} within, and the risk release conduction starts and the new risk conduction path emerges.

Summary

The key paths of disruption risk conduction changes dynamically, as time passes, and it has three stages. In the first stage, the risk transmits to enterprises with low risk resistance capacity, which is the preliminary risk conduction path. In the second stage, strong coupling happens in the risk conduction process, affecting enterprises with greater risk resistance capacity, which is the second risk conduction route. In the third stage, the risk continues to expand, and the original equilibrium in supply chain enterprises gets disrupted in succession, and thus the risk conduction path continues to extend.

The model of supply chain disruption conduction paths established here considers the conduction function among risk elements, and the description approximates the reality. It is conducive to finding the risk elements and node enterprises most threatening in the supply chain network, thus providing support for supply chain disruption risk management.

Risk conduction energy intensity evaluation of supply chain disruptions

Haddon (1970) proposed the energy release theory (ERT) for studying risks, and maintained that every system has a certain carrying limit. As the system energy exceeds the carrying limit, events occur and the system disintegrates. Supply chain disruption risks display the features of energy in the conduction process. To illustrate, the disruption of supply chains results in insufficient sales, which causes capital flows to decline, and thus enterprises find it difficult to operate and may even close down. Supply chain disruption risk can be prevented through energy control. In his PhD thesis entitled, 'Research on the Supply Chain Risk Transmission and Control', Qiu (2010) once constructed a model for analyzing supply chain risk conduction energy, and the functions were as follows. The factors that constitute supply chain risk conduction energy are analyzed; the relationships among affecting elements is simplified; the assessment dimension of supply chain risk conduction energy is reduced; and the vector model related to supply chain risk conduction energy is built on the basis of supply chain risk conduction energy standards to measure the energy volume in the risk conduction process. This can be used as reference to evaluate the supply chain disruption risk conduction energy.

Energy composition of supply chain disruption risk conduction

Energy is a concept in physics, which is universal in nature and every field. Any mechanical movement is displayed in the form of energy. To illustrate, molecule movement displays energy; movement of tangible objects shows mechanical energy; and the movement of particles with electricity displays electric power. By the same token, supply chain disruption risk conduction needs energy support. According to the three elements: risk factors, risk events, and risk results, supply chain disruption risk energy transmission can be represented by three indices: supply chain disruption risk current, the density of supply chain disruption risk current, and the transmitting speed of supply chain disruption risk current.

- Supply chain disruption risk current

  Current refers to the volume of current that flows through the horizontal dimension within units of time. Here, risk current is defined as the potential loss within a specific period of time as enterprises face a risk and do not take any measures. Supply chain disruption risk current refers to the potential loss, including economic loss, and reputation loss for enterprises, which can be represented as supply chain risk current (SCRC).

  As enterprises do not take any measures to effectively control disruption risks and bring loss to the supply chain, this can be called input supply chain disruption risk current, illustrated as $SCRC_I$. If the number of node enterprises that the input disruption risk current flows to is n, then it can be indicated by enterprise risk current (ERC), and the input disruption risk current faced by supply chain node enterprises is:

$$ERC_I = \frac{SCRC_I}{n} \tag{2-8}$$

If the input supply chain disruption risk current is fixed and the number of enterprises that receive input risk current increases, then the risk current is assigned within these enterprises and the disruption risk current faced by a single enterprise declines. As disruption risk transmits to another recipient, the current changes. Here, the remaining risk current after passing an enterprise is defined as output disruption risk current.

Factors that affect input supply chain disruption risk current are various and complicated. The risk current shaped by different disruption risks in different forms differs, but the input supply chain disruption risk current is the sum of each risk current. In terms of output supply chain disruption risk current, it also has a number of factors. For instance, risk resistance of node enterprises affects output supply chain disruption risk current directly. For this reason, three indices of measurement are summarized, as follows.

(1) *Disruption risk rejection rate:* It refers to the ratio between the risk current that enterprises send to risk initiators and the input risk current of risk recipients, illustrated by rejection (R). As risk recipients face the input disruption risk current, they do not accept all of them passively. On the contrary, due to the awareness of self-protection, they manage to feed back the risk current to the original risk initiators to prevent the invasion of risk current. In other words, they will return part of disruption risk to the senders.

(2) *Disruption risk absorption rate:* It refers to the ratio between the absorbed disruption risk current and the input disruption risk current, illustrated as absorption (A). As risk recipients face the input disruption risk current, for one thing, they reflect the risk current to risk senders; for another, the remaining risk current digests part of risk current by itself in order to reduce the risk current by taking some measures.

(3) *Disruption risk deportation ratio:* It refers to the risk current that deports risk recipients. In other words, it is the ratio between output disruption risk current and the input disruption risk current, illustrated by deportation (D). In terms of disruption risk recipients, not all risks can be digested or reflected by themselves in order to prevent supply chain disruption risk current from transmitting continuously, which is associated with risk types and risk resistance of risk recipients. Risk current not digested or reflected transmits continuously and enters the next node enterprise in supply chains.

Based on the preceding analysis, the following will be evidently achieved:

$$R + A + D = 1 \tag{2-9}$$

With respect to the single risk, the disruption risk current related to node enterprises in supply chain is linearly associated with A, R, and D. However, in terms of supply chain system, the risk current cannot add up the simple linear of each risk current. The main reason is that the supply chain system is made up of many member enterprises, and the disruption risk types are numerous and complicated. As such, as disruption risk transmits within the supply chain system, it is linked with risk resistance capacity of node enterprises and the degree of intersection among different disruption risks. To illustrate, various risks intrude supply chain synchronically, and risks affect each other; some risk current forms resonance and thus the input risk current increases significantly. On the contrary, the interaction among some risks might be offset, and the input supply chain risk current may decline. As a result, the supply chain disruption risk current does not completely depend on the risk itself; the organic whole composed of many risk currents also affects the current. In other words, the volume of the input supply chain disruption risk current is not a simple linear addition of various risk currents. If there are no linear correlations among input disruption risk currents, and the total number of disruption risks is m, then the input disruption risk current in a supply chain system can be considered as the vector sum of each input disruption risk current in the space of Dimension m, illustrated as $SCRC_I$. The vector function can be expressed as:

$$SCRC_I = (ERC_I^1, ERC_I^2, \ldots, ERC_I^j, ERC_I^m) \tag{2-10}$$

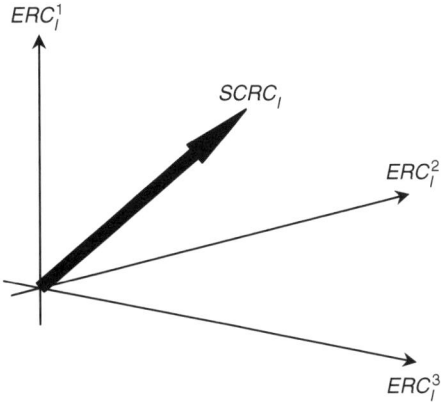

Figure 2.8 An illustration of supply chain disruption risk current vector.

ERC_I^j refers to the input disruption risk current related to Enterprise *J*; *j* can be from 1 to *m*; as *m* = 3, if these three risk currents have the same influence on supply chains, then the vector diagram can be shown as given in Figure 2.8:

- Density of supply chain disruption risk current

  The density of supply chain disruption risk current refers to the average input disruption risk current through supply chain node enterprises within a certain period of time, illustrated as ρ, and the following is achieved:

$$\rho = \frac{ERC_I}{\Delta t} \tag{2-11}$$

In the preceding equation, ERC_I is the input risk current of node enterprises in supply chain, and Δt is the total time. From this, as the time is fixed, if the density of input disruption risk current is significant, then the risk current faced by the node enterprises in supply chain is enormous.

- The transmitting speed of supply chain disruption risk current

  The fundamental principle of supply chain disruption risk current conduction is that there is risk energy gap between risk source and risk accommodation, which drives the risk to move from enterprises with huge risk energy to those with minor energy. The speed of supply chain disruption risk conduction is the number of node enterprises that the disruption risk passes within the unit time, illustrated as:

$$\gamma = \frac{n}{\Delta t} \tag{2-12}$$

In the preceding equation, γ is the transmitting speed of supply chain disruption risk, n is the number of supply chain node enterprises that disruption risk passes through, and Δt is the time spent by supply chain node enterprises for which disruption risk passed.

Input disruption risk current transmits within the supply chain system, whose transmitting speed is closely related to resistance within the system. The system obstruction mainly comes from the resistance of supply chain node enterprises against disruption risk current and the interaction among different risk currents. The conduction speed of supply chain disruption risk currents cannot be determined by the risk current itself; it is determined by the organic whole consisting of numerous risks. The transmitting speed of supply chain disruption risk current cannot be integrated and, therefore, the focus here is the transmitting speed of a certain disruption risk current. If the absorption rate or reflection rate is low, then the deportation rate increases and the radiation power grows, and vice versa. In terms of node enterprises with high disruption risk deportation rate, the risk absorption and reflection power are weak, and the obstacles weaken as the risk moves forward, and thus the speed of risk conduction accelerates.

Measurement of supply chain disruption risk transmission energy

Disruption risk factors contribute to disruption risk events, which result in disruption risk consequence. Supply chain disruption risk conduction brings loss to clients. As a result, energy measurement in disruption risk conduction can be expressed by the loss (L) that supply chain disruption risk brings to the clients, including three aspects: economic loss, the loss of product function, and reputation loss.

- Economic loss
  The economic loss induced by disruption risk can be illustrated by economic loss (L^E). The economic loss is associated with risk current intensity and output risk current, whereas the risk current intensity is linked with the density of risk currents and risk carrying capacity.

  The same disruption risk density has different risk intensities for different enterprises. Enterprises having strong risk resistance may not feel the intensity of the risk even when the risk current is significant, while enterprises with low risk resistance may experience huge risk intensity under similar circumstances.

  The loss brought by supply chain disruption risk to clients depends on the output risk current, and thus the economic loss brought by supply chain disruption risk to clients is as follows:

  $$L^E = \rho D \Delta t \qquad\qquad (2\text{-}13)$$

The meaning of symbols in Equation (2-13) is the same as the Equations (2-11) and (2-12), and D is the deportation rate of the disruption risk current in the supply chain system. The following is achieved:

$$D = \prod_{i=1}^{n} D_I^i \qquad (2\text{-}14)$$

In the equation, D_I^i is the absorption rate related to Node Enterprise i that supply chain disruption risk current passes, and n is the number of node enterprises that supply chain disruption risk current passes.

If the input disruption risk current is fixed, the loss brought to clients largely depends on the output risk current. In the case of different output risk currents and different risk carrying capacities related to node enterprises, the loss brought to clients varies. If carrying limit of disruption risk which a node enterprise can assume reaches the maximum, denoted as RCC. Disruption risk intensity is defined as the ratio between the input disruption risk current and disruption risk carrying capacity of node enterprises, denoted as Q; the input is I; and the output is O; and then:

$$Q_I = \frac{ERC_I}{RCC} \qquad (2\text{-}15)$$

In Equation (2-15), ERC_I is the input disruption risk current of Node Enterprise I, and Q_I is the input disruption risk current intensity of Node Enterprise I.

The intensity of output disruption risk current of node enterprises can be expressed as:

$$Q_O = \frac{ERC_O}{RCC} \qquad (2\text{-}16)$$

In Equation (2-16), Q_o is the intensity of the output disruption risk current, and:

$$Q_O = \frac{ERC_I \times D_I}{RCC} \qquad (2\text{-}17)$$

Based on the preceding analysis, the supply chain output disruption risk current can be expressed as follows:

$$SCRC_O = SCRC_I \times D \qquad (2\text{-}18)$$

The degree of economic loss brought to clients varies with different types of disruption risks, and some disruption risks might bring greater loss to clients while other disruption risks might bring only a minor loss to them. Hence, the loss brought to clients by supply chain risk could be further expressed as:

$$L_i^E = \sum_{j=1}^{m} \omega_i^e L_{ij}^e \tag{2-19}$$

- The loss of product function
  The loss of product function can be denoted as L_i^F, which refers to the negative effects of certain product aspects brought to clients by disruption risks related to supply chain enterprises, and it can show satisfying degrees of some product functions in relation to client demand. Different disruption risk brings different loss of product function to clients, and thus the loss of product function can be expressed as follows.

$$L_i^F = \sum_{h=1}^{m} \omega_i^f L_{ih}^f \tag{2-20}$$

- Reputation loss
  The reputation loss is denoted as L_i^S, which refers to the effects of disruption risk events on client psychology. It shows that clients lose confidence in supply chain enterprises, and they stop buying the products from the enterprises. This psychological influence might not be alleviated within a short period. The degrees of influence related to different disruption risk elements on supply chain enterprise reputation differ, which can be illustrated as:

$$L_i^S = \sum_{k=1}^{m} \omega_i^s L_{ik}^s \tag{2-21}$$

Hence, the supply chain disruption loss can be further expressed as:

$$L_i = (L_i^E, L_i^F, L_i^S)$$
$$= \left(\sum_{j=1}^{m} \omega_i^e L_{ij}^e, \sum_{h=1}^{m} \omega_i^f L_{ih}^f, \sum_{k=1}^{m} \omega_i^s L_{ik}^s \right) \tag{2-22}$$

In Equation (2-22), L_i^E, L_i^F, and L_i^S indicate the economic loss, the loss of production, and reputation loss brought by disruption loss in Type i, respectively; ω_i^e, ω_i^f, and ω_i^s indicate the degree of effects of disruption risk in Type i on economic loss, the loss of production function, and reputation loss, respectively; L_{ij}^e, L_{ih}^f, and L_{ik}^s indicate the economic loss assessed, the loss of product function, and reputation loss brought by disruption risk in Type i, respectively.

In order to have a better understanding of the loss brought by various disruption risks to the supply chain, loss induced by supply chain disruption risk can be expressed as follows, by calculating the length of the module related to disruption risk:

$$
\begin{aligned}
\| L_i \| &= \sqrt{(L_i^E)^2 + (L_i^F)^2 + (L_i^S)^2} \\
&= \sqrt{\left(\sum_{j=1}^{m} \omega_i^e L_{ij}^e\right)^2 + \left(\sum_{h=1}^{m} \omega_i^f L_{ih}^f\right)^2 + \left(\sum_{k=1}^{m} \omega_i^s L_{ik}^s\right)^2}
\end{aligned}
\tag{2-23}
$$

A model of energy vector analysis in supply chain risk transmission

- Introduction to models

Supply chain disruption risks can bring clients economic loss, the loss of production function, and reputation loss, and these three indices can reflect different aspects of loss and there is a positive connection among these three indices. In other words, the change in one index does not mean that the other two indices will change in the same direction.

Based on the preceding analysis, the following hypotheses are proposed:

(1) There is a non-linear connection between the economic loss, the loss of production function, and reputation loss brought by supply chain disruption risk to clients.
(2) As the supply chain disruption risk transmits, it has both volume and direction, i.e., a vector.

As a result of this, the vector diagram related to three-dimensional loss space can be constructed if the economic loss is Axis X; function loss is Axis Y; and reputation loss is Axis Z. Thus, the energy can be measured by loss as supply chain disruption risk transmits, which can be illustrated as $L = \overrightarrow{OA}$ (Figure 2.9).

In Figure 2.9, if the loss brought to clients as supply chain risk disruption in the transmitting process is located at point A, and the intersection angles between OA and X, Y, and Z are α, β, and δ, respectively, then the supply chain loss is expressed as follows:

$$
\begin{aligned}
L = \overrightarrow{OA} &= (x, y, z) \\
&= prj_x \overrightarrow{OA} + prj_y \overrightarrow{OA} + prj_z \overrightarrow{OA} \\
&= \| OA \| (i \cos \alpha + j \cos \beta + k \cos \delta)
\end{aligned}
\tag{2-24}
$$

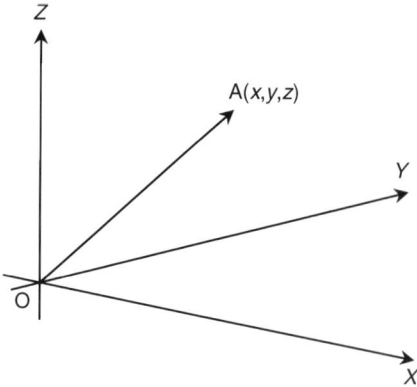

Figure 2.9 An illustration of supply chain disruption risk loss vector.

Therein, $\|OA\| = \sqrt{x^2 + y^2 + z^2}$, $\cos \alpha = \dfrac{x}{\|OA\|}$, $\cos \beta = \dfrac{y}{\|OA\|}$,

$\cos \delta = \dfrac{z}{\|OA\|}$; $prj_x \overrightarrow{OA}$, $prj_y \overrightarrow{OA}$, $prj_z \overrightarrow{OA}$ indicate the economic loss,

production function loss, and reputation loss brought by supply chain disruption risk to clients, namely, the projection of the vector OA in regard to Axes X, Y, and Z.

Therefore, if the economic loss, production function loss, and reputation loss brought by supply chain disruption risk to clients are known, then the loss volume and direction caused by supply chain disruption risk can be determined.

- Vector analytical model

In terms of the uncertain factors such as changes and time shift, the loss caused by supply chain disruption risk is likely to change. To illustrate, if the initial anticipated loss caused by supply chain disruption risk is located at Point A, it will arrive at Point B after a certain period of time, and hence the change of the loss related to supply chain disruption risk is expressed as follows:

$$\Delta L = \overrightarrow{OB} - \overrightarrow{OA} = \overrightarrow{AB} \qquad (2\text{-}25)$$

Therefore, the following is achieved:

$$\Delta L = \|AB\|(i \cos \alpha + j \cos \beta + k \cos \delta)$$

$$= \sqrt{(prj_x b - prj_x a)^2 + (prj_y b - prj_y a)^2 + (prj_z b - prj_z a)^2} \qquad (2\text{-}26)$$

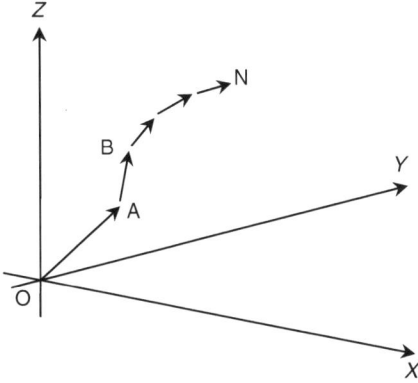

Figure 2.10 A change of supply chain disruption risk loss.

Therein, the conditions are: $\cos \alpha = \dfrac{prj_x b - prj_x a}{\| AB \|}$, $\cos \beta = \dfrac{prj_y b - prj_y a}{\| AB \|}$,

$\cos \delta = \dfrac{prj_z b - prj_z a}{\| AB \|}$.

Connect each point, and a smooth curved line is achieved (Figure 2.10), and the change of supply chain disruption risk loss is achieved. Since the supply chain disruption risk changes dynamically, it is important to ensure the dynamics and directions of supply chain disruption risk loss, and some effective measures can help minimize the disruption risk loss.

• The modification of the model related to supply chain disruption risk energy vector analysis

As mentioned in the preceding text, the input current of supply chain disruption risk is the premise for measuring supply chain disruption risk loss. The main reason is that the formation of risks is associated with various elements. Different elements exercise different effects on the disruption risk current. As analyzed earlier, the loss induced by supply chain disruption risk current in Type i, namely L_i^I, can be expressed as follows:

$$L_i^I = \left(\omega_{ij}^{Ie} L_{ij}^{Ie}, \omega_{ij}^{If} L_{ij}^{If}, \omega_{ij}^{Is} L_{ij}^{Is} \right) \tag{2-27}$$

In the preceding equation, ω_{ij}^{Ie}, ω_{ij}^{If}, and ω_{ij}^{Is} indicate the degree of effects of Type j risk element in Type i disruption risk current on economic loss, production function loss, and reputation loss; L_{ij}^{Ie}, L_{ij}^{If}, and L_{ij}^{Is} show the assessed value of Type j risk element in Type i disruption risk current in relation to economic loss, product function loss, and reputation loss.

Thus, the loss vector model of supply chain input disruption risk current can be modified as follows:

$$L_I = \parallel SCRC_I \parallel \left(\omega_i^{le} L_i^{le}, \omega_i^{lf} L_i^{lf}, \omega_i^{ls} L_i^{ls} \right)$$

$$= \left(prj_x \overrightarrow{SCRC_I} + prj_y \overrightarrow{SCRC_I} + prj_z \overrightarrow{SCRC_I} \right)$$

$$\left(\omega_i^{le} L_i^{le}, \omega_i^{lf} L_i^{lf}, \omega_i^{ls} L_i^{ls} \right) \tag{2-28}$$

In practice, the loss of supply chain disruption risk depends on the output current of supply chain risks, and the output current is associated with the risk deportation rate. Hence:

$$L_O = SCRC_I D_I^i \tag{2-29}$$

The calculation of deportation rate is achieved by fuzzy assessment or based on empirical studies. Consider that the output risk current formed by different types of disruption risk might be the same, but the economic loss, production function loss, and reputation loss induced are different. That is to say, there is a gap as the supply chain output disruption risk current is transformed into economic loss, production function loss, and reputation loss, and the transformation efficiency coefficient can be denoted as μ, and thus a general model of supply chain output disruption risk current loss can be expressed as:

$$L_i^o = SCRC_I D_I^i \left(\mu_{ij}^{oe} \omega_{ij}^{le} L_{ij}^{le}, \mu_{ij}^{of} \omega_{ij}^{lf} L_{if}^{lf}, \mu_{ij}^{os} \omega_{ij}^{ls} L_{ij}^{ls} \right)$$

$$\omega_{ij}^{le} + \omega_{ij}^{lf} + \omega_{ij}^{ls} = 1 \tag{2-30}$$

$$\mu_{ij}^{oe} + \mu_{ij}^{of} + \mu_{ij}^{os} = 1$$

In the preceding equation, the meaning of $\omega_{ij}^{le}, \omega_{ij}^{lf}, \omega_{ij}^{ls}$ and $L_{ij}^{le}, L_{ij}^{lf}, L_{ij}^{ls}$ is the same as Equation (2-27), and μ_{ij}^{oe}, μ_{ij}^{of}, and μ_{ij}^{os} indicate the transformation rate of Type j risk element in Type i output disruption risk current in relation to economic loss, product function loss, and reputation loss.

Summary

This section mainly analyzes the fundamental elements and transmitting energy in relation to supply chain disruption risk conduction. Through direct calculation methods, some relevant concepts are provided, such as risk current, the density of risk current, risk deportation rate, risk absorption rate, risk feedback rate, and enterprise risk carrying capacity. A model of energy vector for measuring supply chain disruption risk conduction is constructed, including the economic loss, product function loss, and reputation loss brought by supply chain disruption risk to clients. As a result of this, the degree of influence of different risk elements and the index of risk current transformation rate are introduced for the reason that there is inconsistency of the risk elements on disruption risk current. The model is modified, and ultimately the general energy vector model in supply chain risk conduction is achieved.

Conclusion

With the global economic integration, the forms of enterprise disruption risk conduction display the features of network, diversity, and complexity. The enterprises are supposed to be aware of the domestic and international disruption risk conduction. They are supposed to dredge disruption risk in macro and micro environments, strengthen and improve the prevention mechanism of disruption risk conduction, and thus enable enterprises to avoid twists and turns and have positive growth.

Supply chain disruption risk might emanate from without the supply chain system, namely, environment risk. The risk might come from the exterior of enterprises and the interior of supply chains: supply risk and demand risk. In addition, the risk might derive from the interior of enterprises: process risk and control risk.

Supply chain disruption risk conduction refers to the process in which the risk is released by the source in the external environment and the internal system. It is attached to tangible objects and intangible effects and passes or spreads to the function node and flow of each business in supply chain through a certain path or channel. It spreads or amplifies gradually as time passes, which might endanger the overall supply chain network, and thus the manufacturing and operational activities in supply chain enterprises deviate from the anticipated target and suffer loss. This is the disruption risk conduction within supply chain enterprises, and it also includes the external conduction of disruption risk among enterprises.

In a narrow sense, supply chain disruption risk refers to the process in which uncertain disruption risk source is attached to risk carriers in the manufacturing and operational processes of enterprises through a certain path or channel and transmit and spread to the node and flow of profit-related functions in enterprises, and thus the supply chain disruption risk expands and results in loss.

In a broad sense, there is a profit relationship among supply chain enterprises, and thus there is definitely correlation of disruption risk among supply chain enterprise groups that constitute profit chains. The disruption risk induced by one enterprise in supply chain affects the associated enterprises, and even spreads to the overall supply chain network, thus forming disruption risk conduction flow among enterprises. Supply chain disruption risk conduction is not only a process of physical activities, but also economic activities. The disruption risk conduction not only transmits risk itself but also spreads risk-related environmental elements, such as concepts, behavior orientation, and network.

Supply chain disruption risk conduction is random, abrupt, connected, non-linear, path-dependent, risk changeable, and irreversible. In the light of different stages of disruption risk conduction, the supply chain disruption risk conduction can be divided into two tiers: disruption risk conduction within and outside enterprises. In terms of different characteristics of disruption risk conduction, supply chain disruption risk can be divided into risk conduction in the form of bubble evaporation, element scarcity, structure collapse, tsunami and waves, chained reaction, and paths. The process of supply chain disruption risk conduction includes the key conduction elements such as risk origins, risk current, risk carriers, risk conduction paths, risk valve value, risk events, and risk subsystems.

The key paths of supply chain disruption risk conduction shift with passage of time and have several stages. In the first stage, the risk conduction occurs in the enterprises with low risk resistance capacity, which becomes the primary risk conduction path. In the second stage, strong coupling takes place in the process of risk conduction, and it spreads to enterprises with stronger risk resistance capacity, which becomes the second risk conduction path. In the third stage, the risk expands continuously, and the original equilibrium in supply chain is damaged continuously, and thus the risk disruption path continues to extend. Here, the path model constructed in relation to supply chain disruption risk conduction considers the conduction function among risk factors, and thus the description of supply chain disruption risk conduction is closer to reality, which is conducive to discovering the most powerful risk elements and node enterprises in the supply chain network, and provides support for the management of supply chain disruption risks.

The energy of supply chain disruption risk conduction represents the loss brought by supply chain disruption risk to enterprises, including the economic loss, production function loss, and reputation loss. The integrated analysis of the structural characteristics of supply chains and the consequence brought by the outbreak of supply chain disruption risk help refine the energy assessment index related to supply chain disruption risk conduction, including the current, the density, and transmitting speed of supply chain disruption risk. These three assessment indices resolve the problem of selecting different indices because of different supply chain enterprises, which are universal.

On the basis of the three dimensions of supply chain economic loss, product function loss, and reputation loss, the fundamental elements and transmitting energy of supply chain disruption risk conduction are analyzed. The relevant concepts such as risk current, the density of risk current, risk deportation rate, risk absorption rate, risk feedback rate, and risk carrying capacity of enterprises are measured through direct calculation methods. The energy vector model for measuring supply chain disruption risk conduction is constructed. At the same time, the degree of effects of risk elements and the transformation efficiency rate index of risk current are introduced, and thus the general energy vector model of supply chain disruption risk conduction has been built.

3 The loss assessment methods of supply chain disruptive events

Introduction

The supply chain comprises the core enterprises which range from purchasing raw materials to manufacturing intermediate products and the finished products, and the network consists of suppliers, manufacturers, distributors, and retailers. There are many links between purchasing, manufacturing, processing, and sales, along with logistics, capital flow, and information flow. With the development of the theory and practice of supply chain management, its complexity and uncertainty is also increasing; vulnerability of supply chains and the disruptions they suffer have attracted increasing attention in recent years.

The lean production and just-in-time theories require enterprises to eliminate waste, reduce inventory, and cut the time of manufacturing and logistics, so that the cost can be reduced and the goal of maximizing profits can be realized. Undoubtedly, this model has its advantages in a stable market environment. However, as the fluctuations of demand and supply and uncertainty increase, the supply chain becomes fragile due to lack of sufficient resilience.

In order to cut the cost, many supply chain enterprises choose to centralize manufacturing. In other words, they produce products with less diversity in a certain place to achieve economies of scale. However, the disruption risk in relation to production and transportation is evident in such cases.

Reduction of the number of suppliers has always been regarded as a major method to optimize supply chain and improve purchasing efficiency, with the purpose of cutting management costs and accelerating information exchange and transmission. This also helps boost the ability for price negotiation, and, therefore, this (lower number of suppliers) has become a tendency. Nonetheless, the reduction in the number of suppliers increases the uncertainty of purchasing. Once there are problems related to product quality or supplies, the manufacturers are passive.

As the vulnerability of the supply chain grows and economic globalization and outsourcing tendency increase, collaboration among supply chain enterprises is strengthening and supply chain network structures are becoming increasingly complicated. Each member in a supply chain network constitutes one node and depends on and influences all others, and hence any disruption event affects all nodes rapidly. In addition, it spreads to the entire network and causes loss to supply chain enterprises.

Here, the focus is on assessment of the loss caused by a supply chain disruption event, and the intrinsic principle of the loss spreading along supply chains is illustrated and the assessment methods are provided. Therefore, supply chain enterprises can assess the loss and relevant effects induced by disruptive events, and effective measures can then be taken to reduce the loss.

The basic loss assessment models of supply chain disruptive events

Features of supply chain disruptive events

- Abruptness
  When supply chain disruptive events occur, the process is extremely rapid. It is difficult to predict and accurately grasp the information related to the time, place, manner, and degree of explosion of supply chain disruptive events. It is hard to anticipate the cause, actual scale, status change, development tendency, and degree and extent of effects in relation to disruptive events.
- Destruction
  Once the supply chain disruptive events occur, they have different degrees of negative effects marked by enterprise property loss, production breakdown, and personal safety. The direct effect induced by supply chain disruptive events is the economic loss, which might endanger the enterprise brands or reputation. If they are not treated properly, they can devastate the enterprises, and even influence the existence and development of the enterprises.
- Urgency
  After the supply chain disruptive events, it is necessary for enterprise decision-makers to take countermeasures swiftly and immediately, and make every effort to reduce the loss and prevent the loss from spreading. As the supply chain disruption event develops and evolves, the negative effects induced increase; as time passes, the supply, production, and sales of enterprises might get disrupted. In the treatment of supply chain disruptive events, time management determines the effectiveness of management to a great extent.
- Spreading
  To some extent, supply chain disruptive events often create huge damage, which can spread to a wider range within a short period of time, and thus give rise to more serious and extensive destruction and secondary disasters. If the supply chain disruptive events are more serious, the range of destruction and effects tend to grow.

- Linkage/diffusivity
  After supply chain disruptive events emerge, their effects cannot be limited within enterprises. Nonetheless, they interact among enterprises within the supply chain network, and extend in the dimensions of time, space, and depth. A supply chain disruption in one single enterprise affects its own industries or other industries. Supply chain disruption risk in regions might evolve into supply chain disruptive events worldwide.
- Complexity
  Supply chain disruptive events have their own characteristics and generating mechanisms, and the relevant affecting factors are numerous. However, the effects of factors are difficult to measure, which brings considerable uncertainty. The process and evolution of supply chain disruptive events are sophisticated, and display the complex features of the dynamic system.
- Difficult to predict
  The probability of supply chain disruption risk is low, and it is difficult to describe its probability and distribution status. Therefore, it is difficult to predict and prevent it effectively.

The characteristics of loss assessment related to supply chain disruptive events

Supply chain disruptive events often have small probability but with huge impact. Some supply chain disruptive events occur and evolve. Although some might follow some known patterns, the event probability is still small, and it is difficult to accurately predict the time of emergence, the range of influence, and duration. Therefore, managers do not have enough understanding about the principles of evolution of supply chain disruptive events. The effects of supply chain disruptive events are extensive, not confined to one enterprise in the supply chain. As the disruptive events are serious, many functions of a number of node enterprises in supply chains might lose effects simultaneously and cause loss.

As supply chain disruptive events have small probability and significant influence, facing the potential loss related to the enterprises, managers in supply chain enterprises are supposed to encounter some uncertain problems.

- No general definite expressions
  The process of incurring of loss caused by supply chain disruptive events to enterprises is affected by changes in supply chain structure and coping strategies. Nonetheless, it is difficult to mathematically express how these factors specifically affect the performance levels.

  These three factors are extremely complicated, without any indices for direct measurement. In specific supply chain disruptive events, these three factors cover different contents. The measurement indices related to supply chain disruptive events in different industries and types might not be the same. To illustrate, in terms of the coping strategy of supply chains, different strategies can affect the potential loss induced by supply chain disruptive events differently. Some need to transfer demand realization and some need to expand supply realization. Therefore, the coping strategies cannot achieve the same results and functions after the objects change. Although these major factors have been examined in the literature, there are very few consistently acknowledged measurement indices.

Furthermore, these three factors are not totally independent. As supply chain disruptive events induce loss to enterprises, a certain factor, which enterprises focus on to take corresponding measures, might change other factors. For instance, to initiate the backup suppliers or the contingent purchase after the supply chain disruptive events happen means that the structure of supply chains has changed: there is one more upstream supplier.

- Continuity
  In the process of supply chain disruptive events bringing loss to enterprises, each factor often has a continuous effect on the loss, which cannot terminate the influence instantly and penetrate the whole process. For instance, if enterprises do not take coping measures in response to a disruptive event within a reasonable time, the measures do not have any effect on the potential loss of enterprises. For example, if a power supply system encounters freezing rain and the power supply is shut off because electric cables are covered with ice, the electricity company will send repairmen to remove the ice on the electric cables. Here, the effects of the measures will continue until the overall attacking process is over.

  The duration of supply chain disruptive events varies. In the process of responding to the event, the starting and terminating times of the three major factors differ, with different durations. In some stages, single factors might take effect; in others, multiple factors might take effect.

- Aftereffects
  Aftereffects mean that once the status of a certain stage is fixed, on the basis of each status and decision in the previous stage, the next stage will spread and evolve. In other words, the future is associated with the past. The process in which supply chain disruptive events affect supply chains can be divided into many stages, and the enterprise performance status, in a later stage, further develops on the basis of the three affecting factors in the previous stage. That is to say, the preliminary performance level in a late stage is the ultimate performance level in the previous stage.

- Information incompleteness
  Characteristics of the supply chain disruptive events with small probability constrain the emergency management capacity of enterprises in relation to identification, judgment, and treatment. Owing to the limitations related to the level of information sharing and collaboration in the node enterprises in supply chains, enterprises obtain incomplete information in the process of the loss caused by supply chain disruptive events. With the derivation of supply chain disruptive events, the information obtained by enterprises will update and increase.

Fundamental models

As supply chain disruptive events have small probability and huge influence, it is difficult to predict their intensity, impact, and duration. Nevertheless, in the light of the current information, it is likely to anticipate and predict the likely future performance within a short period of time by taking appropriate measures. As information gradually increases and updates, the previous prediction can be modulated and approximated for estimating the potential development tendency in the future. Thus, supply chain enterprises can predict the loss induced by disruptive events, and take appropriate measures.

Before assessing the effects induced by disruptive events, some safe hypotheses can be made to construct models of effects brought by supply chain disruptive events to enterprises (as outlined in the master degree thesis entitled, 'Research on the Loss Assessment of Emergencies in Supply Chain' (Dong, 2011)).

1. Except the changes of supply chain structure, coping strategy, and supply chain disruptive events themselves, other factors do not have effects on the loss process related to supply chain disruptive events.
2. Before supply chain disruptive events happen, the performance of supply chain node enterprises is normal.
3. As the node enterprises are in the recovery stage after the disruptive events, the events do not occur in node enterprises again.
4. Each affecting factor might have an impact on enterprises in the same period, but it will not change simultaneously.

Performance targets of supply chain enterprises can be diverse, and they can collide with one another and can also be divided into different stages. In the light of different targets of supply chain enterprises, the assessment with multiple variables can be applied to performance from many perspectives (Choi and Krause, 2006).

Performance evaluation shows the operation level and profitability of supply chain enterprises; assessment indices might include sales volume, sales, production, and profit margin. Performance targets of enterprises affected by disruptive events might differ from targets in normal operational periods. Here, the common target is to make every effort to ensure normal operations.

As enterprises are attacked by supply chain disruptive events, their performance levels might alter and deviate from the normal range. As time passes, supply chain disruptive events might further deteriorate the performance of enterprises. However, they might recover gradually with the efforts made by enterprises, thus reaching a new stable status, as illustrated in Figure 3.1.

In the preceding figure, p is the performance of supply chain enterprises; different enterprises have different and diverse targets, and thus the indices to measure performance are not the same. Production, sales volume, and sales can be used as indices, and sales volume, cost, and other financial targets can be integrated. p_0 is the warning levels of performance; as performance levels are below

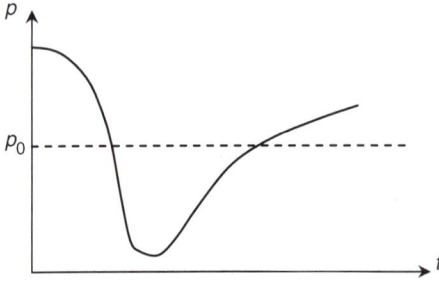

Figure 3.1 Effects of disruptive events.

the warning levels, supply chain enterprises will have early warnings, and the corresponding measures should be taken to deal with supply chain disruptive events, and *t* indicates time.

As mentioned earlier, in the process of being attacked by supply chain disruptive events, three major factors affect the loss, and then the basic loss assessment model of supply chain disruptive events can be expressed as follows:

$$p = f(X,Y,Z) \tag{3-1}$$

In this equation, X is the first type of factor—supply chain structure; Y indicates the second type of factor—coping strategies, including early warning and recovery capability; Z indicates the third type of factor—the development status of supply chain disruptive events themselves.

In reality, the sequence of these three major factors affecting supply chain disruptive events is not the same. On some occasions, the single effect happens; on other occasions, the three factors impact the supply chain simultaneously.

Summary

Supply chain disruptive events are abrupt, destructive, urgent, spreading, chained/diffusive, complicated, and unpredictable. The loss assessment of supply chain disruptive events does not have general definite expressions; it has features of continuity, aftereffects, and information incompleteness. Although supply chain disruptive events have small probability and huge influence, the construction of the loss assessment models of supply chain disruptive events enables supply chain enterprises to anticipate and predict their performance development within a short period of time in future.

The loss assessment methods of supply chain disruptive events—method of superposition

By decomposing the process—in which disruptive events bring loss to enterprises—into several stages, the superposing method can be used to analyze each stage from three aspects: supply chain structure, coping strategy, and the supply chain disruptive events themselves. The time nodes related to the changes in affecting factors are identified. After analysis of single factors within every two time nodes (i.e., within the assessment stages) is implemented, the function expressions related to the performance level that change trajectory in the next stage are further anticipated. Also, the superposition happens based on analysis of the previous assessment stage. At the same time, the information rolls and updates, and the prediction is further modified (Dong, 2011). The flow of this method is illustrated in Figure 3.2.

1. Event stage
    In the method of superposition, supply chain disruptive events of enterprises can be divided into five stages: preparatory stage, reaction stage, coping stage, recovery stage, and termination stage. These five stages are called event stages, illustrated as $S_i, i = 1,2,3,4,5$.
2. Assessment stage
    After the stage of defining events, within each event stage, the starting point is the supply chain structure, coping strategies, and supply chain disruptive events themselves, and the time node is searched when factors change, and then the affecting factor is determined. The duration of every two adjacent time nodes is called the assessment stage, denoted by $S_{i,j}, i = 1,2,3,4,5 \ j = 1,2,3....$ The two adjacent assessment stages are differentiated by the time node when a factor changes, and thus it is possible to analyze the single factor within the assessment stages.

    In stage S_3 of the impact of supply chain disruptive events on enterprises, features and specific circumstances of supply chain disruptive events, the supply chain structure, coping strategies of enterprises, and supply chain disruptive events themselves are analyzed first. Then the time nodes are searched when these factors change, for example, when the backup suppliers are initiated for supply, or when the new pricing strategies of transferring product demand are implemented. These nodes are assessed by examining whether the three affecting factors, the supply chain structure, coping strategies of enterprises, and supply chain disruptive events themselves, change or not. These nodes divide the event stage S_3 into some assessment stages, illustrated as $S_{3,1}, S_{3,2},...,S_{3,j},...,S_{3,n}$, where $n = 1,2,3,....$ The initial status of enterprise performance in assessment stage $S_{3,j+1}$ is the final status of the assessment stage $S_{3,j}$. As the time nodes are sufficient, the event stage S_3 can be divided delicately enough. Therefore, as the assessment stage $S_{3,j}$ develops into assessment stage $S_{3,j+1}$, only one factor influences the loss caused by the disruptive events, and thus it is likely to achieve short-term

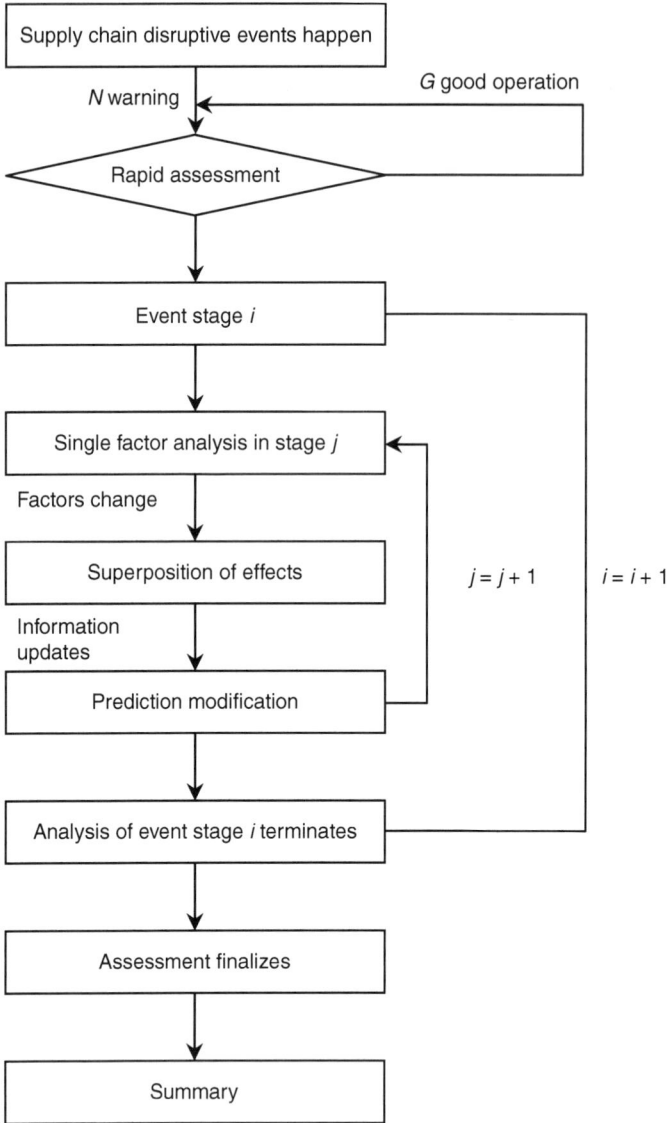

Figure 3.2 The flow of the superposition method.

prediction. If the dividing point between $S_{3,j}$ and $S_{3,j+1}$ is the time node of implementing strategy M, then M is any specific strategy or circumstance of factors: supply chain structure, coping strategy, and supply chain disruptive events themselves, such as the time node when some new pricing strategy is used to transfer the product demand.

3. Rapid assessment

    It is not practical to predict the future tendency over a long period of time. Rapid assessment means the predicted time is divided into extremely short periods. The division of assessment stages makes it possible to analyze the single factor. Rapid assessment means it is likely to have short-term predictions. Here, supply chain enterprises may select appropriate indices to measure their own performance levels and fluctuation range in light of their own industries.

4. Superposition

    The division of assessment stages makes it possible to analyze the single factors in the assessment stages. The aftereffects in relation to loss assessment of supply chain disruptive events are then used to superpose the results of the single factor analysis in a late assessment stage with the assessment results in the previous stage, and thus the short-term prediction in relation to enterprise performance is achieved. As discussed earlier, in the process of supply chain disruptive events affecting enterprises, performance level affected by supply chain structure is X, enterprise coping strategy is Y, and supply chain disruptive events themselves are Z within $S_{i,\,j+1}$, and it is associated with the status in the previous assessment stage $S_{i,j}$, as illustrated in Figure 3.3.

$$p_{i,j+1} = f_{i,j+1}(f_{i,j}, \theta_1 X + \theta_2 Y + \theta_3 Z) \tag{3-2}$$

Therein, i indicates the serial number of the event stage; j indicates the serial number of assessment stage; $p_{i,j+1}$ indicates the enterprise performance level of the event stage i in assessment stage j; θ_1, θ_2, and θ_3 are coefficients, in which only one coefficient is 1 and the other two coefficients are both 0. The reason is that only one factor changes in the two adjacent assessment stages.

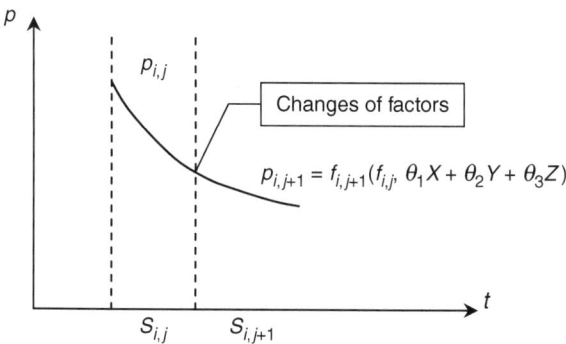

Figure 3.3 An illustration of superposition.

5. Information scrolling and updating
    Scrolling is the continuity of short-term prediction. There is a gap between
    the prediction functions and the actual tendency of performance levels of
    supply chain enterprises. Within each assessment stage, enterprises can
    obtain the information regarding the status of disruptive events, operation
    of enterprises themselves, and other node enterprises in supply chains, with
    the development of supply chain disruptive events. Supply chain enterprises
    can update the operating data (such as inventory volume) and productivity of
    suppliers and transportation time, among others. In the light of the updated
    information, the function expression $f_{i,j}$ regarding the short-term prediction
    trajectory of the current operating status in enterprises can be modified, and
    then the new prediction function $g_{i,j}$ is achieved.
    On the basis of superposition of single factors, the information scrolls and
    updates, and the short-term prediction function of the performance related to
    supply chain enterprises are modified. Thus, the short-term prediction func-
    tion can be appropriate in terms of the actual tendency of the performance
    levels of supply chain enterprises, as illustrated in Figure 3.4. According to
    the real-life circumstances, supply chain enterprises can update their data and
    determine their scrolling periods by themselves.

The loss assessment procedures of supply chain disruptive events

As disruptive events bring loss to supply chain enterprises, the loss process can
be divided into several stages. The event stages can be further divided into
many delicate assessment stages, with the purpose of analyzing single factors
in the target assessment stages. They can be superposed with the analytical
results of the previous assessment stage, and thus the performance tendency of
supply chain enterprise over a short period of time can be predicted. The mathematical expressions of performance-level trajectory of changes can be
achieved (Dong, 2011). Supply chain enterprises can update information by

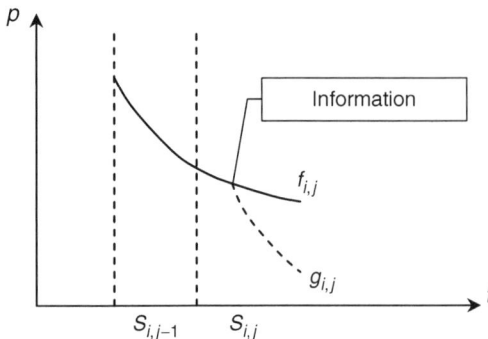

Figure 3.4 An illustration of rolling and updating.

Division stage	Short-term assessing	Scroll and update	Loss analysis	Summary

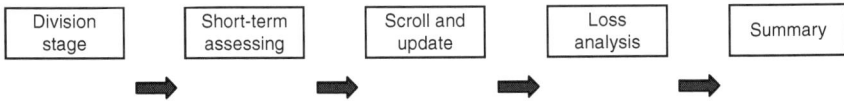

Figure 3.5 Loss assessment stage in supply chain disruptive events.

themselves according to the real circumstances. The mathematical expressions can be further modified, and thus more accurate prediction function can be achieved.

Loss assessment of supply chain disruptive events can be decomposed into five stages: division stage–short-term assessment–scrolling and updating–loss analysis–summary, as illustrated in Figure 3.5.

Stage one—division stage

The process in which supply chain disruptive events affect enterprises can be divided into five stages, whose terminating point might be within the reaction period or the coping period. These five stages are called event stages and are illustrated as S_i, $i = 1,2,3,4,5$, according to chronological sequence. The specific division varies with the gap among supply chain disruptive events, as illustrated in Figures 3.6 and 3.7.

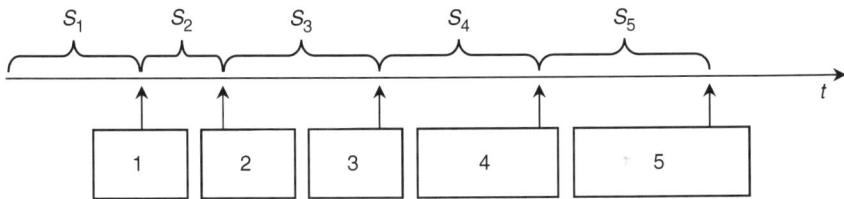

Figure 3.6 Type one of division of event stages (1: outbreak of disruptive events; 2: termination of disruptive events; 3: early warnings of enterprises; 4: the increased range and speed of performance of enterprise have reached the standards; 5: the performance of enterprises recovers and reaches the new stable level).

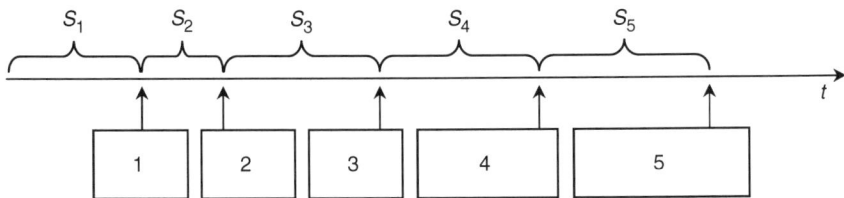

Figure 3.7 Type two of division of event stages (1: outbreak of disruptive events; 2: early warnings of enterprises; 3: termination of disruptive events; 4: the increased range and speed of performance of enterprise have reached the standards; 5: the performance of enterprises recovers and reaches the new stable level).

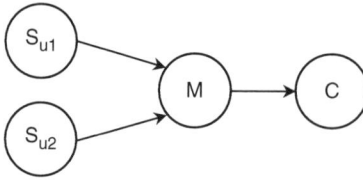

Figure 3.8 An illustration to supply chain structure.

Here, consider two suppliers, a single manufacturer, and terminal consumers as a simple supply chain, as shown in Figure 3.8.

Where S is supplier; M is manufacturer, and C is client. Manufacturer M has two suppliers: S_{u1} and S_{u2}; the terminal clients of the supply chain is C; and each node indicates one enterprise in the supply chain. Manufacturer M purchases 80% of its raw materials from supplier S_{u1} and the remaining 20% is purchased from supplier S_{u2}. Its primary performance target is to ensure production.

Fire broke out in the factory of supplier S_{u1} in relation to manufacturer M, but was extinguished by the supplier on the same day. However, 70% of the machinery was destroyed, and thus productivity was considerably affected. It was impossible to offer manufacturer M raw materials as per the original plan. Supplier S_{u1} did not inform manufacturer M in time. The manufacturer has some stored materials, and, as a result, its production was not prominently affected. Here, manufacturer M did not feel the impact of the disruptive event. As the inventory drops, manufacturer M sends warnings and starts to take coping measures and contacts supplier S_{u2} swiftly. It sends rush orders to purchase urgently. In the case of coping strategy, which has nothing to do with supply chain structure, the supply of raw materials for enterprises can be guaranteed to some extent. As the productivity of supplier S_{u1} starts to recover, recovery of raw material supply for manufacturer M speeds up, and ultimately the production returns to normal range.

Here, the supply chain disruptive event is the outbreak of fire in the factory of supplier S_{u1}, whose impact on the manufacturer can be decomposed into five event stages, illustrated as S_i, $i = 1,2,3,4,5$, and the unit time is defined as days, as shown in Figure 3.9.

Stage two—short-term assessment

In stage one, the loss induced by the supply chain disruptive event can be divided over five event stages, and from three factors: supply chain structure, enterprise coping measures, and supply chain disruptive events themselves. In each event stage, the time is regarded as the node when factors change. Each event stage is further decomposed into many assessment stages, and the short-term assessment is implemented in the assessment stage, which is superposed with the analytical results of the previous assessment stage. Thus, the loss processes related to supply chain disruptive events are analyzed accordingly.

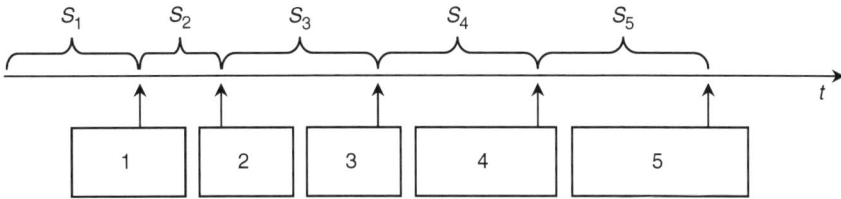

Figure 3.9 Stages of supply chain disruptive events (1: outbreak fire in supplier S_{u1}; 2: the fire extinguished; 3: the warnings by manufacturer M; 4: the increased range and speed of performance of manufacturer M have reached the standards; 5: the performance of manufacturer M recovers and reaches the new stable level).

At first, the three major factors affecting loss can be analyzed to establish whether they change in the five event stages. If a factor does not change in a stage, then it is not considered in the following analysis in this stage. Take the fire as an illustration. The five event stages can be further analyzed from the supply chain structure, enterprise coping measures, and supply chain disruptive events themselves. Not each factor will have an effect in each event stage, and the details can be found in Table 3.1.

In the light of the analysis of factors of loss in supply chain disruptive events, the event stage with √ can be further analyzed to ensure the specific factors or to search for specific measurable manners or indices, as shown in Table 3.2.

(1) Event stage S_1

Here, the event stage S_1 before the happening of the supply chain disruptive event is not examined. In this stage, the production of manufacturer M is $p_1 = p_0$, where p_0 is the mean stable production per day, before the disruptive event occurs.

(2) Event stage S_2

In the event stage S_2, only supply chain disruptive events themselves change. The fire broke out and then was extinguished rapidly, and only 70% of

Table 3.1 Analysis of factors of supply chain disruptive events

Factors	Event Stages				
	S_1	S_2	S_3	S_4	S_5
X	—	×	√	√	×
Y	—	×	×	√	√
Z	—	√	×	×	×

Notes: — indicates the range of superposition methods in this stage; √ indicates that the corresponding factors change in this event stage; × indicates that the corresponding factors do not change in this event stage.

Table 3.2 Analysis of specific factors in supply chain disruptive events

Factors	Event Stages				
	S_1	S_2	S_3	S_4	S_5
X	/	/	Inventory emergency	Inventory depletion	/
Y	/	/	/	Capacity recovery; Emergent purchase	Capacity recovery
Z	/	Rapid completion	/	/	/

machinery of the supplier was destroyed, which did not have a direct impact on the production of manufacturer M. In this stage, the production of manufacturer M is: $p_2 = p_0$.

(3) Event stage S_3

In the event stage S_3, although the supply of raw materials for manufacturer M cannot catch up with production, the inventory serves as a buffer. On entering the event stage S_3, if the inventory level of manufacturer M is S, the daily consumption level of raw materials is θ_0 to maintain the normal daily production, of which 80% comes from supplier S_{u1}, and 20% from supplier S_{u2}. The critical inventory of the manufacturer is defined as $2\theta_0$. Supplier S_{u1} fails to supply raw materials according to the order from manufacturer M in time. Although supplier S_{u2} continues to supply the raw material, the supply volume is small, and thus the inventory of manufacturer M reduces at $0.8\theta_0$ each day. After $\left[\dfrac{s - 2\theta_0}{0.80} \right]$ days' consumption, the inventory drops to the critical level, and the manufacturer immediately starts taking coping measures, entering event stage S_4, as illustrated in Figure 3.10.

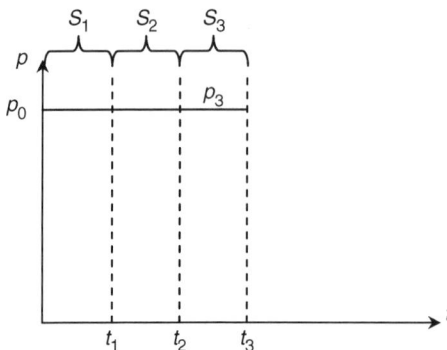

Figure 3.10 Event stage S_3.

In this stage, production of manufacturer M is as follows:

$$p_3 = p_0$$

$$\text{and } t_3 = t_2 + \left[\frac{s - 2\theta_0}{0.80}\right]$$

(4) Event stage S_4

According to the analysis, the three major factors—supply chain structure, enterprise coping measures, and supply chain disruptive events themselves—are defined as the demarcation standards, and then the three dividing points can be determined. Thus, the event stage S_4 can be decomposed into four assessment stages, illustrated as $S_{4,1}$, $S_{4,2}$, $S_{4,3}$, and $S_{4,4}$.

- Assessment stage $S_{4,1}$

  On entering event stage S_4, manufacturer M continues to use the small inventory left, until it runs out of the materials. This is the first assessment stage $S_{4,1}$. In this assessment stage $S_{4,1}$, the production of manufacturer M is:

  $$p_{4,1} = p_0 \text{ and } t_{4,1} = t_3 + 2$$

- Assessment stage $S_{4,2}$

  After 2 days, the factor X of supply chain structure changes—manufacturer M runs out of inventory, which means that it is only supplied by supplier S_{u2}. Once the buffering effect of the inventory is over, the daily production of enterprises will drop significantly to $0.2p_0$. In the assessment stage $S_{4,2}$, production of the manufacturer is:

  $$p_{4,2} = 0.2 p_0$$

- Assessment stage $S_{4,3}$

  After the early warnings of supply chain enterprises, manufacturer M starts to select the appropriate coping strategy and contacts supplier S_{u2} to purchase the raw materials urgently, in order to compensate for the loss of raw materials, and thus the effect of this supply chain disruptive event can be reduced. Manufacturer M at time $t_{4,2}$ begins to receive the urgent order of raw materials. If supplier S_{u2} can slowly increase the daily supply volume to the original level, then factor Y of enterprise coping strategy changes. Therefore, this time node can be defined as time node $S_{4,3}$ of the third assessment stage in event stage S_4, as shown in Figure 3.11. In assessment stage $S_{4,3}$, the production of manufacturer M is:

  $$p_{4,3} = f_{4,3}\left(f_{4,3}, \theta_1 X + \theta_2 Y + \theta_3 Z\right) = f_{4,3}(f_{4,3}, Y)$$

  where $\theta_1 = 0, \theta_2 = 1, \theta_3 = 0$

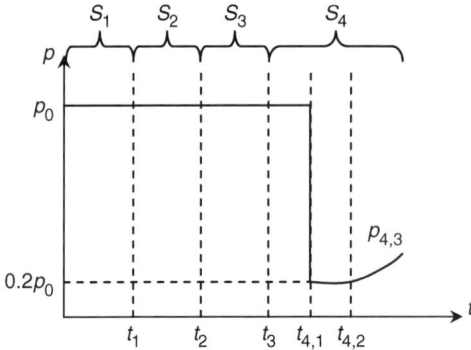

Figure 3.11   Assessment stage $S_{4,3}$.

$$p_{4,3} = f_{4,3}\left(f_{4,3}, \theta_1 X + \theta_2 Y + \theta_3 Z\right) = f_{4,3}\left(f_{4,3}, Y\right)$$

where $\theta_1 = 0, \theta_2 = 1, \theta_3 = 0$

Where t_1 indicates that the fire broke out in the factory of supplier S_{u1}; t_2 indicates that the fire was extinguished; t_3 indicates that the manufacturer sent out early warnings; $t_{4,1}$ indicates the exhaustion of the inventory; and $t_{4,2}$ indicates the urgent purchase.

- Assessment stage $S_{4,4}$

  After the machinery was damaged in the fire, supplier S_{u1} ordered new machines, which arrived. At the same time, the machines that were repaired could be used again in production. The productivity that this supplier lost in the fire gradually recovered, and supplier S_{u1} restarted supplies to manufacturer M at time $t_{4,3}$, as shown in Figure 3.12. In the assessment stage $S_{4,4}$, production of manufacturer M is:

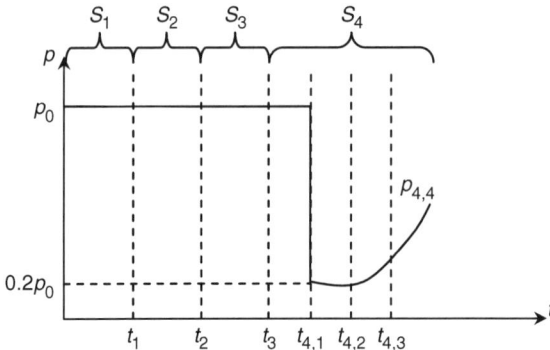

Figure 3.12   Assessment stage $S_{4,4}$.

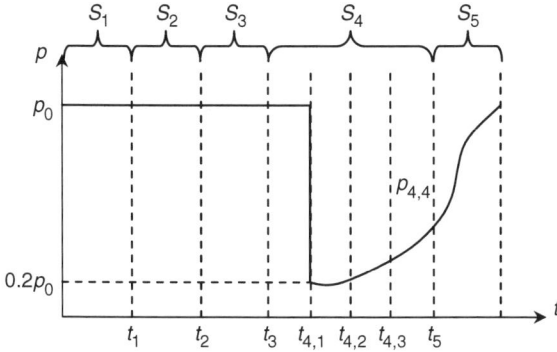

Figure 3.13 Event stage S_5.

$$p_{4,4} = f_{4,4}\left(f_{4,4}, \theta_1 X + \theta_2 Y + \theta_3 Z\right) = f_{4,4}(f_{4,4}, Y)$$

where $\theta_1 = 0, \theta_2 = 1, \theta_3 = 0$

Where t_1 indicates that the fire broke out in the premises of supplier S_{u1}; t_2 indicates that the fire was extinguished; t_3 indicates that the manufacturer sent out early warnings; $t_{4,1}$ indicates the exhaustion of the inventory; $t_{4,2}$ indicates the urgent purchase; and $t_{4,3}$ indicates the recovery of productivity.

(5) Event stage S_5

As both the increased range and speed of production of supply chain enterprises reach the critical value defined by the enterprises themselves, they enter the event stage S_5, as shown in Figure 3.13.

Where t_1 indicates that the fire broke out in the premises of supplier S_{u1}; t_2 indicates that the fire was extinguished; t_3 indicates that the manufacturer sent out early warnings; $t_{4,1}$ indicates the exhaustion of the inventory; $t_{4,2}$ indicates the urgent purchase; $t_{4,3}$ indicates the recovery of productivity; and t_5 indicates that the increased range and speed related to the performance of manufacturer M achieved the target.

Stage three—information update

The function expression of the performance tendency predicted is modified, and the function expression of the accurate operational status trajectory is provided.

For instance, in the second assessment stage $S_{3,2}$ of the event stage S_3, as the supply chain disruptive event evolves, the information concerning the event and the enterprises and other node enterprises in the supply chain have increased gradually. In light of the known information, it is likely to modify the function expression of predictable operational status trajectory in the short term.

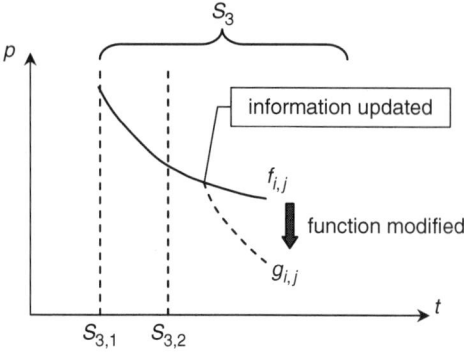

Figure 3.14 The modification of mathematical expression relating to status trajectory.

If $p_{3,2} = f_{3,2}\left(f_{3,1}, X, Y, Z\right)$ is known, the function expression after modification is $p'_{3,2} = g_{3,2}\left(f_{3,1}, X', Y', Z'\right)$, which approximates the future tendency. In other words, the prediction is more accurate, as shown in Figure 3.14.

Stage four—loss analysis

In the assessment stage, as the predicted performance tendency function is achieved, effects of affecting factors in supply chain disruptive events are assessed.

From assessment stage $S_{i,j}$ to $S_{i,j+1}$, the slope of enterprise performance curve changes, which defines the effects of factors in assessment stage $S_{i,j}$ and $S_{i,j+1}$. As Δf is bigger, namely, if the curve slope changes significantly, their effects are greater, as shown in Figure 3.15.

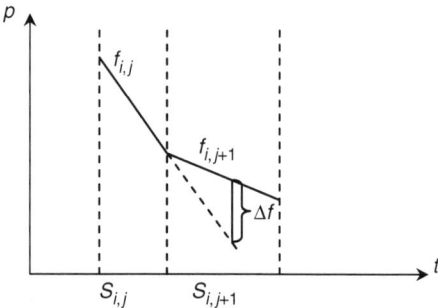

Figure 3.15 Slope comparison.

Stage five—summary

After the supply chain disruptive event is over, the process of the overall assessment can be reviewed, and the method or indices in the treatment and assessment of supply chain disruptive events can be summarized for future use.

Summary

The loss assessment of supply chain disruptive events can be decomposed into five stages: stage division–short-term assessment–scrolling and updating–loss analysis–summary. The process by which supply chain disruptive events create the loss can be divided into five event stages, and in each event stage, the three major factors—the supply chain structure, enterprises coping measures, and supply chain disruptive events themselves—are considered first, and the time when factors change is viewed as nodes. Each event stage can be further decomposed into many assessment stages. The short-term assessment is implemented in the assessment stage, and is superposed with the analytical result of the previous assessment stage. The loss process relating to supply chain disruptive events is analyzed stage by stage. The information updating stages of the loss assessment process relating to supply chain disruptive events can facilitate modification of function expressions of the predictable performance tendency. Thus, function expression of accurate operational status trajectory is achieved.

Conclusion

Supply chain disruptive events are complicated and can happen in each field or in one node enterprise in supply chains, or they may emerge in many links in supply chains. Supply chain disruptive events are abrupt, destructive, urgent, spreading, chained/diffusive, sophisticated, and difficult to predict. The loss caused by a supply chain disruptive event cannot generally have definite expressions. Such losses often have the features of continuity, aftereffects, and information incompleteness. Supply chain disruptive events are minor in terms of probability, but are enormous in influence.

In terms of the effects caused by supply chain disruptive events to enterprises, it is difficult to predict the loss induced in the long term due to the uncertainty of disruptive events. However, the multiple factors can be decomposed into single factors, and the long term can be decomposed into several short periods of time. The prediction is grounded on this, which is superposed and scrolled. The short terms are extended into long terms, and single factors are superposed to multiple factors. Thus, it is likely to assess the loss. In the superposition method of loss assessment in supply chain disruptive events, the process by which supply chain disruptive events bring loss to enterprises can be divided into several stages. The three aspects—supply chain structure, coping strategies, and supply chain disruptive events themselves—are considered. The time node is searched when the factors change. After the analysis of a single factor in every two time nodes (i.e., in the assessment stages), the function expressions of performance level changing trajectory in the next stage are predicted and superposed on the basis of analysis in the previous assessment stage. At the same time, information scrolls and updates, and the prediction is further modified.

Loss assessment of supply chain disruptive events can be disintegrated into five stages: division stage–short-term assessment–scrolling and updating–loss analysis–summary. The process in which supply chain disruptive events induce loss can be decomposed into five event stages. The information updating stages of the loss assessment process relating to supply chain disruptive events can help modify the function expressions of the predictable performance tendency. Thus, the function expressions of accurate operational status trajectory are provided.

4 Supply chain coordinated models under the risk of demand disruptions

Introduction

Coordinated management of supply chains emphasizes collaboration among supply chain enterprises. Although supply chain coordinated management can achieve partial or overall optimization, performance can improve significantly because of coordination. More importantly, obstacles caused by a centralized management can be overcome.

Coordinated management of supply chain can improve core competitiveness of the enterprises and enhance the overall competitive advantage of the supply chain as a whole. Rapid reaction to demand can become more agile, and thus the demands of economic globalization can be met more effectively. Supply chain coordinated management is the key factor in the creation of supply chain value, and the lack of collaboration in supply chains leads to bullwhip effects and low efficiency. The main method of supply chain coordination is to establish the rational and scientific mechanisms of motivation and supervision related to information symmetry or asymmetry.

Here, two stages of supply chain models are investigated, and the issues of production and pricing of short-term products are studied. In the first stage, the manufacturing plan has already been fixed, when the demand is still unknown. In the second stage, when demand is known, products that have already been accommodated in the original production are sold in the market.

In practice, there is no such thing as complete market information; it is difficult to grab the circumstance of demand disruption, and the manufacturing plan of short-term products in particular. When the central decision-makers manage production and sales in supply chains, this problem can be resolved by the newsvendor model (Khouja, 1999; Qi et al., 2004). The fundamental newsvendor model has only one stage, and all the decisions have already been made before the demand information is completely known. Here, the model with centralized decision-makers is studied, and the difference is that the two stages are considered with a focus on the second stage. After the plans of manufacturing in the first stage are fixed, it is hoped that, under the premise that the demand circumstance is known, modification of production planning in the first stage can increase the profits and reduce the cost.

Generally, in terms of the probable demand disruption, modulation of manufacturing decisions can help achieve anticipated profits. In reality, demand disruption might occur and the cost created by demand disruption and redundant inventory are unknown. With respect to these circumstances, the cost is constant in the general hypothesis. Hence, in terms of centralized decision-makers, the unknown demand situation in the second stage is understood, and it is still necessary to adjust the original plan of production. As the suppliers and retailers act independently, an effective method is necessary to deal with the issue of demand disruption.

Introduction to supply chain models

The model of cooperation lot size in supply chains

The evolution of enterprise relationship challenges the traditional economic lot size. In the model of conventional economic lot size, demand and supply are in antagonistic relations. The suppliers consider their own profits and pursue the lot size of the order under the condition of low cost. This lot size of order might not be optimal for the suppliers. In other words, in the conventional model of economic lot size, there is no link between demand and supply. Thus, the overall cost of demand and supply cannot be the lowest. For buyers, an excessively large lot size increases inventory charges. For suppliers, increase of lot size of production means lower cost of equipment adjustment and thus lower manufacturing cost. Buyers and suppliers are thus in antagonistic relations. From the perspective of supply chain management, the buyers and suppliers form a relationship of cooperative game, with the win-win consequence, and thus higher profits and efficiency are achieved compared with the non-cooperative game.

Before the model of lot size of supply and demand is constructed, it is necessary to hypothesize the applicable range of the model.

1. Suppliers encounter a number of clients, and the products the clients require vary significantly. Here, the discussion focuses on the relationship between suppliers and one client.
2. The demand quantity of this client is unit Q annually, and the demand within 1 year is distributed evenly.
3. The productivity of suppliers is unit R, plus $R > Q$.
4. The transportation time and charges are proportional, and it has nothing to do with volume. The transportation charges are paid by suppliers.

Given that condition (1) is in line with reality, in a purchaser's market, clients pursue individual products and suppliers must satisfy varying demand from different clients. Thus, the study of suppliers and one single client does not lose universality or representation. Since suppliers encounter many clients, production R is far greater than demand quantity Q of a single client, and thus hypothetical condition (3) is consistent with reality. The hypothetical condition (2) is grounded on the design of the model related to classic economic lot size. The hypothetical condition (4) is designed for the simplified model, and the form of transportation charges will not affect the validity of the model (see the master degree thesis entitled, 'Suppy Chain Model with Demand Disruptions' (Shen, 2007)).

The decision of the individual lot size of purchasers and suppliers under the condition of non-cooperative game

The model of economic lot size of buyers

The total cost of annual orders of buyers can consist of three parts: purchasing cost, order treatment and transportation cost, and annual inventory charges. C_d refers to the total cost of annual orders, and the following is achieved:

$$C_d = pQ + \left(\frac{Q}{q_d}\right)(s_d + z_d) + \left(\frac{q_d}{2}\right)h_d p \qquad (4\text{-}1)$$

In the preceding equation, p indicates commodity price; q_d indicates the annual demand quantity of buyers; s_d indicates the order lot size of buyers; z_d indicates the treatment cost of each order of buyers; h_d indicates the transportation cost for each order; and Q indicates the annual inventory charge rate (%) of buyers. Equation (4-1) is the calculation of q_d, and the optimal lot size of order can be achieved as follows.

$$q_d = \sqrt{\frac{2Q(s_d + z_d)}{h_d p}} \qquad (4\text{-}2)$$

Equation (4-2) can be substituted into Equation (4-1), and the total cost C_d relating to minimal orders of suppliers can be derived as follows:

$$C_d = pQ + \sqrt{\frac{2Q(s_d + z_d)}{h_d p}} \qquad (4\text{-}3)$$

The optimal order times N_d of buyers are as follows:

$$N_d = \sqrt{\frac{Q h_d p}{2(s_d + z_d)}} \qquad (4\text{-}4)$$

The model of the optimal manufacturing lot size of suppliers

The total cost of suppliers consists of four parts: manufacturing cost, manufacturing preparatory cost, order treatment cost, and opportunity cost. C_s indicates the total cost of supply by suppliers, and the following is achieved:

$$C_s = (1 - m_s)pQ + \frac{Q}{q_s(s_{s1} + s_{s2})} + \frac{\dfrac{q_s}{2}(1 - m_s)ph_s Q}{R} \qquad (4\text{-}5)$$

In this equation, m_s indicates the profit rate of suppliers; q_s indicates the manufacturing lot size; S_{s1} indicates the production preparatory cost of suppliers each time; S_{s2} indicates the treatment cost of each order of suppliers; and h_s indicates the opportunity cost (%) of suppliers. Equation (4-5) is calculated in relation to q_s, and the optimal manufacturing lot size q_s of suppliers can be derived as follows:

$$q_s = \sqrt{\frac{2R(s_{s1} + s_{s2})}{(1 - m_s)ph_s}}$$

(4-6)

Equation (4-6) is substituted into Equation (4-5) and then the total cost C_s of the minimal supply of suppliers is:

$$C_s = (1 - m_s)pQ + \frac{Q}{R\sqrt{\frac{2R(s_{s1} + s_{s2})}{(1 - m_s)ph_s}}}$$

The optimal manufacturing times of suppliers are as follows:

$$N_s = Q\sqrt{\frac{(1 - m_s)ph_s}{2R(s_{s1} + s_{s2})}}$$

The consequence analysis of individual decisions of buyers and suppliers

As the buyers and suppliers determine their respective optimal lot sizes individually, their information is in the non-equivalent state. Thus, the lack of stock or redundant inventory may reduce the profits of the overall supply chain. If suppliers fail to meet the demand of buyers, then buyers shift to other suppliers, and thus the suppliers lose the opportunity. If the suppliers have much redundant inventory, their cost increases. In the independent non-cooperative relationship, suppliers are passive in the market competition.

The optimal decision model of suppliers under the condition of buyers' optimal decision

If there is no collaboration between buyers and suppliers, suppliers will pursue maximal profits under the condition that the buyers have already made decisions. If buyers have made the optimal decisions, the decision models of suppliers can be categorized into two types. One is that suppliers make the make-to-order decisions. The other is that suppliers pursue the minimal cost and then they can make make-to-stock decisions.

The decision model of manufacturing lot size of suppliers in the make-to-order form

In the make-to-order form, suppliers can serve clients well, and reduce the inventory, and thus gradually achieve just-in-time form. Here, the manufacturing times of suppliers are equal to the ordering times of buyers, and the manufacturing lot size of suppliers is equal to that of buyers, namely:

$$q_s = q_d = \sqrt{\frac{2Q(s_d + z_d)}{h_d p}}$$

$$N_s = N_d = \sqrt{\frac{Qh_d p}{2(s_d + z_d)}}$$

$$C_s = (1 - m_s)pQ + (s_{s1} + s_{s2})\sqrt{\frac{Qh_d p}{2(s_d + z_d)}} + (1 - m_s)h_s\sqrt{\frac{Qp(s_d + z_d)}{2h_d}}$$

In the just-in-time form, the key for the suppliers to reduce cost and increase service level is to improve the flexibility of the machinery and to respond quickly to the clients' demand with the lowest cost. As such, the zero stock and zero production preparatory time and cost are achieved.

The decision model of pursuing minimal cost by suppliers

As suppliers produce the unit product nq_d each time, if suppliers arrange the production at time T_0, ensuring that stockout does not occur and the minimal cost is achieved, the quantity that the suppliers finish producing at time T_1 is q_d, and the remaining production $(n-1)q_d$ is continued within the time $\dfrac{(n-1)q_d}{R}$. If the time of finishing production is set as T_e, then $T_e = \dfrac{nq_d}{R}$. The total inventory K within 1 week by suppliers is as follows:

$$K = \frac{nq_d^2}{2}\left[\frac{(n-1)}{Q} - \frac{(n-2)}{R}\right]$$

The average inventory of suppliers is as follows:

$$\bar{K} = \frac{q_d}{2\left[(n-1) - \dfrac{n-2}{R}\right]}$$

The total cost of suppliers is as follows:

$$C_s = Qp(1 - m_s) + \left(\frac{Q}{nq_d}\right)s_{s1} + \left(\frac{Q}{q_d}\right)s_{s2} + \left(\frac{q_d}{2}\right)\left[(n-1) - \frac{(n-2)Q}{R}\right]h_s(1 - m_s)p$$

In the preceding equation, n is calculated as follows:

$$n = \sqrt{\left[\frac{s_{s1}}{s_d + z_d}\right]\left(\frac{h_d}{h_s\left[\frac{1}{(1 - m_s)}\right]\left[\frac{R}{(R - Q)}\right]}\right)}$$

Therefore, the optimal lot size of production for suppliers is as follows:

$$q_s = nq_d = \sqrt{\left[\frac{2Qs_{s1}}{h_s(1-m_s)p}\right]\left[\frac{R}{(R-Q)}\right]}$$

The lot size model of cooperative game between buyers and suppliers

In the analysis of the preceding models, it is clear that suppliers are passive, and they make decisions after buyers have already decided. The cost of suppliers is relatively higher, but buyers are in an advantageous position in terms of decision. As such, the supply chain does not achieve overall optimization. In theory, supply chain members are in the supply chain subsystems, and they can carry out manufacturing and decision-making activities for optimal efficiency and profits of supply chains. Thus, supply chains can achieve the maximal efficiency and profits.

This is difficult to achieve in reality because the relationship between supply and demand is asymmetrical, and their modified results are also asymmetrical. In the case of non-cooperative games, buyers are in an optimal state, but suppliers are in a non-optimal state. If buyers increase their lot size, then the inventory charges increase and the buyers' profits are hurt. Nonetheless, suppliers can reduce their cost. As a result, in the process of realizing optimization of supply chains, it is important to consider redistribution of profits of buyers and suppliers. While suppliers reduce their cost, the buyers' cost is either reduced or remains unchanged. The discount models of prices here can increase the profits of suppliers and reduce the cost of buyers. As such, both buyers and suppliers can benefit in the cooperative game.

If the suppliers request buyers to increase their lot size to the original optimal economic lot size x ($x \geq 1$), namely, xq_d, then the total cost of buyers is as follows:

$$C_d(xq_d) = pQ + \sqrt{\frac{2Q(s_d + z_d)}{h_d p}}\left[1 + \frac{(x-1)^2}{2x}\right]$$

If $x \geq 1$, then $C_d(xq_d) \geq C_d(q_d)$, and the order cost of buyers increases to:

$$C_d(xq_d) - C_d(q_d) = \frac{\sqrt{\frac{2Q(s_d + z_d)}{h_d p}}(x-1)^2}{2x}$$

If suppliers provide buyers with a price discount of a, and the savings on the purchasing cost of suppliers and the increase in amount of inventory charges are greater than the increase in the total ordering cost of buyers, then the following is achieved:

$$apQ + \frac{axq_d}{2}ph_d > \frac{\sqrt{\frac{2Q(s_d + z_d)}{h_d p}}(x-1)^2}{2x}$$

The preceding equation is simplified as follows:

$$a > \frac{\sqrt{\frac{2Q(s_d + z_d)}{h_d p}}(x-1)^2}{2xpQ + x^2 q_d h_d p}$$

From the perspectives of suppliers, if the profit before discounts is Y_s, then the following is achieved:

$$Y_s = Qm_s p - \frac{Q}{nq_d}s_{s1} - \frac{Q}{q_d}s_{s2} - \frac{q_d}{2}\left[(n-1) - \frac{(n-2)Q}{R}\right]h_s(1-m_s)p$$

As the profits are maximized:

$$n = \sqrt{\left[\frac{s_{s1}}{s_d + z_d}\right]\left(\frac{h_d}{h_s\left[\frac{1}{1-m_s}\right]\left[\frac{R}{R-Q}\right]}\right)}$$

After discounts, if the suppliers' profits are Y_t, then the following is achieved:

$$Y_t = Q(m_s - a)p - \frac{Q}{nxq_d}s_{s1} - \frac{Q}{xq_d}s_{s2} - \frac{xq_d}{2}\left[(n-1) - \frac{(n-2)Q}{R}\right]h_s(1-m_s)p$$

As the profits are maximized:

$$n = \left(\frac{1}{x}\right)\sqrt{\left[\frac{s_{s1}}{s_d + z_d}\right]\left(\frac{h_d}{h_s\left[\frac{1}{1-m_s}\right]\left[\frac{R}{R-Q}\right]}\right)}$$

The profits Y_t after discounts by suppliers are greater than profits Y_s before discounts, that is, $Y_t > Y_s$, and the following can be achieved:

$$a < \frac{s_{s2}(x-1)}{q_d px} + \frac{q_d}{2Q}h_s(1-m_s)(x-1)\frac{R-2Q}{R}$$

If the additional ordering cost of buyers is less than that of the profits of suppliers—that is, the overall profit level in supply chain can increase through collaboration—then the following must be correct:

$$\frac{s_{s2}(x-1)}{q_d px} + q_d h_s(1-m_s)(x-1)\frac{R-2Q}{R} > \frac{\sqrt{\frac{2Q(s_d + z_d)}{h_d p}}(x-1)^2}{2xpQ + x^2 q_d h_d p}$$

Therefore, here, as long as:

$$a \in \left\{ \begin{array}{l} \dfrac{\sqrt{\dfrac{2Q(s_d + z_d)}{h_d p}}(x-1)^2}{2xpQ} + x^2 q_d h_d p, \\[4mm] \dfrac{s_{s2}(x-1)}{q_d px} + \dfrac{q_d}{2Q} h_s (1 - m_s)(x-1) \dfrac{R - 2Q}{R} \end{array} \right\}$$

Summary

In the non-cooperative game, passive results may be due to lot size decisions being taken individually by buyers and suppliers, but the model of the optimal production lot size can be constructed by suppliers, if buyers have already made decisions. In the cooperative game, the optimal lot size can be constructed by suppliers and buyers, and the issue of profit distribution can be solved by price discounts. Thus, overall optimal profits can be achieved in supply chains.

Supply chain coordination without disruption

In terms of supply chain coordination, research focuses on decisions related to price and order quantity. This method of quantity discount is commonly applied in research and reality (Jeuland and Shugan, 1983; Maqbool and Srikanth, 1987; Abad, 1988; Sheffi, 2003). If the demand price relations are fixed and known, the study can start from the models of single suppliers and single retailers. The supplier manufactures one product and sells it to retailers, and then retailers sell them in the market. The unit production cost is fixed, and the cost of retailers is determined by the strategy of quantity discount. The Stackelberg game hypothesizes the leading role of suppliers, but the retailers are considered as supportive. Here, suppliers first propose the strategy of quantity discount, and then on the basis of the preceding strategy, the ordering quantity and retailing price are determined. Thus, suppliers must satisfy the ordering demand of suppliers (Shen, 2007).

In this game, suppliers and retailers are independent decision-makers, with the aim to maximize their own profits. $\bar{f}^s$ and $\bar{f}^r$ are profits of suppliers and retailers, respectively, and then $\bar{f}^{sc} = \bar{f}^s + \bar{f}^r$ indicate the profits of supply chains. If the unit production cost of suppliers is C, the price and demand relationship is expressed as $d = \bar{D} - KP$, where $\bar{D}$ refers to the market volume (potential maximum demand); K refers to the price sensitive factor; P refers to the unit retail price; and d refers to the real demand under retail price P (the product quantity that suppliers must provide). Finally, s_b and r_b refer to the unit inventory cost of suppliers and retailers, respectively. If the retail price is defined as P, then the profits of the supply chain are as follows:

$$\bar{f}^{sc}(p) = (\bar{D} - KP)(P - C) - \frac{r_b}{2}(\bar{D} - KP) - \frac{s_b}{2}(\bar{D} - KP) \tag{4-7}$$

The first derivative is achieved in the preceding equation, and it is easy to achieve the following:

$$\bar{P} = \frac{\bar{D} + KC}{2K} + \frac{r_b + s_b}{4} \tag{4-8}$$

Here, the profits of supply chains reach their maximum. Equation (4-7) is substituted into Equation (4-8), and the following is achieved:

$$\bar{f}_{max}^{sc} = \left[\frac{\bar{D} - KC}{2\sqrt{K}} - \frac{\sqrt{K}}{4}(r_b + s_b) \right]^2 \tag{4-9}$$

The corresponding retail price and manufacturing quantity are as follows:

$$\bar{P} = \frac{\bar{D} + KC}{2K} + \frac{r_b + s_b}{4}, \bar{Q} = \frac{\bar{D} - KC}{2} - \frac{K}{4}(r_b + s_b) \tag{4-10}$$

As supply chain coordination is achieved and profits reach their maximum, the following two problems arise:

1. How to distribute profits between suppliers and retailers?
2. How do suppliers make buyers order quantity $\bar{Q}$, and achieve retail price $\bar{P}$?

The common method to solve the preceding problems is that the retailers establish an appropriate scheme of quantity discount (Lee and Rosenblatt, 1986). There are two forms of quantity discounts: the overall quantity discount form and added quantity discount form. Here, only the overall quantity discount form is adopted.

The strategy of the overall quantity discount is defined as $AQDP(W_1, W_2, Q)$, where $W_1 > W_2$, and it means that if the ordering quantity of retailers is $q < Q$, then the unit price at which suppliers sell their products to retailers is W_1; if the ordering quantity of retailers is $q \geq Q$, then the unit price that suppliers charge to retailers is W_2.

If $\bar{f}^s$ refers to the profits that suppliers hope to achieve, where $\bar{f}^s = \eta \bar{f}_{max}^{sc}$, $0 < \eta < 1$, suppliers formulate the appropriate $AQDP(W_1, W_2, Q)$ and retailers order product quantity $\bar{Q}$. Thus, the suppliers get the profit $\bar{f}^s$, and the maximum profit of the supply chain can be achieved.

Lemma 1: If $\bar{f}^s = \eta \bar{f}_{max}^{sc}$, $0 < \eta < 1$, then, in the strategy of $AQDP(\bar{W}_1, \bar{W}_2, \bar{Q})$, the following can be achieved under supply chain coordination.

$$\bar{W}_1 > \frac{\bar{D}}{K} - \sqrt{1-\eta}\left(\frac{\bar{D} - KC}{K} - \frac{1}{2}(r_b + s_b) \right) - \frac{1}{2K}r_b$$

$$\bar{W}_2 = C - \frac{r_b}{2} + \frac{\eta}{K}\frac{\bar{D} - KC}{2} + \left(\frac{1}{2} - \frac{\eta}{4} \right)(r_b + s_b)$$

It proves that, if the order quantity is greater than $\bar{Q}$, then the purchasing price is $\bar{W}_2$ and thus the profit function of retailers is as follows:

$$f_1^r(Q) = Q\left(\frac{\bar{D}-Q}{K} - \bar{W}_2\right) - \frac{Q}{2}r_b, \; Q \geq \bar{Q} \tag{4-11}$$

It is easy to understand that the profit in Equation (4-11) in $Q_1 = \dfrac{\bar{D}-\bar{W}_2 K}{2} - \dfrac{K}{4}r_b$ reaches the maximum. Nevertheless, as $Q_1 < \bar{Q}$, retailers cannot order quantity Q_1 from suppliers at the purchasing price $\bar{W}_2$. Therefore, in this case, retailers cannot achieve maximum profits. In addition, it is easy to understand that $f_1^r(Q)$ is the convex function of Q. Therefore, in the possible range $Q \geq \bar{Q}$, if the retailers intend to achieve maximum profits at purchasing price $\bar{W}_2$, then it can be achieved only by ordering quantity $\bar{Q}$. Here, the profits of retailers are as follows:

$$(1-\eta)\bar{f}_{\max}^{sc}$$

If the order quantity of retailers is less than $\bar{Q}$, then the product is purchased at price $\bar{W}_1$. Here, the profit function of retailers is as follows:

$$f_2^r(Q) = Q\left(\frac{\bar{D}-Q}{K} - \bar{W}_1\right) - \frac{Q}{2}r_b \tag{4-12}$$

It is easy to understand that Equation (4-12) in $Q_2 = \dfrac{\bar{D}-\bar{W}_1 K}{2} - \dfrac{K}{4}r_b < \bar{Q}$ reaches the maximum profits, but as:

$$\bar{W}_1 > \frac{\bar{D}}{K} - \sqrt{1-\eta}\left(\frac{\bar{D}-KC}{K} - \frac{1}{2}(r_b + s_b)\right) - \frac{1}{2K}r_b \tag{4-13}$$

The following is achieved:

$$f_2^r(Q_2) = \frac{1}{K}\left(\frac{\bar{D}-\bar{W}_1 K}{2} - \frac{K}{4}r_b\right)^2 < f_1^r(\bar{Q}) \tag{4-14}$$

The preceding equation shows that the maximum profits of retailers must be achieved by ordering quantity $\bar{Q}$ of products. Up to now, the profits of suppliers can also reach the maximum.

The strategy *AQDP* in Lemma 1 is determined by suppliers, who understand that the maximal profits in supply chains are $\bar{f}_{\max}^{sc}$. Through the strategy *AQDP*, suppliers can allocate first to themselves, and the remaining can be allocated to retailers. In a similar vein, the strategy *AQDP* can also be set up from the perspective of retailers. If suppliers understand that retailers participate in this game, the bottom line of profits obtained is $\bar{f}^r$. Thus, suppliers can achieve the desired results through setting up $\bar{f}^s = \bar{f}_{\max}^{sc} - \bar{f}^r$.

Supply chain models with central decision-makers under the risk of demand disruptions

Supply chain models in demand disruptions

There are two stages in demand disruption models. In the first stage, the relationship between price and demand is $d = \bar{D} - KP$. In the second stage, the real demand is $d = \bar{D} + \Delta D - KP$, and demand disruption is indicated by ΔD (Shen, 2007). Apparently, as $\Delta D > 0$, it is likely that either production or retail price will be increased to raise the profits; and $\Delta D < 0$, vice versa.

In the demand disruption model, if the disruption is resolved, the major decision-makers will search for the maximum profits for the supply chain. Again, if the real demand in the price and demand relationship is Q, and P is the new retail price, here, $P = \dfrac{\bar{D} + \Delta D - Q}{K}$, the corresponding production deviation is $\Delta Q = Q - \bar{Q}$. As $\Delta Q < 0$, it is evident that the ultimate production will result in redundant inventory, or the surplus products will sell at a price much lower than price P in the market. As $\Delta Q > 0$, in order to meet the new demand, production needs to be increased. In the case of additional demand, the charges of using resources often go up; therefore, the unit cost of this part of production will be higher than C.

From the perspective of major decision-makers, if the manufacturing quantity Q is fixed, then the profit function of supply chain in demand disruption is as follows:

$$f(Q) = Q\left[\frac{\bar{D} + \Delta D - Q}{K} - C\right] - \lambda_1(Q - \bar{Q})^+ - \lambda_2(\bar{Q} - Q)^+ - \frac{Q}{2}(r_b + s_b)$$
$$(4\text{-}15)$$

Here, the parameter $\lambda_1 > 0$ is the marginal cost when the superadded demand increases; $\lambda_2 > 0$ is the marginal cost when the superadded demand decreases; $(x)^+ = \max[x, 0]$. To be more exact, λ_1 is the added cost of suppliers, excluding C, as $\Delta Q > 0$; nevertheless, λ_2 is the treatment cost as $\Delta Q < 0$. In order to calculate λ_2, it is necessary to consider the preliminary unit production cost C. As $0 < \lambda_2 < C$, the model indicates that the surplus products $\bar{Q} - Q$ may sell at a price lower than C in the market. As $C \leq \lambda_2$, the model indicates that, in the surplus production, the treatment cost is $\lambda_2 - C$. In practice, the treatment cost is generally lower than the unit production cost. Therefore, the following is achieved:

Hypothesis 1. $\lambda_2 \leq 2C$

In Equation (4-15), if $f(Q)$ in Q^* reaches the maximum, namely, Q^* is the optimal manufacturing level, then it is known that, as market volume increases, the production volume will expand. On the contrary, as the market volume decreases, manufacturing volume will drop. Thus, the following lemmas are achieved:

Lemma 2. In Equation (4-15), if f(Q) in Q = Q* reaches the maximum, then as $\Delta D > 0, Q^* \geq \bar{Q}$; as $\Delta D < 0, Q^* \leq \bar{Q}$.

This proves that, as $\bar{Q} = \dfrac{\bar{D} - KC}{2} - \dfrac{K}{4}(r_b + s_b)$ is known, substitute this equation into (4-15), and the following can be achieved:

$$f(\bar{Q}) = \bar{Q}\left(\frac{\bar{D} + \Delta D - \bar{Q}}{K} - C\right) - \frac{\bar{Q}}{2}(r_b + s_b)$$

$$= \left[\frac{\bar{D} - KC}{2\sqrt{K}} - \frac{\sqrt{K}}{4}(r_b + s_b)\right]^2 + \bar{Q}\frac{\Delta D}{K} \tag{4-16}$$

With the preceding definition, as $\Delta D = 0$, $f(Q)$ in $Q = \bar{Q}$ reaches the maximum, with any $Q > 0$, the following is achieved:

$$\left[\frac{\bar{D} - KC}{2\sqrt{K}} - \frac{\sqrt{K}}{4}(r_b + s_b)\right]^2 \geq Q\left(\frac{\bar{D} - Q}{K} - C\right) - \frac{Q}{2}(r_b + s_b) \tag{4-17}$$

If $\Delta D > 0$, but $Q^* < \bar{Q}$, then the following is achieved:

$$f(Q^*) = Q^*\left[\frac{\bar{D} - Q}{K} - C\right] + Q^*\frac{\Delta D}{K} - \lambda_2(\bar{Q} - Q^*) - \frac{Q^*}{2}(r_b + s_b)$$

$$\leq \left[\frac{\bar{D} - KC}{2\sqrt{K}} - \frac{\sqrt{K}}{4}(r_b + s_b)\right]^2 + Q^*\frac{\Delta D}{K} - \lambda_2(\bar{Q} - Q^*)$$

$$< f(\bar{Q})$$

With hypothetical inconsistency, it shows that as $\Delta D > 0$, here $Q^* \geq \bar{Q}$. Likewise, it proves that as $\Delta D < 0$, here $Q^* \leq \bar{Q}$.

The optimality in demand expanding

In Lemma 2, as $\Delta D > 0$, the optimal $f(Q)$ is simplified as the following strict concave function:

$$f_1(Q) = Q\left(\frac{\bar{D} + \Delta D - Q}{K} - C\right) - \lambda_1(Q - \bar{Q}) - \frac{Q}{2}(r_b + s_b), Q \geq \bar{Q} \tag{4-18}$$

Considering the preceding optimality issue of the absence of restriction, the first derivative $f_1'(Q)$ is applied, and the following is achieved:

$$f_1'(Q) = \frac{\bar{D} + \Delta D - Q}{K} - C - \frac{Q}{K} - \lambda_1 - \frac{1}{2}(r_b + s_b) = 0$$

Calculate the preceding equation in relation to Q:

$$Q_1 = \frac{\bar{D}-KC}{2} - \frac{K}{4}(r_b + s_b) + \frac{\Delta D - K\lambda_1}{2} \tag{4-19}$$

Under the condition of $Q \geq \bar{Q}$, Q_1 is discussed in Equation (4-19), in two scenarios.

In scenario one: $\Delta D > \lambda_1 K$, here, if $Q_1 \geq \bar{Q}$, it means that $f_1(Q)$ in $Q = \bar{Q}$ achieves optimization, letting $Q^*_{case1} = Q_1$.

In scenario two: $0 < \Delta D < \lambda_1 K$, and evidently, here $Q_1 < \bar{Q}$, and Q_1 is not the optimality of the equation. Thus, $f_1(Q)$ in $\bar{Q} = \frac{\bar{D}-KC}{2} - \frac{K}{4}(r_b + s_b)$ reaches the maximum, letting $Q^*_{case2} = \frac{\bar{D}-KC}{2} - \frac{K}{4}(r_b + s_b)$.

Consider all the preceding circumstances, and the following is achieved:

$$Q^* = \begin{cases} Q^*_{case1} = \dfrac{\bar{D}-KC}{2} - \dfrac{K}{4}(r_b + s_b) + \dfrac{\Delta D - K\lambda_1}{2} \\[3mm] Q^*_{case2} = \dfrac{\bar{D}-KC}{2} - \dfrac{K}{4}(r_b + s_b) \end{cases}$$

So far, it can be seen that, if the increased quantity ΔD of market volume is greater than $K\lambda_1$, production will grow on the basis of the original manufacturing plan. In addition, Q_1 in the equation can be seen as two parts: the preliminary optimal manufacturing plan $\bar{Q} = \frac{\bar{D}-KC}{2} - \frac{K}{4}(r_b + s_b)$ and the increased production level $\frac{\Delta D - K\lambda_1}{2}$. The latter can be considered as the optimal production in another new market, in which the relationship of price and demand is $d = \Delta D - KP$, and the unit production cost is λ_1. In terms of the form of Q^*, it is clear that, if the new market volume is large enough ($\Delta D \geq \lambda_1 K$), it will be profitable to adjust the manufacturing plan to meet the demand of the new market.

Nevertheless, as long as the market volume increases, the optimal retail price P^* increases, too. In scenario two, the following is achieved:

$$P^*_{case2} = \frac{1}{K}(\bar{D} + \Delta D - Q^*_{case2}) = \bar{P} + \frac{\Delta D}{K}$$

With regard to this retail price, the optimal profits in supply chains are as follows:

$$f^{sc}_{case2} = \bar{f}^{sc}_{max} + \Delta D \frac{\bar{Q}}{K}$$

It can be seen from the preceding equation that, as the marginal market volume increases, the optimal profit of the supply chain is in proportion with the increased volume ΔD in market, and the proportional factor is $\frac{\bar{Q}}{K}$.

In scenario one, the following is achieved:

$$P^*_{case1} = \frac{1}{K}(\bar{D} + \Delta D - Q^*_{case1}) = \bar{P} + \frac{\Delta D + \lambda_1 K}{2K}$$

The corresponding optimal profit is as follows:

$$f^{sc}_{case1} = Q^*_{case1}(P^*_{case1} - C) - \lambda_1(Q^*_{case1} - \bar{Q}) - \frac{Q^*_{case1}}{2}(r_b + s_b)$$

$$= \left(\frac{\bar{D} - KC}{2} - \frac{K}{4}(r_b + s_b) + \frac{\Delta D - K\lambda_1}{2}\right)\left(\frac{\bar{D} + KC}{2K} + \frac{r_b + s_b}{4} + \frac{\Delta D + K\lambda_1}{2K} - C\right)$$

$$- \lambda_1 \frac{\Delta D - K\lambda_1}{2} - \frac{r_b + s_b}{2}\left(\frac{\bar{D} - KC}{2} - \frac{K}{4}(r_b + s_b) + \frac{\Delta D - K\lambda_1}{2}\right)$$

$$= \left(\frac{\bar{D} - KC}{2} - \frac{K}{4}(r_b + s_b) + \frac{\Delta D - K\lambda_1}{2}\right)\left(\frac{\bar{D} - KC + \Delta D + K\lambda_1}{2K} + \frac{r_b + s_b}{4}\right)$$

$$- \lambda_1 \frac{\Delta D - K\lambda_1}{2} - \frac{r_b + s_b}{2}\left(\frac{\bar{D} - KC}{2} - \frac{K}{4}(r_b + s_b) + \frac{\Delta D - K\lambda_1}{2}\right)$$

$$= \bar{f}^{sc}_{max} + \frac{\Delta D}{K}\bar{Q} + \frac{(\Delta D - K\lambda_1)^2}{4K}$$

It can be seen from the preceding equation that the profits of supply chains increase twice as much as the additional quantity ΔD of the market volume.

The optimality of the decreasing demand

Next, consider the scenario as $\Delta D < 0$. For the convenience of discussion, the market volume is considered to be large enough, and thus the following hypothesis is proposed:

Hypothesis 2: $\bar{D} + \Delta D - CK - \frac{K}{2}(r_b + s_b) > 0$

As $\Delta D < 0$, the optimality $f(Q)$ can be simplified as the following function:

$$f_2(Q) = Q\left(\frac{\bar{D} + \Delta D - Q}{K} - C\right) - \lambda_2(\bar{Q} - Q) - \frac{Q}{2}(r_b + s_b), \quad \bar{Q} \geq Q \qquad (4\text{-}20)$$

Similar to $\Delta D > 0$, there are two scenarios: the scenario of $3(-\lambda_2 K \leq \Delta D < 0)$ and the scenario of $4(\Delta D < -\lambda_2 K)$. In Equation (4-20), $f_2(Q)$ in the following $Q = Q^*$ reaches optimality:

$$Q^* = \begin{cases} Q^*_{case3} = \dfrac{\bar{D} - KC}{2} - \dfrac{K}{4}(r_b + s_b) \\[2ex] Q^*_{case4} = \dfrac{\bar{D} - KC}{2} - \dfrac{K}{4}(r_b + s_b) + \dfrac{\Delta D + \lambda_2 K}{2} \end{cases}$$

In scenario three, the optimal retail price and the corresponding profits in supply chain can be expressed as:

$$P^*_{case3} = \bar{P} + \frac{\Delta D}{K}, f^{sc}_{case3} = \bar{f}^{sc}_{max} + \Delta D \frac{\bar{Q}}{K}$$

In scenario four, the optimal retail price and the corresponding profits in supply chain can be expressed as:

$$P^*_{case4} = \bar{P} + \frac{\Delta D - \lambda_2 K}{2K}, f^{sc}_{case4} = \bar{f}^{sc}_{max} + \Delta d \frac{\bar{Q}}{K} + \frac{(\Delta D + \lambda_2 K)^2}{4K}$$

Summary

Synthesize all the preceding circumstances, and the following theorems can be achieved.

In Theorem 1, if the demand disruption ΔD is fixed, and the demand function of the market price is $d = \bar{D} + \Delta D - KP$, then the optimal retail price is P^*. As the optimal production Q^* is provided by the following two equations, the profits in the supply chain reach the maximum.

$$P^* = \begin{cases} \bar{P} + \dfrac{\Delta D - \lambda_2 K}{2K}, & \Delta D \leq -\lambda_2 K \\[2mm] \bar{P} + \dfrac{\Delta D}{K}, & -\lambda_2 K \leq \Delta D \leq \lambda_1 K \\[2mm] \bar{P} + \dfrac{\Delta D + \lambda_1 K}{2K}, & \lambda_1 K \leq \Delta D \end{cases} \tag{4-21}$$

$$Q^* = \begin{cases} \bar{Q} + \dfrac{\Delta D + \lambda_2 K}{2}, & \Delta D \leq -\lambda_2 K \\[2mm] \bar{Q}, & -\lambda_2 K \leq \Delta D \leq \lambda_1 K \\[2mm] \bar{Q} + \dfrac{\Delta D - \lambda_1 K}{2}, & \lambda_1 K \leq \Delta D \end{cases} \tag{4-22}$$

It can be seen from Theorem 1 that the original manufacturing plan $\bar{Q}$ is robust in the disruption of market volume. As market demand disruption is comparatively small, it is not necessary to adjust the original manufacturing plan. In this case, the adjustment of retail price can compensate for the loss because of the cost. If the change of market volume exceeds $\lambda_1 K$, it is necessary to modify the original manufacturing plan and the retail price.

In terms of the increased profits in supply chain in the case of demand disruption, for the convenience of comparison, if the retail price is $\bar{P}$, in this hypothesis, as $\bar{D} + \Delta D - K > 0$, the quantity sold by retailers is $\hat{Q} = \bar{D} + \Delta D - K\bar{P}$. Here, the profit function is as follows:

$$\hat{f}^{sc}(\hat{Q}) = \hat{Q}(P - C) - \lambda_1 (\Delta D)^+ - \lambda_2 (\Delta D)^- - \frac{r_b + s_b}{2} \hat{Q} \tag{4-23}$$

As $\bar{D}+\Delta D-K\bar{P}\leq 0$, no sales are feasible. Equation (4-23) can be simplified into two scenarios: $\Delta D>0$ and $\Delta D<0$. The following is achieved:

$$
\hat{f}^{sc}=\begin{cases}
\left[\dfrac{\bar{D}-KC}{2\sqrt{K}}-\dfrac{\sqrt{K}}{4}(r_b+s_b)\right]^2+\Delta D\left(\dfrac{\bar{D}-KC}{2K}-\dfrac{r_b+s_b}{4}\right)-\lambda_1\Delta D, \Delta D>0\\[4mm]
\left[\dfrac{\bar{D}-KC}{2\sqrt{K}}-\dfrac{\sqrt{K}}{4}(r_b+s_b)\right]^2+\Delta D\left(\dfrac{\bar{D}-KC}{2K}-\dfrac{r_b+s_b}{4}\right)+\lambda_2\Delta D, \Delta D<0,\\[4mm]
\bar{D}+\Delta D-K\bar{P}>0-(\lambda_2+s_b)\left(\dfrac{\bar{D}-KC}{2K}-\dfrac{K}{4}(r_b+s_b)\right), \bar{D}+\Delta D-K\bar{P}>0
\end{cases}
$$

Compare the profits before and after demand disruptions, as shown in Table 4.1.

It can be seen from this table that if $\Delta D\neq 0$, the preceding strategies are adopted, and the profits in the supply chain increase. As the demand disruption ΔD is relatively small, the profit gap increases as the line of ΔD; as the demand disruption increases, the profit gap increases twice ΔD.

Experiments of quantitative values

First, consider the fundamental circumstance, in which the model of supply chain is without demand disruption. Let the unit production cost of suppliers be $c=1$, $\bar{D}=11$, $K=1$, $s_b=0.5$, $r_b=0.5$, and the relationship between price and demand be $d=11-P$. The corresponding optimal retail price is $\bar{P}=6.25$; the

Table 4.1 Profit comparison before and after demand disruption

Scenarios	Demand disruption ΔD	Profit gap: $f^{sc}_{casei}-\hat{f}^{sc}$
1	$\Delta D>\lambda_1 K$	$\dfrac{(\Delta D-\lambda_1 K)^2}{4K}+\lambda_1\Delta D$
2	$0<\Delta D<\lambda_1 K$	$\lambda_1\Delta D$
3	$-\lambda_2 K\leq\Delta D<0, \bar{D}+\Delta D-K\bar{P}>0$	$-\lambda_2\Delta D$
	$-\lambda_2 K\leq\Delta D<0, \bar{D}+\Delta D-K\bar{P}\leq 0$	$f^{sc}_{max}+[\Delta D+(\lambda_2+s_b)K]$
		$\left[\dfrac{\bar{D}-KC}{2K}-\dfrac{r_b+s_b}{4}\right]$
4	$\Delta D<-\lambda_2 K, \bar{D}+\Delta D-K\bar{P}>0$	$\dfrac{(\Delta D+\lambda_2 K)^2}{4K}-\lambda_2\Delta D$
		$\left[\bar{D}+\Delta D-\dfrac{K}{2}(r_b+s_b)-(C-\lambda_2)K\right]^2$

optimal manufacturing plan is $\bar{Q} = 4.75$; and the optimal profits in supply chains are $f_{max}^{sc} = 22.5625$. Next, consider the profit allocating factor η in Lemma 1; in terms of the complicated coordinated relationship between suppliers and retailers, for simplicity, if the minimal profit anticipated by retailers in this activity is $\bar{f}^r = 8.1225$, suppliers will refuse to participate if the profit is lower than $\bar{f}^r$. Again, the point is that suppliers know the minimal profits that retailers expect to obtain from this activity and agree with the requirements of retailers. Here, optimal profits in supply chains can be divided into two parts, where suppliers get 14.44 and retailers get 8.1225. That is to say, suppliers get 64% and retailers get 36%, which means $\eta = 0.64$. By substituting this value into Lemma 1, the following can be achieved: $\bar{W}_1 > 5.1$, $\bar{W}_2 = 6.53$. Therefore, suppliers may use the strategy of quantity discount: $AQDP(6, 6.53, 4.75)$. Through Lemma 1, it can be known that supply chain has reached coordination. In other words, the quantity of orders by retailers is $\bar{Q} = 4.75$, and let the retail price be $\bar{P} = 6.25$.

In stage two, if the actual demand is different from the predicted demand, then it is necessary to adjust the original retail price. For simplicity, let the marginal cost adjusted in relation to the original manufacturing plan be $\lambda_1 = \lambda_2 = 1$. In this case, consider the profits of supply chains in demand disruption.

If the market volume is greater than expected, that is, $\Delta D > 0$, for instance, $\Delta D = 3$. It can be achieved from the lemma that the optimal retail price is $P^* = 8.25$; the optimal production is $Q^* = 5.75$; and the supply chain can reach the maximum profits $f^{sc} = 37.8125$. From this perspective, if the demand disruption is not treated properly, for instance, if retailers maintain the optimal retail price at $\bar{P} = 6.25$; the commodity quantity that can be sold is $\bar{Q} = 7.75$; then the profit in the supply chains is $f^{sc} = 36.8125$, which is less than the profit in supply chains in the optimal scenario.

As the next step, consider a scenario where the market volume drops, $\Delta D < 0$. For instance, let $\Delta D = -3$. Accordingly, here the optimal retail price is $P^* = 4.25$, and the market demand is $d = 3.75$. Consider one unit commodity is not sold, and the profit of supply is $f^{sc} = 11.1875$. If the optimal retail price remains stable at $\bar{P} = 6.25$, then only 1.75 units of commodities will be sold. However, 3 units of the product will remain unsold, that is, they shall be in the inventory, and here the profit of the supply chain is $f^{sc} = 6.1875$.

Therefore, in the model constructed, the profit in supply chains will increase anyway.

Supply chain models without central decision-makers under the risk of demand disruptions

In a market with demand disruptions, if suppliers and retailers make decisions independently, in order to achieve maximum profits in the supply chain, the preceding results must be modified. In the models without disruptions in the supply chain, it is already known that suppliers may make retailers order $\bar{Q}$ and set the retail price at $\bar{P}$ through setting up a strategy of the complete quantity discount. If there are no central decision-makers, it proves that the supply chain can achieve coordination when a similar strategy of overall quantity discount is adopted (Shen, 2007). For simplicity, the inventory cost is not considered here.

The optimality in demand increased

Above all, consider $\Delta D \geq \lambda_1 K$. If suppliers expect the profits to be f^s, then f^s may be expressed as follows:

$$f^s = \frac{\left(\bar{D}+\Delta D-\left(C+\lambda_1\right)K\right)^2}{4K}+\lambda_1\bar{Q}$$

Here, there are two scenarios. First, if $f^s \geq \lambda_1\bar{Q}$, then the following equation can be achieved:

$$f^s = \eta\frac{\left(\bar{D}+\Delta D-\left(C+\lambda_1\right)K\right)^2}{4K}+\lambda_1\bar{Q} \tag{4-24}$$

Where the parameter $0<\eta<1$ is determined by suppliers.

In Lemma 3, if $\Delta D \geq \lambda_1 K$ and $f^s \geq \lambda_1\bar{Q}$, then supply chains achieve coordination in $AQDP\left(W_1,W_2,Q^*_{case1}\right)$.

$$W_1 > \frac{\bar{D}+\Delta D}{K}-\sqrt{1-\eta}\left(\frac{\bar{D}+\Delta D}{K}-C-\lambda_1\right)$$

$$W_2 = C+\lambda_1+\eta\frac{\bar{D}+\Delta D-\left(C+\lambda_1\right)K}{2K}$$

It proves that, if retailers accept the price at W_2, then the profit function is $f_1^r(Q) = Q\left(\frac{\bar{D}+\Delta D-Q}{K}-W_2\right)$. It is easy to understand that this function achieves optimality at $Q_1 = \frac{\bar{D}+\Delta D-W_2K}{2}$. Again, as $Q_1 \leq Q^*_{case1}$, retailers must order Q^*_{case1} to achieve the optimal profits. Here, the profit function of retailers is as follows:

$$f_1^r\left(Q^*_{case1}\right)=Q^*_{case1}\left(P^*_{case1}-W_2\right)=(1-\eta)\frac{\left(\bar{D}+\Delta D-\left(C+\lambda_1\right)K\right)^2}{4K}$$

If the quantity ordered by retailers is less than Q^*_{case1}, and the price is W_1, then the profit function of retailers is $f_2^r(Q)=Q\left(\frac{\bar{D}+\Delta D-Q}{K}-W_1\right)$, and this function achieves optimality at $Q_2 = \frac{\bar{D}+\Delta D-W_1K}{2}$. Similar to Lemma 1, here, $f_2^r(Q)<f_1^r(Q)$. Therefore, in order to achieve the maximal profits, the optimal ordering quantity for the retailers is Q^*_{case1}, and the supply chain achieves coordination.

Next, consider $f^s < \lambda_1 \bar{Q}$, let $f^s = \eta \lambda_1 \bar{Q}, 0 < \eta < 1$. Here, the following Lemma 4 can prove that the supply chain cannot achieve coordination.

Lemma 4. If $\Delta D \geq \lambda_1 K$ and $f^s = \eta \lambda_1 \bar{Q}, 0 < \eta < 1$, then for any $AQDP(W_1, W_2, Q)$, the supply chain cannot achieve coordination.

It proves that if, in te rms of (W_1, W_2, q_0), the supply chain achieves coordination, then retailers must order quantity Q^*_{case1}, and the profits of suppliers are as follows:

$$f^s = \eta \lambda_1 \frac{\bar{D} - CK}{2} \frac{\left(\bar{D} + \Delta D - (C + \lambda_1)K\right)}{2} W_2 - C \frac{\bar{D} - CK}{2} - (C + \lambda_1) \frac{\Delta D - \lambda_1 K}{2}$$

As such, the following can be achieved:

$$W_2 = C + \lambda_1 + (\eta - 1) \frac{\lambda_1 (\bar{D} - CK)}{(\bar{D} + \Delta D - (C + \lambda_1)K)}$$

Nevertheless, in the preceding W_2, the profits of retailers will achieve optimality at $Q_2 = \frac{\bar{D} + \Delta D - W_2 K}{2}$, and it is easy to know $Q_2 > Q^*_{case1}$ through calculation. Therefore, the ordering quantity by retailers will be Q_2, but the supply chain will not achieve coordination.

Next, consider $0 < \Delta D < \lambda_1 K$. In this case, to achieve the maximum profits in the supply chain, it is understood from the preceding content that retailers must order quantity $Q^*_{case2} = \frac{\bar{D} - KC}{2}$. If suppliers expect to obtain profits $f^s = \eta f^{sc}_{case2}$, then here is the following Lemma 5.

Lemma 5. If $0 < \Delta D < \lambda_1 K$ and $f^s = \eta f^{sc}_{case2}$, then, as $\eta > \frac{2\Delta D}{(\bar{D} + \Delta D - CK)}$, the coordination of supply chain can be achieved in $AQDP(W_1, W_2, \bar{Q})$; as $\eta \leq \frac{2\Delta D}{(\bar{D} + \Delta D - CK)}$, for any $AQDP(W_1, W_2, Q)$, the supply chain cannot achieve coordination.

This proves that, if retailers accept price W_2, then the profit is $f_1^r(Q) = Q\left(\frac{\bar{D} + \Delta D - Q}{K} - W_2\right)$. It is easy to understand that this function achieves optimality at $Q_1 = \frac{\bar{D} + \Delta D - W_2 K}{2}$. As $\eta > \frac{2\Delta D}{(\bar{D} + 2\Delta D - CK)}$, apparently, here, $Q_1 < \bar{Q}$. However, in $AQDP(W_1, W_2, \bar{Q})$, retailers must order quantity $\bar{Q}$ in order to achieve optimal profits, and thus the supply chain achieves coordination. As $\eta > \frac{2\Delta D}{(\bar{D} + 2\Delta D - CK)}$, then, here, $Q_1 \geq \bar{Q}$. It can be understood from the preceding discussion that the supply chain cannot achieve coordination.

The optimal solution of demand reduced

First of all, consider $-\lambda_2 K \le \Delta D < 0$. In this case, it has already been proved earlier that, as $\bar{D} + \Delta D > KC$, the overall profit of the supply chain is positive. If the preceding equation is established, and the profit that the suppliers expect to obtain is $f^s = \eta f^{sc}_{case3}$, then Lemma 6 is achieved as follows:

Lemma 6. If $-\lambda_2 K \le \Delta D < 0$ and $\bar{D} + \Delta D > KC$, then, as $\eta > \dfrac{2\Delta D}{\left(\bar{D} + 2\Delta D - CK\right)}$, supply chains achieve coordination under the strategy of the overall quantity discount: $AQDP\left(W_1, W_2, \bar{Q}\right)$; as $\eta \le \dfrac{2\Delta D}{\left(\bar{D} + 2\Delta D - CK\right)}$, for any $AQDP\left(W_1, W_2, Q\right)$, the supply chain cannot achieve coordination.

This proves that it is evident to achieve it, similar to the test in Lemma 5, and thus it is omitted.

Finally, consider $\Delta D < -\lambda_2 K$. In this case, the maximum profits in supply chains have already been known as follows:

$$f^{sc}_{case4} = \frac{\left(\Delta D + \bar{D} - (C - \lambda_2)K\right)^2}{4K} - \lambda_2 \frac{\Delta D - CK}{2}$$

If retailers expect to obtain the minimal profits as follows:

$$f^{sc}_{case4} = \frac{\left(\Delta D + \bar{D} - (C - \lambda_2)K\right)^2}{4K} - \eta\lambda_2 \frac{\Delta D - CK}{2}, \quad \eta > 0 \tag{4-25}$$

Then, Lemma 7 is achieved as follows:

Lemma 7. If $\Delta D < -\lambda_2 K$, then, as $\eta > 0$, supply chains achieve coordination with the strategy: $AQDP\left(W_1, W_2, Q^*_{case4}\right)$.

$$W_2 = C - \lambda_1 + \frac{\eta\lambda_2\left(\bar{D} - CK\right)}{\left(\bar{D} + \Delta D - (C + \lambda_1)K\right)}$$

W_1 is big enough, and $\eta > 0$ is determined by Equation (4-25).

It proves that, if retailers accept price W_2, and the profit function is $f_1^r(Q) = Q\left(\dfrac{\bar{D} + \Delta D - Q}{K} - W_2\right)$, this profit function achieves optimality at $Q_1 = \dfrac{\bar{D} + \Delta D - W_2 K}{2}$. As $W_2 > C - \lambda_1$, $Q_1 < Q^*_{case4}$ can be achieved, retailers cannot achieve their optimal profits; the ordering quantity must be Q^*_{case4}; here it is:

$$f_1^r\left(Q^*_{case4}\right) = \frac{\left(\Delta D + \bar{D} - (C - \lambda_2)K\right)^2}{4K} - \lambda_2 \frac{\Delta D - CK}{2}$$

However, this is expected by retailers. In addition, the substantially higher retail price W_1 set here cannot help retailers achieve profits larger than $f_1^r(Q^*_{case4})$.

Conclusion

There is a sophisticated relationship among member enterprises in supply chains, and the essence is the relationship between supply and marketing among enterprises. Any two members can constitute a two-stage supply chain structure. Under the premise that the relationship between demand and price is predicted, to achieve the maximum profits, suppliers will manufacture a certain quantity of the product, determined by their own perspectives, and then sell them to retailers. Retailers will also consider their own maximum profits, and will order a certain quantity and settle the optimal retail price. The mismatch between the optimal production of suppliers and the optimal ordering quantity of retailers can be solved by the strategy of appropriate quantity discount. As such, supply chains achieve coordination and also the optimal profits.

Here, the focus is the analysis of the model of two-stage supply chains in demand disruption. As the market information is changeable and consumers' demands are diverse, manufacturing decisions according to prediction may not be consistent with the market, which may lead to two scenarios. That is to say, overstock is created by overproduction, and the production is not sufficient, so that the opportunity of making profits is lost. The models discussed here are based on these two scenarios. Through quantitative analysis, in demand disruptions, suppliers and retailers will achieve the maximal profits by adjusting their own strategies. The quantitative experiments show that, unlike the previous supply chain models, the models constructed here can achieve maximal profits.

5 Supply chain coordinated models under the risk of supply disruptions

Introduction

Generally, the probability of supply chain disruptive events occurring is relatively small. However, once they happen, they bring enormous loss to supply chains. Management methods and approaches used for addressing supply chain disruptive events can be called *coping strategies*. Here, supply chain disruptive events are mainly defined from the perspective of supply chain management, including raw material supply disruptions, substantial demand growth, strong fluctuations of prices, and abrupt decrease of productivity, excluding the events themselves that lead to supply chain disruptive events.

Tang (2006) maintained that risk management of supply chains refers to the effective supply chain risk management that allows it to run safely, reduce the cost, and improve operational performance through coordination and cooperation among supply chain members to ensure profitability and continuity. Kleindorfer and Saad (2005) pointed out that the aim of supply chain risk management is to improve the validity and robustness of supply chains in the context of different risks, which can be categorized into two types—one is normal risk of supply chains, and the other is disruption risk of supply chains.

Hallikas *et al.* (2004) studied risk evaluation of supply chains quantitatively, from the probability of risk events and influence perspective, and disintegrated the probability and effects into five stages, for making the most significant risk attract the most attention. They also point out that the method of reducing risks is integration of reducing probability and effects.

Nagurney *et al.* (2004) designed a network of the three-stage super network structure of the supply chain, including a three-stage decision of manufacturers, distributors, and retailers. They considered supply risk and demand risk, optimized according to multiple-property decision, achieve profit maximization, and risk minimization, and derive the equilibrium conditions of the model and conclusion.

Xu *et al.* (2003) studied and discussed the influence of sudden demand changes on supply chains consisting of suppliers and retailers. Gan *et al.* (2005) discussed the issue of supply chain risk sharing, considering coordination of supply chains composed of one risk-neutral supplier and one risk-averse retailer, and designed the coordination of supply chain system by a risk-sharing contract.

Supply chain disruptive events often involve the processes of emergence, spreading, and recovery. Disruptive events occur in different supply chain structures, and their spreading and recovery processes vary. However, there is a general pattern for the process and phenomenon of the spreading and recovery of disruptive events in different supply chain structures.

The treatment of supply chain disruptive events often covers the beforehand, intermediate, and afterward measures. Nevertheless, in practice, few enterprises take coping measures at a certain stage; most take coping measures in many stages. In other words, they implement the complete coping strategies in several steps.

Here, two coordinated methods of assistance and penalty are discussed to investigate the conditions that coordinated methods must satisfy to achieve the overall optimality of supply chains. Since the coping process mainly means that enterprises take preventive measures to deal with disruptive events urgently, with the purpose of minimizing the effects of disruptive events on enterprises or supply chains, the model decision variables here include two aspects—the relevant decision variables of previous preventive measures and afterward recovery process, namely, two-stage model—beforehand and afterward stages.

Here, three supply chain structures are analyzed: supply chains of one supplier and one distributor, supply chains of one supplier and many distributors, and supply chains of many suppliers and one distributor. When disruptive events happen and suppliers cannot provide products to downstream distributors, how distributors and suppliers coordinate in supply chains is discussed. In the case of one supplier and one distributor, the two conditions of risk-neutral and risk-averse are discussed. The fundamental coordinated method can be divided into two types—one is that distributors provide aid for suppliers affected by disruptive events, and the other is that suppliers pay the penalty to downstream suppliers to compensate for the loss of distributors.

Since the coping measures taken by supply chain enterprises in each stage may not be mutually isolated, the coping strategy of supply chain disruptive events in the complete process is discussed here. On the basis of calculation of the probability of supply chain disruptive events occurring because of natural disasters, from the perspective of supply chain management, the issue concerning what conditions related to the coordinating method can allow supply chain enterprises to take preventive and recovery measures to optimize the overall supply chain is considered. The coordinated methods include assistance and penalty. At the same time, the influence of risk-averse effects of suppliers on preventive strategies and recovery process in supply chains is also examined.

Probability of disruptive events

For addressing supply chain disruptive events, it is necessary to study preventive measures in advance, considering the probability of the events occurring. If the occurring probability of disruptive events and the impact scale are understood, it is possible to take preventive measures to make the profits of enterprises or the overall supply chain to achieve optimality by the traditional mathematical models. If there is no understanding of probability of supply chain disruptive events or the mathematical models of influence scale, then when the preventive measures are taken, the decision will be made by subjective experience, which makes it difficult to achieve the optimality in objectivity (see the PhD thesis entitled, 'Research on Countermeasures of Supply Disruption' (Sheng, 2008)).

In terms of the probability and impact of supply chain disruptive events, it is important to discuss the incentive of disruptive events occurring. Supply chain disruptive events can be classified in relation to material flow, information flow, and capital flow. It is important to note that this typology is based on the supply chain disruptive events themselves, and this is not the incentive of supply chain disruptive events. The causes of supply chain disruptive events vary, including earthquakes, tsunamis, strikes, and terrorist attacks, among others. If the occurring probability and influence scale of supply disruptive events are ensured, then it is necessary to discuss the incentives that induce supply chain disruptions.

It is difficult to discuss these incentives because the incentives inducing supply chain disruptions are various. The relevant studies on different incentives may belong to different disciplines, including natural science (earthquakes, tsunamis, etc.) and social science (strikes, terrorist attacks, etc.). Here, the study of supply chain disruptive events is mainly from the perspective of supply chain management, and the definition of disruptive events does not include the events inducing supply chain disruptive events themselves. In other words, the focus here is on supply chain management, and thus the occurring mechanism of earthquakes and strikes is not discussed in depth.

Based on the preceding discussion, here the focus is on the discussion about the occurring probability of supply chain disruptive events caused by natural disasters. However, other types of incentives of disruptive events are not analyzed in depth.

The occurring probability of three basic types of disruptive event incentives

Here, the incentives of supply chain disruptive events can be categorized into three basic types: natural disasters, group disasters, and contingency.

- Natural disasters
  The typical examples of incentives in supply chain disruptive events are earthquakes, floods, blackouts, typhoons, and other serious natural disasters. It is found that the study of events caused by natural disasters may apply the self-organized criticality. Satisfying the complicated system of self-organized criticality, natural disasters satisfy the power law relations between the occurring frequency (N) and scale (R: the effects of natural disasters): $N = cR^{-D}$, where c, D are constants that can be calculated by historic data. Therefore, this provides the theoretical base and evidence for calculating the mathematical models that can describe the occurrence probability and impact scales of disruptive events created by natural disasters.

- Group disasters

The basic difference between incentives of supply chain disruptive events and other types of disruptive events is that group disasters mix with subjective dynamic factors. In terms of incentives related to this type of supply chain disruptive events, it is impossible to estimate the occurring probability and influence scales. Take terrorist attacks as an illustration. At the moment, it is difficult to predict the occurring probability and effects caused by this event. It is difficult to use mathematical models to describe group disasters. One main cause is that this type of events have a certain feature of being self-adaptive. When some preventive measures are taken to enhance some links, the group (such as terrorists) that intends to initiate group disasters may launch group disasters in some unexpected links. In addition, group disasters often happen at times when there is least preventive preparations, and in the weakest places. The decision on this type of incentives of disruptive events in relation to advance prediction and preventive measures depends more on the experience and subjective feelings of decision-makers.

- Contingency

In terms of this type of incentives for disruptive events, in some cases, the historic data can provide an approximate judgment. For instance, in studying the occurring probability of the working machines, the hypothesis that the service time of machines is subject to a certain index distribution is often based on historic data. Nonetheless, it is difficult to predict the occurring probability of some contingency, such as the probability of fires in workshops. In this case, preventive decisions are more likely to be determined by the subjective judgment of decision-makers.

Here, the focus is to construct mathematical models and deduction in relation to the occurring probability and effects of disruptive events caused by natural disasters, but group disasters and contingency are not considered here. The main reason is that, in group disasters and contingency, it is impossible to estimate occurring probability. Furthermore, although the occurring probability of some contingency can be described by mathematical models, in terms of different types of contingency, different mathematical models are required to describe them. With respect to the contingency of machine malfunction, the probability of machine malfunction of different machines in their operation processes varies, and thus it is difficult to use the unified mathematical methods to describe it.

The determination of the occurring probability of supply chain disruptive events induced by natural disasters

Self-organized criticality is applied for explaining the behavior of the dynamic systems related to the extensive dissipation. This dissipated dynamic system includes the numerous components that have short-range functions and evolves toward the criticality spontaneously. In the critical state, a tiny disturbance in the exterior induces avalanche events of different sizes in the system. If these avalanche events display the structure of different shapes in space, and the noise $\frac{1}{f}$ occurs in time, then the distribution of Power Law emerges, which shows that the system has self-organized criticality. The self-organized criticality is one pattern of the complicated behavior in nature, which has been effectively applied in many aspects such as earthquakes, meteorology, and blackouts. Consider that many disruptive events in reality are caused by various factors such as earthquakes and meteorological disasters, and thus the self-organized criticality is introduced into the study of supply chain disruptive events.

Extreme value theory is applied for constructing models and statistically analyzing the random variables with extreme variability related to those events that occur rarely but have enormous effects. In terms of the objects of extreme value theory, it is suitable for disruptive events. At the moment, the extreme value theory has been widely applied in hydrology, meteorology, earthquakes, and power accidents. In order to use the extreme value theory, it is necessary to understand the extreme distribution of natural disasters causing supply chain disruptive events.

If the system has self-organized criticality, then the power law distribution is satisfied, and the extreme distribution of natural disasters can be derived. Furthermore, it can be further derived that the occurring probability of natural disasters will exceed a certain scale within a period of time. Thus, the occurring probability of supply chain disruptive events is achieved, and the related method of supply chain management can be applied for coordinating the operation of supply chains.

Based on the previous research, serious disasters such as earthquakes, floods, blackouts, and typhoons have the self-organized criticality, namely, the distribution of power law. Here, consider the issue of supply chain coordination related to disruptive events under the condition of satisfying the self-organized criticality. On the basis of this, consider that the supply chain achieves the overall optimality through the mechanism of supply chain coordination.

It is worth mentioning that the probability of all disruptive events cannot be derived. The most important reason is that there is no evidence showing that, as disruptive events occur, the relevant system has the self-organized criticality. Therefore, the premise here is that the system of disruptive events occurred has self-organized criticality, which is suitable for the supply chain disruptions induced by natural disasters and blackouts.

The extreme value theory is a branch of the order statistics theory, which is concerned with the extreme value distribution of sample size.

If $X_1, X_2, \cdots, X_n$ are the random variable sequence of independent identical distribution, and $F(x)$ is the probability distribution function $i = 1, 2, \cdots, n$ of $F(x)$, letting $Y_n = \max(X_1, X_2, \cdots, X_n)$, the distribution function of Y_n is as follows:

$$F_{Yn}(y) = \Pr\{Y_n \le y\} = \Pr\{X_1 \le y, X_2 \le y, \cdots, X_n \le y\} = \left[F(x)\right]^n \qquad (5\text{-}1)$$

It can be seen from Equation (5-1) that as $0 \le F(x) < 1$, $\lim_{n \to \infty} F_{Y_n}(y) = 0$; as $F(x) = 1$, $F_{Y_n}(y) = 1$. Thus, the extreme distribution is the degenerate distribution. From the extreme theory of Fisher-Tippett, the distribution of the random variable $Z_n = \dfrac{Y_n - b_n}{a_n}$ after standardization of Y_n is not degenerate distribution any more. After standardization, regardless of the original distribution of the sample data, as n is large enough, the extreme distribution has the following three forms: Gumbel distribution (Type I), Frechet distribution (Type II), and Weibull distribution (Type III), and the relevant mathematical description is as follows:

(1) Gumbel distribution (Type I)

$$H(x) = \exp\{-\exp(-x)\} \quad x \in (-\infty, +\infty)$$

(2) Frechet distribution (Type II)

$$H(x) = \begin{cases} 0 & x \in (-\infty, 0) \\ \exp(-x^{-k}) & x \in (0, +\infty), k \in (0, +\infty) \end{cases}$$

(3) Weibull distribution (Type III)

$$H(x) = \begin{cases} \exp\{-(-x^k)\} & x \in (-\infty, 0), k \in (0, +\infty) \\ 1 & x \in (0, +\infty) \end{cases}$$

In terms of the natural disasters that have happened in the system that satisfies self-organized criticality, the power law relationship between the occurring frequency N and scale R (the effects of natural disasters): $N = cR^{-D}$. In the statistical data, if the maximum and minimum of scales are r_{max} and r_{min}, let $X = \ln R$ and then $N = ce^{-DX}$ and $x_{min} = \ln r_{min}$. Transfer the frequency into probability, and then the distribution function of X is achieved as follows:

$$F(x) = \Pr\{X \le x\} = \dfrac{\displaystyle\int_{x_{min}}^{x} ce^{-Dt}\, dt}{\displaystyle\int_{x_{min}}^{\infty} ce^{-Dt}\, dt} = 1 - e^{-D(x - x_{min})} \tag{5-2}$$

Apply the theory of maximum domains of attraction in the extreme value theory, and the extreme form of extreme value distribution in Equation (5-2) can be judged to be the gradual distribution of convergence to Type I, and the maximum extreme distribution can be achieved and is equal to:

$$G(x) = \exp\{-\exp[-\alpha(x - \mu)]\} \tag{5-3}$$

In Equation (5-3), the parameters of α, μ can be determined by the least squares method. Specifically, given observation data in unit time (such as n years), in each unit time select the maximum influence and loss (such as the area or number of people affected) caused by the natural disaster (such as typhoon); if the effect logarithm caused is x_i $(i=1,2,\cdots,n)$, put them in ascending order as follows: $x_1 \le x_2 \le \cdots \le x_i \le \cdots \le x_n$. In terms of x_i, $E\big[G(x_i)\big]=\dfrac{i}{n+1}$. Consider $\dfrac{i}{n+1}$ as the estimation of $G(x_i)$, and substitute it into Equation (5-3).

$$\frac{i}{n+1}=\exp\left\{-\exp\left[-\alpha\left(x_i-\mu\right)\right]\right\}$$

namely: $-\ln\left(-\ln\dfrac{i}{n+1}\right)=\alpha\left(x_i-\mu\right)$

n linear equation can be achieved from n value observed, and then compute the parameters α, μ by using least squares method. The relevant extreme distribution of Equation (5-3) can be achieved. If the scale of the maximal disadvantageous event that suppliers can carry in supply chains is r_0 (such as the maximal scales of typhoons and earthquakes), then the scale of disadvantageous events exceeds r_0, which will result in disruptive events (referring to the events that affect suppliers significantly, such as production disruptions caused by the factory destruction) and have a great effect on the normal operation of suppliers. The occurring probability of these disruptive events (the disadvantageous events whose scale exceeds r_0) within a period of time can be computed from Equation (5-3).

$$p=1-G\left(\ln r_0\right)=1-\exp\left\{-\exp\left[-\alpha\left(\ln r_0-\mu\right)\right]\right\} \qquad (5\text{-}4)$$

If the occurring probability of disruptive events in the next stage is known, then the model of preventive measures before the disruptive events can be studied and constructed, and the optimal strategy about preventive measures can be computed.

The two-stage coordinated model between a supplier and a distributor

The focus here is the supply chain composed of one supplier and one distributor. As disruptive events happen for suppliers, it is impossible to provide products to distributors without the conditions of coordinated methods, which allow the suppliers to take preventive measures, and afterward the recovery process, to achieve the overall optimality in supply chains (Sheng, 2008).

Two coordinated mechanisms are considered here:

(1) The coordinated mechanisms that provide aid—namely, the distributors in downstream supply chains provide aid for suppliers suffering from disruptive events.
(2) The coordinated mechanism of paying penalty—namely, the distributors in downstream supply chains pay penalty for suppliers suffering from disruptive events.

Here, the two-stage coordinated models of supply chains in two circumstances are considered: risk-neutral and risk-averse suppliers. Above all, the two-stage coordinated model of supply chains is discussed in the case of suppliers with a risk-neutral attitude and one distributor.

The two-stage coordinated model of supply chains in the case of suppliers with a risk-neutral attitude and one distributor

Consider the supply chain composed of one supplier and one distributor here, and the supplier might suffer from the effects of disruptive events and fails to satisfy the demand of distributors. The supplier is risk-neutral. Firstly, consider the first coordinated mechanism—distributors provide aid to suppliers suffering from the impact of disruptive events in order to accelerate the recovery process of suppliers.

The coordinated method in supply chains based on aid

Here, the coordinated method of supply chains is used after the disruptive events, where distributors provide aid for the suppliers suffering from disruptive events. The typical circumstance of this coordinated mechanism in which distributors provide aid for suppliers is that this supplier is the only one for the distributor, or at least distributors cannot find other suppliers as substitutes in a short period of time. Here, the model can be disintegrated into two stages chronologically. In the first stage, suppliers take preventive measures to guard against disruptive events. In the second stage, as disruptive events emerge, the backorder cost is related with orders of distributors. Thus, distributors expect that suppliers will resume manufacturing soon and provide aid for suppliers. After a period of recovery, suppliers will resume their production.

(1) The basic hypothesis, decision process, and the illustrations of parameters in models

In supply chain models, consider the relevant circumstances in different stages. In the first stage, in order to prevent the disruptive events in the second stage (next period), suppliers will take preventive measure τ_0. The occurrence of disruptive events will make suppliers fail to satisfy the demand of distributors, who will start to provide aid t for suppliers. In the second stage, suppliers resume manufacturing; the cost is $C(\tau_0, \tau)$; the duration is τ; the backorder cost by distributors is $\theta\tau$; and suppliers' production has completely recovered.

Illustrations of the relevant parameters are as follows:

τ_0 indicates the number of preventive measures suppliers take before disruptive events happen, with the purpose of preventing the occurrence of disruptive events or reducing the loss caused by disruptive events. The items of preventive measures include formulating plans to deal with disruptive events, purchasing and allocating emergency materials, and staff training for tackling disruptive events, among others. In addition, τ_0 can be understood as the preventive measures adopted beforehand in order to deal with different levels of disruptive events, the severity of disruptive events, or the capacity to cope with disruptive events beforehand in relation to enterprises. For the convenience of description, τ_0 here is called preventive measures.

τ indicates the time that suppliers take to resume manufacturing after the disruptive event occurs.

t indicates that distributors provide aid for suppliers suffering from disruptive events to help them resume manufacturing (shortening τ), which can be seen as the capital that suppliers provide for distributors or the human resources and equipment that suppliers provide.

$C(\tau_0, \tau)$ indicates the relevant cost of suppliers in the process between the time after the occurrence of disruptive event and the recovery of production. The cost is supposed to include two major elements: the first is the cost that the suppliers incur for resuming production, and the second is that, as suppliers cannot provide products normally and they may lose some orders, it is possible to produce the cost of order loss. The relevant cost $C(\tau_0, \tau)$ of suppliers is supposed to be the synthesis of the two cost factors. Since the cost factor of supply chain recovery might play a leading role in these factors, $C(\tau_0, \tau)$ is called the recovery cost of suppliers. Evidently, $C(\tau_0, \tau)$ is supposed to be associated with τ_0 and τ.

θ indicates the time (τ) when suppliers resume manufacturing and the backorder cost in the unit time. Since the backorder cost is associated with the operation status of distributors when disruptive events happen, the hypothesis of θ is the random variable that is subject to the identical probability distribution, and the probability density function is $f(\theta)$. θ value is definite after disruptive events in the second stage.

$g(\tau_0)$ indicates the cost that suppliers incur for preventive measures at τ_0.

p indicates the occurring probability of disruptive events, which can be computed according to Equation (5-4).

Hypothesis 1: $\dfrac{\partial^2 C(\tau_0, \tau)}{\partial \tau^2} \geq 0$. This hypothesis shows that $C(\tau_0, \tau)$ is the convex function of τ. In terms of recovery cost of suppliers, the shorter recovery time generally means a higher cost of recovery. As the recovery time τ reduces, the recovery time accelerates.

Hypothesis 2: $\dfrac{\partial C(\tau_0, \tau)}{\partial \tau_0} \leq 0$, $\dfrac{\partial^2 C(\tau_0, \tau)}{\partial \tau_0^2} \geq 0$. This hypothesis shows that $C(\tau_0, \tau)$ is the convex function of τ_0. If suppliers take more

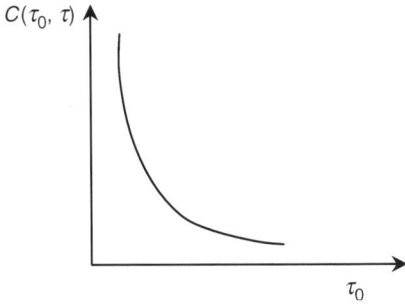

Figure 5.1 The shape of $C(\tau_0,\tau)$.

preventive measures in the first stage, then the recovery cost will be less in the second stage. As the preventive measures decrease, the recovery cost $C(\tau_0,\tau)$ will rise. The relationship between $C(\tau_0,\tau)$ and τ_0 can be found in Figure 5.1.

Hypothesis 3: $\dfrac{\partial g(\tau_0)}{\partial \tau_0} \geq 0$, $\dfrac{\partial^2 g(\tau_0)}{\partial \tau_0^2} \geq M$. M is a positive number big enough to ensure that the target function of optimization is the convex function. This hypothesis shows that $g(\tau_0)$ is the convex function of τ_0. This means that if suppliers take more preventive measures in the first stage, the preventive cost will grow. As the preventive measures τ_0 increase, the preventive cost rises. This suggests that the preliminary preventive cost is usually relatively lower; however, as the preventive measures increase, the preventive cost tends to go up. The relationship between $g(\tau_0)$ and τ_0 can be found in Figure 5.2.

(2) The study of decisions in centralized supply chains
    First, consider risk-neutral suppliers and distributors as centralized supply chains. Compute the optimal preventive measures in the first stage of the

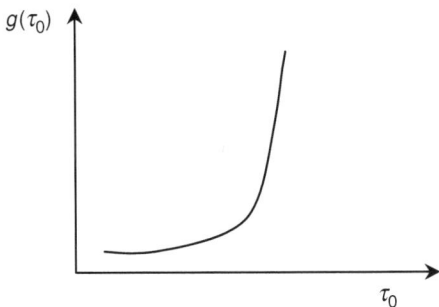

Figure 5.2 The shape of $g(\tau_0)$.

centralized supply chains τ_0 and the optimal recovery time τ in the second stage. As the decision of centralized supply chains can be disintegrated into two stages, it can start from the decision procedure (decision variable is τ) in the second stage at first for computing.

In terms of centralized supply chains, the cost of disruptive events in the second stage is as follows:

$$\min_{\tau} C_1(\tau_0, \tau) = C(\tau_0, \tau) + \theta \tau \tag{5-5}$$

In Equation (5-5), there is no cost of consortium, which means that the cost of consortium is the quantity in relation to the recovery time τ, similar to the sunk cost. Here, in the process of building models and solutions, inclusion of consortium cost has no effects.

Let the first derivative in Equation (5-5) be equal to 0.

$$\frac{\partial C_1(\tau_0, \tau)}{\partial \tau} = \frac{\partial C(\tau_0, \tau)}{\partial \tau} + \theta = 0$$

Therefore:

$$\frac{\partial C(\tau_0, \tau)}{\partial \tau} = -\theta$$

Compute the second derivative in Equation (5-5) and apply Hypothesis 1:

$$\frac{\partial^2 C_1(\tau_0, \tau)}{\partial \tau^2} = \frac{\partial^2 C(\tau_0, \tau)}{\partial \tau^2} \geq 0$$

Therefore, the optimal recovery time τ must satisfy the following:

$$\frac{\partial C(\tau_0, \tau)}{\partial \tau} = -\theta \tag{5-6}$$

As a second step, consider the decision τ_0 of the centralized supply chain in the first stage. Here, θ is the random variable, and the probability density is $f(\theta)$. The target function of the centralized supply chain in the first stage is as follows:

$$\min_{\tau_0} C_2(\tau_0, \tau) = g(\tau_0) + pE_\theta\left[C(\tau_0, \tau) + \theta \tau\right] \tag{5-7}$$

Where p indicates the probability of disruptive events affecting suppliers in the second stage, which can be solved through Equation (5-4). $E_\theta\left[C(\tau_0, \tau) + \theta \tau\right]$ indicates the expected cost to be incurred in the second stage in centralized supply chains, if disruptive events happen in the second stage.

$$\frac{\partial C_2(\tau_0, \tau)}{\partial \tau_0} = \frac{\partial g(\tau_0)}{\partial \tau_0} + pE_\theta\left[\frac{\partial C(\tau_0, \tau)}{\partial \tau_0} + \frac{\partial C(\tau_0, \tau)}{\partial \tau}\frac{\partial \tau}{\partial \tau_0} + \theta\frac{\partial \tau}{\partial \tau_0}\right]$$

Substitute it into Equation (5-6), and the following can be achieved:

$$\frac{\partial C_2(\tau_0,\tau)}{\partial \tau_0} = \frac{\partial g(\tau_0)}{\partial \tau_0} + pE_\theta \left[\frac{\partial C(\tau_0,\tau)}{\partial \tau_0} \right] = 0 \tag{5-8}$$

Compute the second derivative in Equation (5-8):

$$\frac{\partial^2 C_2(\tau_0,\tau)}{\partial \tau_0^2} = \frac{\partial^2 g(\tau_0)}{\partial \tau_0^2} + pE_\theta \left[\frac{\partial^2 C(\tau_0,\tau)}{\partial \tau_0^2} + \frac{\partial^2 C(\tau_0,\tau)}{\partial \tau_0 \partial \tau} \frac{\partial \tau}{\partial \tau_0} \right] \tag{5-9}$$

According to Hypothesis 3, Equation (5-9) is greater than 0, and thus the optimal preventive measure has the only optimal solution in the first stage of centralized supply chains, making the first derivative equal to 0. Therefore, the optimal preventive measure τ_0 taken in the first stage of centralized supply chains must satisfy the following:

$$\frac{\partial g(\tau_0)}{\partial \tau_0} + pE_\theta \left[\frac{\partial C(\tau_0,\tau)}{\partial \tau_0} \right] = 0 \tag{5-10}$$

Based on the preceding analysis, it can be established that, in the case of centralized supply chains, the following conclusions can be achieved:

In the case of centralized supply chains, the optimal recovery time τ of supply chains and the optimal preventive measure τ_0 must satisfy:

$$\left[\begin{array}{l} \dfrac{\partial C(\tau_0,\tau)}{\partial \tau} = -\theta \\[2ex] \dfrac{\partial g(\tau_0)}{\partial \tau_0} + pE_\theta \left[\dfrac{\partial C(\tau_0,\tau)}{\partial \tau_0} \right] = 0 \end{array} \right.$$

In addition, if the probability p of disruptive events increases in the second stage, then the optimal τ_0 rises.

This conclusion shows that, if disruptive events occur in the second stage as predicted by manufacturers in the first stage, then, in order to prevent the disruptive events from happening, more preventive measures might be taken in the first stage. It can be seen from Equation (5-4) that probability p depends on parameters α, μ, and r_0 where α and μ are determined by the scale and frequency of the previous natural disasters, whereas r_0 rests on the disaster resistance of suppliers. In other words, the intensity of the optimal preventive measures taken by the centralized supply chain in the first stage is associated with the scale and frequency of previous natural disasters and the disaster resistance capacity of suppliers themselves.

(3) The study of the decision of scattered supply chains

In this model, consider the risk-neutral suppliers, who are affected by disruptive events and cannot satisfy the demand of distributors. Here, suppliers and distributors optimize their target function in their own interest.

However, in order to achieve supply chain coordination, distributors provide aid t for suppliers with the purpose of affecting decisions τ_0 and τ of suppliers. Here, the conditions that must be satisfied by aid t are calculated to allow the scattered supply chains to achieve coordination, namely, to achieve overall optimality.

Hypothesis 4: $\dfrac{\partial^2 C(\tau_0, \tau)}{\partial \tau^2} - \dfrac{\partial^2 t}{\partial \tau^2} \geq 0$. Hypothesis 4 shows that, after t increases,

the total cost function of suppliers C_s can still satisfy the property of the convex function.

Above all, consider that the scattered supply chains satisfy the conditions of coordination, and here the following conclusions can be drawn:

If distributors provide aid for suppliers t, and the scattered supply chains achieve the overall optimization in the second stage after the disruptive event (i.e., the suppliers' decisions τ in the scattered supply chains are the same as those in the centralized supply chains), then the conditions that aid t must satisfy are as follows:

$$\frac{\partial t}{\partial \tau} = -\theta$$

It proves that, in the case of t, the target cost function of decisions in the second stage for suppliers is as follows:

$$\min_{\tau} C_s = C(\tau_0, \tau) - t \tag{5-11}$$

Compute the first and second derivatives of τ in Equation (5-11), and let the first derivative be equal to 0.

$$\frac{\partial C_s(\tau_0, \tau)}{\partial \tau} = \frac{\partial C(\tau_0, \tau)}{\partial \tau} - \frac{\partial t}{\partial \tau} = 0 \tag{5-12}$$

$$\frac{\partial^2 C_s(\tau_0, \tau)}{\partial \tau^2} = \frac{\partial^2 C(\tau_0, \tau)}{\partial \tau^2} - \frac{\partial^2 t}{\partial \tau^2} \tag{5-13}$$

As $\dfrac{\partial^2 C(\tau_0, \tau)}{\partial \tau^2} - \dfrac{\partial^2 t}{\partial \tau^2} \geq 0$, $\dfrac{\partial^2 C_s(\tau_0, \tau)}{\partial \tau^2} \geq 0$, the optimal decisions by the suppliers in the scattered supply chain in the second stage must be satisfied, and the following can be achieved:

$$\frac{\partial C(\tau_0, \tau)}{\partial \tau} = \frac{\partial t}{\partial \tau} \tag{5-14}$$

Comparing Equations (5-6) and (5-14), it can be established that, as $\dfrac{\partial t}{\partial \tau} = -\theta$, the scattered supply chain achieves coordination. The decision τ in the recovery time taken after disruptive events in the scattered supply chains is the same as that in the centralized supply chains.

Next, consider the conditions under which the suppliers achieve coordination in the first stage, and then the following conclusions can be drawn.

If distributors supply aid for suppliers t, and the scattered supply chains achieve the overall optimization in the first stage after the disruptive events (i.e., the suppliers' decisions τ_0 in the scattered supply chains are the same as those in the centralized supply chains), then the conditions that aid t must satisfy are as follows:

$$\frac{\partial t}{\partial \tau_0} = 0$$

This proves that the target function of decision τ_0 in the first stage for suppliers is as follows:

$$\min_{\tau_0} C_s\left(\tau_0,\tau\right) = g\tau_0 + pE_\theta\left[C\left(\tau_0,\tau\right)-t\right] \tag{5-15}$$

Compute the first and second derivatives in Equation (5-15), and let the first derivative be equal to 0.

$$\frac{\partial C_s\left(\tau_0,\tau\right)}{\partial \tau_0} = \frac{\partial g\left(\tau_0\right)}{\partial \tau_0} + pE_\theta\left[\frac{\partial C\left(\tau_0,\tau\right)}{\partial \tau_0} + \frac{\partial C\left(\tau_0,\tau\right)}{\partial \tau}\frac{\partial \tau}{\partial \tau_0} - \frac{\partial t}{\partial \tau_0} - \frac{\partial t}{\partial \tau}\frac{\partial \tau}{\partial \tau_0}\right] \tag{5-16}$$

As $\dfrac{\partial C\left(\tau_0,\tau\right)}{\partial \tau} = \dfrac{\partial t}{\partial \tau}$, Equation (5-16) is equal to:

$$\frac{\partial g\left(\tau_0\right)}{\partial \tau_0} + pE_\theta\left[\frac{\partial C\left(\tau_0,\tau\right)}{\partial \tau_0} - \frac{\partial t}{\partial \tau_0}\right] = 0 \tag{5-17}$$

$$\frac{\partial^2 C\left(\tau_0,\tau\right)}{\partial \tau_0^2} = \frac{\partial^2 g\left(\tau_0\right)}{\partial \tau_0^2} + pE_\theta\left[\frac{\partial^2 C\left(\tau_0,\tau\right)}{\partial \tau_0^2} + \frac{\partial^2 C\left(\tau_0,\tau\right)}{\partial \tau\partial \tau_0}\frac{\partial \tau}{\partial \tau_0} - \frac{\partial^2 t}{\partial \tau_0^2} - \frac{\partial^2 t}{\partial \tau_0\partial \tau}\frac{\partial \tau}{\partial \tau_0}\right]$$

From Hypothesis 3, $\dfrac{\partial^2 C\left(\tau_0,\tau\right)}{\partial \tau_0^2} \geq 0$ can be derived. Comparing Equation (5-10) and (5-17), it can be established that, as $\dfrac{\partial t}{\partial \tau_0} = 0$, the decisions on preventive measures in the scattered supply chains in the first stage are the same as those in the centralized supply chains.

It is worth mentioning that $\dfrac{\partial t}{\partial \tau_0} = 0$ does not mean that t has nothing to do with τ_0. On the contrary, if the preventive measures taken by suppliers in the first stage are in place, then the aid by distributors is likely to drop. The key issue is that this tendency is based on the premise that recovery time τ must be ensured to satisfy the distributors. The reason is that, for distributors, the recovery time is the ultimate variable concerned. If the recovery time of suppliers can satisfy the distributors, then the aid by distributors will not vary with the number of preventive measures taken by suppliers. Therefore, the relationship between t and τ_0 is established through τ, but there is no direct relationship between t and τ_0.

From the preceding analysis, it can be established that, as the aid function t of distributors in relation to suppliers satisfied the condition $\begin{cases} \dfrac{\partial t}{\partial \tau} = -\theta \\ \dfrac{\partial t}{\partial \tau_0} = 0 \end{cases}$, scattered supply chains can achieve coordination, and the decisions on τ_0 and τ by suppliers are the same as those by suppliers in centralized supply chains.

Consider the specific expressions that satisfy the preceding conditions and the following function:

$$t = \alpha - \theta\tau$$

Where $u \geq \alpha \geq \theta\tau$, and u is the reserved utility of distributors, namely, the maximum loss that the distributors can carry. This function obviously satisfies $\dfrac{\partial t}{\partial \tau} = -\theta$. In addition, the disruptive events occur after θ is determined by $\dfrac{\partial t}{\partial \tau_0} = 0$

distributors: the longer the recovery time τ, the smaller t is. Therefore, this function can drive the suppliers to resume manufacturing as soon as possible. α depends on the comparative bargaining power of distributors and suppliers. The size of α value does not affect the cost of the overall supply chain but the cost of suppliers and distributors themselves.

A point to note is that t is determined before τ is specified. In other words, it is impossible to determine τ when the disruptive events occur in the second stage, and thus it is unlikely to obtain t by computing according to the function $t = \alpha - \theta\tau$. In practice, distributors can first reach an agreement $t = \alpha - \theta\tau$ with suppliers, and then provide aid T for suppliers, and generally here $T \neq t$. After suppliers have resumed manufacturing (here it has already been determined), if the aid, which will be repaid because of being insufficiently paid or returned because of being overpaid, is calculated, the amount is $|T - (\alpha - \theta\tau)|$. Another practical method is that, after suppliers resume manufacturing, distributors determine the amount of aid according to the contract $t = \alpha - \theta\tau$. Suppliers and distributors can choose according to the real circumstances.

The coordinated method in supply chains based on penalty

Here, the assumption is still a supply chain composed of risk-neutral suppliers and downstream distributors, where it is impossible for suppliers to provide raw materials or products because of disruptive events. Here, the coordinated mechanism adopted is penalty. In this coordinated mechanism, suppliers with disruptive events must pay the penalty to the distributors with backorder cost. In this case, it is common that distributors and suppliers have already reached an agreement when they sign their business contract. If the suppliers fail to provide products to distributors, then they must pay a penalty to the distributors.

Here, the model can be disintegrated into two stages chronologically. In the first stage, suppliers take preventive measures to address disruptive events. In the second stage, the disruptive events happen, and it is impossible for suppliers to provide products to distributors, who will suffer loss. Suppliers then pay penalty to distributors to compensate for the loss and, after a period of time, suppliers' production recovers.

(1) The basic hypothesis of penalty model, decision procedures, and illustrations of parameters

Here, in the models of supply chains, the relevant circumstances related to each stage are illustrated. In the first stage, suppliers take preventive measures τ_0 that may occur in the second stage (next stage). The disruptive events happen, and then suppliers cannot satisfy the demand of distributors, and pay penalty t to distributors. In the second stage, suppliers resume manufacturing; the cost is $C(\tau_0, \tau_0)$; the duration is τ; and, afterward, suppliers' production recovers completely.

Here, the hypotheses and the illustrations of parameters are similar to those discussed in the preceding text. The major difference is that t represents that suppliers suffering from the effects of disruptive events cannot provide products to distributors, and thus distributors suffer loss. In order to compensate for the loss of distributors, suppliers pay penalty t to distributors.

Hypothesis 5: $\dfrac{\partial^2 C(\tau_0, \tau)}{\partial \tau^2} + \dfrac{\partial^2 t}{\partial \tau^2} \geq 0$. Hypothesis 5 shows that, after t increases, the total cost function C_s of suppliers can still satisfy the property of convex function.

When penalty is used for coordination, the study of modeling centralized supply chains is completely the same as the content discussed earlier. Therefore, the coordination measures of the scattered supply chains are directly considered here.

(2) The study of decisions of the scattered supply chains

Here, suppliers and distributors optimize the target functions in their own interests. Nevertheless, in order to achieve coordination in supply chains, distributors claim penalty t from suppliers, with the aim of affecting the decisions τ_0 and τ of suppliers. Here, the conditions that penalty t must satisfy are computed to allow the scattered supply chains to achieve coordination; namely, to achieve the overall optimality.

First of all, consider the conditions under which scattered supply chains achieve coordination, and the following conclusions can be drawn. If suppliers can provide penalty t for distributors, and the scattered supply chains achieve the overall optimality after the disruptive events in the second stage, then the conditions that the penalty t must satisfy are as follows:

$$\frac{\partial t}{\partial \tau} = 0$$

This proves that, in the case of t, the target cost function in the second stage for suppliers is as follows:

$$\min_{\tau} C_s = C(\tau_0, \tau) + t \qquad (5\text{-}18)$$

Compute the first and second derivatives in Equation (5-18), and let the first derivative be equal to 0.

$$\frac{\partial C_s(\tau_0, \tau)}{\partial \tau} = \frac{\partial C(\tau_0, \tau)}{\partial \tau} + \frac{\partial t}{\partial \tau} = 0 \qquad (5\text{-}19)$$

$$\frac{\partial^2 C_s(\tau_0, \tau)}{\partial \tau^2} = \frac{\partial^2 C(\tau_0, \tau)}{\partial \tau^2} + \frac{\partial^2 t}{\partial \tau^2} \qquad (5\text{-}20)$$

As $\dfrac{\partial^2 C(\tau_0, \tau)}{\partial \tau^2} + \dfrac{\partial^2 t}{\partial \tau^2} \geq 0, \dfrac{\partial^2 C_s(\tau_0, \tau)}{\partial \tau^2} \geq 0$, the optimal decision of suppliers in

the scattered supply chains in the second stage must satisfy $\dfrac{\partial C_s(\tau_0, \tau)}{\partial \tau} = 0$, and the following can be achieved:

$$\frac{\partial C(\tau_0, \tau)}{\partial \tau} = -\frac{\partial t}{\partial \tau} \qquad (5\text{-}21)$$

On comparing Equations (5-6) and (5-21), it can be known that the scattered supply chain achieves coordination as $\dfrac{\partial t}{\partial \tau} = 0$.

In order to achieve the coordinated conditions for the supply chain in the first stage, the following aspects can be considered.

If suppliers can provide penalty t to distributors, and the scattered supply chains achieve the overall optimality after the disruptive events in the first stage, then the conditions that penalty t must satisfy are as follows:

$$\frac{\partial t}{\partial \tau_0} = 0$$

This proves that the target function of decision τ_0 in the first stage for suppliers is:

$$\min_{\tau_0} C_s(\tau_0, \tau) = g\tau_0 + pE_\theta\left[C(\tau_0, \tau) + t\right] \qquad (5\text{-}22)$$

Compute the first and second derivatives of τ_0 in Equation (5-22), and let the first derivative be equal to 0.

$$\frac{\partial C_s(\tau_0,\tau)}{\partial \tau_0} = \frac{\partial g(\tau_0)}{\partial \tau_0} + pE_\theta \left[\frac{\partial C(\tau_0,\tau)}{\partial \tau_0} + \frac{\partial C(\tau_0,\tau)}{\partial \tau} \frac{\partial \tau}{\partial \tau_0} + \frac{\partial t}{\partial \tau_0} + \frac{\partial t}{\partial \tau} \frac{\partial \tau}{\partial \tau_0} \right]$$

$$(5\text{-}23)$$

As $\dfrac{\partial C(\tau_0,\tau)}{\partial \tau} = -\dfrac{\partial t}{\partial \tau}$, Equation (5-23) is equal to:

$$\frac{\partial g(\tau_0)}{\partial \tau_0} + pE_\theta \left[\frac{\partial C(\tau_0,\tau)}{\partial \tau_0} + \frac{\partial t}{\partial \tau_0} \right] = 0 \qquad\qquad (5\text{-}24)$$

$$\frac{\partial^2 C(\tau_0,\tau)}{\partial \tau_0^2} = \frac{\partial^2 g(\tau_0)}{\partial \tau_0^2} + pE_\theta \left[\frac{\partial^2 C(\tau_0,\tau)}{\partial \tau_0^2} + \frac{\partial^2 C(\tau_0,\tau)}{\partial \tau \partial \tau_0} \frac{\partial \tau}{\partial \tau_0} + \frac{\partial^2 t}{\partial \tau_0^2} + \frac{\partial^2 t}{\partial \tau_0 \partial \tau} \frac{\partial \tau}{\partial \tau_0} \right]$$

From Hypothesis 3, $\dfrac{\partial^2 C(\tau_0,\tau)}{\partial \tau_0^2} \geq 0$ can be derived. Compare Equations (5-10)

and (5-24), as $\dfrac{\partial t}{\partial \tau_0} = 0$, and it can be found that the decisions on preventive

measures in the first stage in scattered supply chains and those in centralized supply chains are the same.

Based on the preceding analyses, it can be known that, in order to make the scattered supply chains achieve overall coordination, the following conditions must be satisfied in relation to the penalty that suppliers provide for distributors:

$$\left| \begin{array}{l} \dfrac{\partial t}{\partial \tau} = \theta \\[2mm] \dfrac{\partial t}{\partial \tau_0} = 0 \end{array} \right.$$

The explanation of $\dfrac{\partial t}{\partial \tau_0} = 0$ is actually similar to the preceding circumstances.

In terms of distributors, the recovery time is the ultimate variable concerned. The reason is that the recovery time increases by the unit each time, and the distributors suffer redundant loss. If suppliers can satisfy the demand of distributors, then distributors are not generally concerned with how many preventive measures suppliers have actually taken in the first stage. Thus, it is concluded that there is no direct relationship between the penalty that suppliers pay to distributors and the preventive measures that suppliers take in the first stage.

The model for coordination of two-stage supply chain comprising one supplier with risk aversion and a distributor

In the previous sections, suppliers are risk-neutral, which means that, in some cases, some problems can be solved, but in practice, in most cases, the hypothesis regarding enterprises with risk-neutral attitudes is not very rational. The reason is that many enterprises hate operations risks and financial risks, in the context of disruptive events that exert great influence on enterprises. In general, enterprises dislike this kind of events. Roughly, in the case where enterprises have risk aversion, they use strategies that are different from the measures taken by risk-neutral enterprises, and thus the models constructed in the case of risk-neutral entities might not be applicable for enterprises that have risk aversion. For this reason, it is necessary to investigate the decisions for addressing disruptive events in relation to enterprises that have risk aversion.

Here, consider the supply chain with one supplier and one distributor, where suppliers have risk aversion. Suppliers might not satisfy the demand due to the influence of disruptive events. Here, the study aims to look for a method to coordinate decisions for optimization of the overall supply chains. Here, the decision procedure of supply chains includes two stages: preventive measures that suppliers take before disruptive events, and the recovery time taken after a disruptive event occurs.

Here, the two coordinated mechanisms mentioned earlier are studied to consider what conditions the decision-making procedures of two-stage supply chains, in which enterprises have risk aversion, are able to satisfy. In order to help understand the models constructed, the mechanism in which suppliers pay penalty for distributors is discussed first, and then, after the conclusions are drawn, the mechanism in which distributors provide aid for suppliers is considered.

The coordinated method in supply chains based on penalty

(1) The basic hypotheses of penalty models, decision procedures, and the illustrations of parameters

Here, the process of decision-making for enterprises is similar to the preceding discussion, but the suppliers have risk aversion.

The illustrations of parameters and the hypothetical conditions are similar to the preceding discussions, and the additional parameters are considered in the following text.

X represents the indicative variables of whether the disruptive events occur to suppliers in the second stage, which is a random variable and subject to the distribution of 0–1. If $X = 1$ represents that disruptive events occur in the second stage, then $X = 0$ indicates that the disruptive events do not happen. Let $P\{X = 1\} = p$, in which p represents the probability of disruptive events occurring in the second stage, and the method of computation refers to the discussion in the preceding text.

Likewise, in order to compute the coordination mechanism in the case of risk-averse suppliers, the focus here is on the centralized supply chain composed of suppliers and distributors first.

(2) The study of decisions of the centralized supply chains

First of all, consider the case in which disruptive events occur to one supplier and one distributor in a centralized supply chain, and compute the optimal preventive measure τ_0 for the centralized supply chain in the first stage and the optimal recovery time τ in the second stage. Consider the decision procedure in the second stage (τ is the decision variable) first.

In terms of the centralized supply chain, the cost of the disruptive event in the second stage is as follows.

$$\min_{\tau} C_1(\tau_0,\tau) = C(\tau_0,\tau) + \theta\tau$$

Therefore, this target function is the same as the corresponding target function discussed earlier, and thus the solution can be referred to the above equation.

The optimal recovery time τ must satisfy the following:

$$\frac{\partial C(\tau_0,\tau)}{\partial \tau} = -\theta \tag{5-25}$$

In terms of decision τ_0 for centralized supply chain in the first stage, consider the case in which the centralized supply chain has risk aversion. In the first stage, as disruptive events do not happen, θ is a random variable. If disruptive events happen in the second stage, then after the disruptive events, the cost expectation (referring to the expectation of θ) that disruptive events affect centralized supply chains is $E_\theta\left[C(\tau_0,\tau) + \theta\tau\right]$. Let $\tilde{C} = \begin{cases} E_\theta\left[C(\tau_0,\tau) + \theta\tau\right] & X = 1 \\ 0 & X = 0 \end{cases}$. Therefore $E(\tilde{C}) = pE_\theta\left[C(\tau_0,\tau) + \theta\tau\right]$.

$$D(\tilde{C}) = E(\tilde{C}^2) - E^2(\tilde{C}) = (p - p^2)E^2\left[C(\tau_0,\tau) + \theta\tau\right]$$

Based on the average value of risk aversion–variance model, the target function of centralized supply chain in the first stage is as follows:

$$\min_{\tau_0} C_2(\tau_0,\tau) = g(\tau_0) + E(\tilde{C}) + AD(\tilde{C})$$

$$= g(\tau_0) + pE_\theta\left[C(\tau_0,\tau) + \theta\tau\right] + A(p - p^2)E_\theta^2\left[C(\tau_0,\tau) + \theta\tau\right] \tag{5-26}$$

Where parameter A represents the extent of annoyance of risk in the centralized supply chain. In terms of supply chains with risk annoyance, if there is $A > 0$, the larger $A > 0$ is in relation to the greater extent of risk annoyance. In Equation (5-26), the first derivative is computed by letting it be 0.

$$\frac{\partial C_s(\tau_0,\tau)}{\partial \tau_0} = \frac{\partial g(\tau_0)}{\partial \tau_0} + \left\{p + 2A(p - p^2)E_\theta\left[C(\tau_0,\tau) + \theta\tau\right]\right\} \times$$

$$E_\theta\left[\frac{\partial C(\tau_0,\tau)}{\partial \tau_0} + \frac{\partial C(\tau_0,\tau)}{\partial \tau}\frac{\partial \tau}{\partial \tau_0} + \theta\frac{\partial \tau}{\partial \tau_0}\right]$$

By substituting it into $\dfrac{\partial C(\tau_0,\tau)}{\partial \tau} = -\theta$, the following can be achieved:

$$\frac{\partial C_s(\tau_0,\tau)}{\partial \tau_0} = \frac{\partial g(\tau_0)}{\partial \tau_0} + \left\{ p + 2A\left(p - p^2\right)E_\theta\left[C(\tau_0,\tau)+\theta\tau\right]\right\} \times E_\theta\left[\frac{\partial C(\tau_0,\tau)}{\partial \tau_0}\right]$$

$$(5\text{-}27)$$

As $\dfrac{\partial^2 g(\tau_0)}{\partial \tau_0{}^2} > M$ (Hypothesis 3), $\dfrac{\partial^2 C_s(\tau_0,\tau)}{\partial \tau_0{}^2} > 0$. The optimal τ_0 must satisfy

that the target function of the first derivative is 0, namely:

$$\frac{\partial g(\tau_0)}{\partial \tau_0} + \left\{ p + 2A\left(p - p^2\right)E_\theta\left[C(\tau_0,\tau)+\theta\tau\right]\right\} \times E_\theta\left[\frac{\partial C(\tau_0,\tau)}{\partial \tau_0}\right] = 0 \quad (5\text{-}28)$$

In terms of preventive measures taken by the centralized supply chain in the case of risk aversion, the following conclusions can be drawn:

Compared with the centralized supply chain with a risk-neutral attitude, more preventive measures are taken with risk aversion in the first stage. In other words, τ_0 will increase.

The next step is to prove by reduction to absurdity. Suppose the preventive measures are small for the centralized supply chain with risk aversion in the first stage. It can be derived from the preceding text that the optimal decision satisfies Equation (5-28) for the centralized supply chain with risk aversion in the first stage. Nevertheless, the optimal strategies (referred to as τ_{s0} in order to differentiate from the case of risk aversion) for the centralized supply chain ($A = 0$) with risk neutrality in the first stage must satisfy the following:

$$\frac{\partial g(\tau_{s0})}{\partial \tau_{s0}} + pE_\theta\left[\frac{\partial C(\tau_{s0},\tau)}{\partial \tau_{s0}}\right] = 0 \qquad\qquad (5\text{-}29)$$

If the preventive measures taken for the centralized supply chain with risk aversion in the first stage are small, namely, $\tau_0 < \tau_{s0}$, then the following can be achieved according to Hypotheses 2 and 3:

$$0 < \frac{\partial g(\tau_0)}{\partial \tau_0} < \frac{\partial g(\tau_{s0})}{\partial \tau_{s0}} \qquad\qquad (5\text{-}30)$$

$$\frac{\partial C(\tau_0,\tau)}{\partial \tau_0} < \frac{\partial C(\tau_{s0},\tau)}{\partial \tau_{s0}} < 0 \qquad\qquad (5\text{-}31)$$

In addition, $A\left(p - p^2\right)E_\theta\left[C(\tau_0,\tau)+\theta\tau\right] > 0$ is achieved, and therefore:

$$\left\{ p + 2A\left(p - p^2\right)E_\theta\left[C(\tau_0,\tau)+\theta\tau\right]\right\} \times E_\theta\left[\frac{\partial C(\tau_0,\tau)}{\partial \tau_0}\right] < pE_\theta\left[\frac{\partial C(\tau_{s0},\tau)}{\partial \tau_{s0}}\right] < 0$$

According to Equations (5-28) and (5-29), in order to achieve the first condition, the following must be satisfied:

$$\frac{\partial g(\tau_0)}{\partial \tau_0} > \frac{\partial g(\tau_{s0})}{\partial \tau_{s0}} > 0 \tag{5-32}$$

Evidently, Equations (5-30) and (5-32) are contradictory, and thus more preventive measures must be taken by the centralized supply chain with risk aversion in the first stage; namely, τ_0 will increase.

This conclusion shows that the centralized supply chain with risk aversion dislikes the risk caused by disruptive events in the second stage and the loss brought by disruptive events to supply chains, and thus they would rather take more preventive measures in the first stage. This is a relatively direct conclusion.

(3) The study of decisions of the scattered supply chains

Here, suppliers and distributors are two independent enterprises. As suppliers fail to provide commodities for distributors, they must pay penalty t to the distributors. Here, consider that the scattered supply chains achieve the conditions of coordination in the second stage first, and then the following conclusions can be drawn.

If suppliers pay penalty t to distributors, and the scattered supply chains achieve the overall optimization after disruptive events in the second stage (referring to the hypothesis that decisions τ of suppliers in the scattered supply chains are the same as those in the centralized supply chains), then penalty t must satisfy the following conditions:

$$\frac{\partial t}{\partial \tau} = \theta$$

In the case of penalty t, the target cost function of decisions of suppliers in the second stage can be expressed as follows:

$$\min_{\tau} C_s = C(\tau_0, \tau) + t$$

Therefore, the suppliers' target function in the second stage is the same as the discussion in the preceding text, and thus the following can be achieved. As $\frac{\partial t}{\partial \tau} = \theta$, the scattered supply chains achieve coordination. The decision of the relevant recovery time taken by suppliers after the disruptive events is the same as that in the case of centralized supply chains.

Next, consider the conditions for the scattered supply chains to achieve coordination in the first stage. The following can be achieved: if suppliers pay penalty t to distributors, and $t = \theta\tau$, then the scattered supply chains can achieve coordination in the first stage.

It proves that the target function of the scattered supply chains in the first stage is as follows:

$$\min_{\tau_0} C_2(\tau_0, \tau) = g(\tau_0) + E(\tilde{C}) + AD(\tilde{C})$$

$$= g(\tau_0) + pE_\theta \left[C(\tau_0, \tau) + t \right] + A\left(p - p^2 \right) E_\theta^2 \left[C(\tau_0, \tau) + t \right] \tag{5-33}$$

Compute the first and second derivatives of τ_0 in Equation (5-33), letting the first derivative be 0, and then:

$$\frac{\partial C_s(\tau_0,\tau)}{\partial \tau_0} = \frac{\partial g(\tau_0)}{\partial \tau_0} + \left\{ p + 2A(p-p^2)E_\theta \left[C(\tau_0,\tau)+t\right] \right\} \times$$

$$E_\theta \left[\frac{\partial C(\tau_0,\tau)}{\partial \tau_0} + \frac{\partial C(\tau_0,\tau)}{\partial \tau}\frac{\partial \tau}{\partial \tau_0} + \frac{\partial \tau}{\partial \tau_0} + \frac{\partial t}{\partial \tau}\frac{\partial \tau}{\partial \tau_0} \right]$$

Substitute it into $\dfrac{\partial C(\tau_0,\tau)}{\partial \tau} = -\dfrac{\partial t}{\partial \tau}$, and the following can be achieved:

$$\frac{\partial C_s(\tau_0,\tau)}{\partial \tau_0} = \frac{\partial g(\tau_0)}{\partial \tau_0} + \left\{ p + 2A(p-p^2)E_\theta \left[C(\tau_0,\tau)+t\right] \right\} \times E_\theta \left[\frac{\partial C(\tau_0,\tau)}{\partial \tau} + \frac{\partial \tau}{\partial \tau_0} \right]$$

$$(5\text{-}34)$$

Compare Equations (5-28) and (5-34), and the following can be achieved. As $t=\theta\tau$ and $\dfrac{\partial t}{\partial \tau_0}=0$, the scattered supply chains achieve coordination in the first stage. In practice, if condition $t=\theta\tau$ is satisfied, then condition $\dfrac{\partial t}{\partial \tau_0}=0$ will be satisfied naturally. Thus, it is fine that only condition $t=\theta\tau$ is satisfied.

It can be seen from the preceding analysis that if the penalty that suppliers in the scattered supply chains pay to the distributors satisfies $t=\theta\tau$, then the scattered supply chains may achieve coordination. Here, the decision of τ_0,τ by suppliers in the scattered supply chains is the same as that in the centralized supply chains.

It is clear that, regarding suppliers with risk aversion, in practice, if distributors expect that suppliers can achieve optimization of supply chains by taking preventive measures beforehand and the recovery procedures after disruptive events, they only request penalty $t=\theta\tau$ from suppliers. In other words, the penalty that suppliers must pay is the function of direct proportion of the recovery time needed.

Compare the results of the preceding analysis with the case of suppliers with risk-neutral attitude. As suppliers prefer risk-neutral attitude, the conditions in which supply chains can achieve coordination are $\begin{cases} \dfrac{\partial t}{\partial \tau}=\theta \\ \dfrac{\partial t}{\partial \tau_0}=0 \end{cases}$. The function expressions that can satisfy this condition have many forms. For instance, in $t=\theta\tau+\beta$, β is the constant. Nonetheless, as suppliers have risk aversion, only in function $t=\theta\tau$ can the supply chains achieve optimization. Evidently, $t=\theta\tau$ satisfies the condition $\begin{cases} \dfrac{\partial t}{\partial \tau}=\theta \\ \dfrac{\partial t}{\partial \tau_0}=0 \end{cases}$. Therefore, the coordinated mechanism of supply chain for suppliers that prefer risk neutrality does not completely apply to the cases of suppliers with risk aversion. Nonetheless, the coordinated mechanism of supply chain for suppliers with risk aversion may apply to risk-neutral suppliers.

The coordination method of supplier chains based on aid

Here, the focus is on analysis of the case in which distributors provide aid to suppliers suffering from disruptive events, after the disruptive events occur, in which suppliers still have risk aversion. The analytical methods here are similar to the discussions in the preceding text. Starting from the overall supply chain, the decision procedures of the scattered supply chains are considered.

In terms of hypotheses and backdrop, the preceding sections have already provided detailed explanations. In addition, analysis of the overall supply chains is the same as the discussions in the preceding text. Thus, it is not necessary to provide additional discussion.

In the case of scattered supply chains, compute the solution and here the coordination methods can be disintegrated into several stages.

First of all, consider the conditions for the scattered supply chains to achieve coordination in the second stage. In the case of aid t, the target cost function for suppliers in the second stage can be expressed as follows:

$$\min_{\tau} C_s = C(\tau_0, \tau) - t$$

Now, this target function of suppliers is the same as that in the preceding discussions. Thus, as $\dfrac{\partial t}{\partial \tau} = -\theta$, the scattered supply chains achieve coordination, and the decision τ of recovery time is the same as that in the centralized supply chains.

Next, consider the condition in which the scattered supply chains achieve coordination in the first stage. The target function of suppliers in the scattered supply chains in the first stage is as follows:

$$\min_{\tau_0} C_2(\tau_0, \tau) = g(\tau_0) + E(\tilde{C}) + AD(\tilde{C})$$

$$= g(\tau_0) + pE_\theta \big[C(\tau_0, \tau) - t \big] + A\big(p - p^2\big) E_\theta^2 \big[C(\tau_0, \tau) - t \big] \qquad (5\text{-}35)$$

Compute the first and second derivatives of τ_0 in Equation (5-35), letting the first derivative be 0; then:

$$\frac{\partial C_s(\tau_0, \tau)}{\partial \tau_0} = \frac{\partial g(\tau_0)}{\partial \tau_0} + \Big\{ p + 2A\big(p - p^2\big) E_\theta \big[C(\tau_0, \tau) - t \big] \Big\} \times$$

$$E_\theta \left[\frac{\partial C(\tau_0, \tau)}{\partial \tau_0} + \frac{\partial C(\tau_0, \tau)}{\partial \tau} \frac{\partial \tau}{\partial \tau_0} - \frac{\partial \tau}{\partial \tau_0} - \frac{\partial t}{\partial \tau} \frac{\partial \tau}{\partial \tau_0} \right]$$

Substitute it into $\dfrac{\partial C(\tau_0,\tau)}{\partial \tau} = \dfrac{\partial t}{\partial \tau}$, and then the following can be achieved:

$$\frac{\partial C_s(\tau_0,\tau)}{\partial \tau_0} = \frac{\partial g(\tau_0)}{\partial \tau_0} + \left\{ p + 2A(p-p^2)E_\theta\left[C(\tau_0,\tau)-t\right] \right\} \times E_\theta \left[\frac{\partial C(\tau_0,\tau)}{\partial \tau} - \frac{\partial \tau}{\partial \tau_0}\right]$$

$$(5\text{-}36)$$

Compare Equations (5-28) and (5-36), and then the following can be achieved. As $t = -\theta\tau$ and $\dfrac{\partial t}{\partial \tau_0} = 0$, the scattered supply chains achieve coordination in the first stage. Here, the aid the distributors pay is negative. In other words, as the aid that distributors provide for suppliers are negative, this type of supply chain may achieve overall optimization. The conclusion that the aid is negative is apparently absurd. However, alternatively, if the symbols here can be seen as the direction of transferred payment between suppliers and distributors, then it shows that the distributors are not supposed to provide aid to suppliers. Instead, suppliers pay the penalty to distributors. That is to say, in the latter circumstance, the supply chain may achieve coordination. This conclusion again proves that the relevant conclusions in the preceding discussion are correct.

Finally, consider why decisions of suppliers cannot achieve optimization of the overall supply chain as distributors provide aid to suppliers. Considering Equation (5-36), as the supply chains described in the preceding sections achieve coordination, substitute the second condition $\dfrac{\partial t}{\partial \tau_0} = 0$ t that must be satisfied, and the following can be achieved:

$$\frac{\partial C_s(\tau_0,\tau)}{\partial \tau_0} = \frac{\partial g(\tau_0)}{\partial \tau_0} + \left\{ p + 2A(p-p^2)E_\theta\left[C(\tau_0,\tau)-t\right] \right\} \times E_\theta \left[\frac{\partial C(\tau_0,\tau)}{\partial \tau_0}\right] = 0$$

As $E_\theta\left[\dfrac{\partial C(\tau_0,\tau)}{\partial \tau_0}\right] < 0$, the disruptive events have an unfavorable impact on suppliers. Thus, generally, here it is $E_\theta\left[C(\tau_0,\tau)-t\right] > 0$; otherwise it means that suppliers can benefit from the disruptive events, and the suppliers expect the disruptive events to happen. However, this is evidently irrational, and here $\theta\tau > 0$ and $0 < p < 1$. If distributors provide aid to suppliers, namely, $t > 0$, then the following is achieved:

$$\left\{ p + 2A(p-p^2)E_\theta\left[C(\tau_0,\tau)-t\right] \right\} < \left\{ p + 2A(p-p^2)E_\theta\left[C(\tau_0,\tau)+\theta\tau\right] \right\}$$

Multiply the two sides of the equation $E_\theta\left[\dfrac{\partial C(\tau_0,\tau)}{\partial \tau_0}\right]$, and the following can be achieved:

$$\left\{ p + 2A(p-p^2)E_\theta\left[C(\tau_0,\tau)-t\right] \right\} \times E_\theta \left[\frac{\partial C(\tau_0,\tau)}{\partial \tau_0}\right] >$$

$$\left\{ p + 2A(p - p^2)E_\theta \left[C(\tau_0, \tau) + \theta\tau \right] \right\} \times E_\theta \left[\frac{\partial C(\tau_0, \tau)}{\partial \tau_0} \right]$$

Hence, it can be seen that $\left. \dfrac{\partial g(\tau_0)}{\partial \tau_0} \right|_{\tau_0 = \tau_{01}} < \left. \dfrac{\partial g(\tau_0)}{\partial \tau_0} \right|_{\tau_0 = \tau_{02}}$, where τ_{01} indicates the

decision on preventive measures by suppliers as distributors provide aid to suppliers. However, τ_{02} refers to the preventive measures by suppliers as supply chains achieve optimization. According to the property of the function $g(\tau_0)$, here $\tau_{01} < \tau_{02}$. In other words, once suppliers with risk aversion obtain the aid from the distributors, preventive measures taken by suppliers in the first stage are smaller than those in the centralized supply chains. This is why it is impossible for supply chains to achieve coordination when there is aid. Thus, the following conclusions can be drawn.

In terms of the supply chain consisting of suppliers and distributors with risk aversion, if the mechanism in which distributors provide aid to suppliers is adopted, then it is impossible for the supply chains to achieve coordination. The reason is that the preventive measures that suppliers take in the first stage are definitely smaller than those in the centralized supply chains.

The coordinated model of two-stage supply chains with one supplier and many distributors

The previous section discussed the coordinated two-stage supply chain with one supplier and one distributor before and after the disruptive events. Here, the focus is on a coordinated two-stage supply chain with one supplier and many distributors. Above all, consider the conditions that this mechanism must be satisfied with in the supply chain with one supplier and many distributors as distributors provide aid for suppliers suffering from disruptive events (Sheng, 2008).

The coordinated method of supply chains based on aids

The hypothesis and basic backdrop of models

Here, the relevant parameters in the model are basically similar to the preceding discussions, and other parameters are added as follows.

θ_i represents the backorder cost that becomes applicable within the recovery time τ taken by suppliers in relation to distributor i ($i = 1, 2, \cdots, n$). The backorder cost varies with the event in relation to different distributors, and it is associated with such factors as the time of the event and the status of distributors. If the distributors fail to satisfy the demand of important clients when a disruptive event occurs, then the backorder cost is supposed to be higher. However, it is difficult to know whether the backorder demand is related to important clients before the disruptive event occurs. Therefore, if θ_i in the first stage is a random variable and has an identical probability distribution, the probability density function is $f(\theta)$. The value of θ_i can be achieved after the disruptive events for suppliers in the second stage, and it becomes the definite value.

Here, the hypothesis is that the information about θ_i is shared by distributors and suppliers. In other words, in the first stage, both distributors and suppliers understand that the probability density function θ_i is $f(\theta)$, and after the disruptive event, both distributors and suppliers understand that the value of θ_i has already been achieved in the second stage.

t_i represents the aid provided by distributors to suppliers in order to allow suppliers to resume manufacturing after disruptive events.

Hypothesis 6: $\dfrac{\partial^2 C(\tau_0,\tau)}{\partial \tau^2} - \sum_{i=1}^{n} \dfrac{\partial^2 t_i}{\partial \tau^2} \geq 0$. This hypothesis shows that the supplier's total cost function C_s can still satisfy the convex function after t_i increases.

The optimal models of centralized supply chains

First of all, consider the supplier with disruptive event and the downstream distributor n as a whole enterprise, and compute the optimal preventive measure τ_0 of the whole enterprise in the first stage and the optimal recovery time τ in the second stage. Since the decision of the whole enterprise can be disintegrated into two stages, computation of the solution must start from the decision procedure in the second stage (τ is the decision variable). The process of computation of the solution related to the model in the decision process in the second stage has already been analyzed in detail in the preceding sections, and thus only the relevant conclusions are discussed here.

Considering the supplier with disruptive events and its downstream distributors as a whole enterprise, the optimal recovery time τ of the enterprise in the second stage satisfies the following:

$$\frac{\partial C(\tau_0,\tau)}{\partial \tau} = -\sum_{i=1}^{n} \theta_i$$

Next, consider decision τ_0 of the whole enterprise in the first stage, and the back-order cost θ_i in the second stage is not achieved. Nevertheless, the enterprise understands that the probability density distribution of θ_i is $f(\theta)$. Furthermore, the enterprise in the first stage knows that the probability of disruptive events occurring in the second stage is p, and thus the target function of the whole enterprise in the first stage is as follows:

$$\min_{\tau_0} C_2(\tau_0,\tau) = g(\tau_0) + pE_\theta \left[C(\tau_0,\tau) + \sum_{i=1}^{n} \theta_i \tau \right] \tag{5-37}$$

Where $E_\theta \left[C(\tau_0, \tau) + \sum_{i=1}^{n} \theta_i \tau \right]$ indicates that if the disruptive events occur in the second stage, then after the disruptive events, the cost expectation occurs in the second stage for the whole enterprise, and the value of the optimal τ_0 must satisfy the following conclusion.

Considering the supplier with disruptive events and its downstream distributors as a whole enterprise, the optimal recovery time τ of the enterprise in the first stage satisfies the following:

$$\frac{\partial g(\tau_0)}{\partial \tau_0} + pE_\theta \left[\frac{\partial C(\tau_0, \tau)}{\partial \tau_0} \right] = 0$$

Proof: compute the first derivative in Equation (5-37) and let the first derivative be 0.

$$\frac{\partial C_2(\tau_0, \tau)}{\partial \tau_0} = \frac{\partial g(\tau_0)}{\partial \tau_0} + pE_\theta \left[\frac{\partial C(\tau_0, \tau)}{\partial \tau_0} + \frac{\partial C(\tau_0, \tau)}{\partial \tau} \frac{\partial \tau}{\partial \tau_0} + \sum_{i=1}^{n} \theta_i \frac{\partial \tau}{\partial \tau_0} \right]$$

As $\dfrac{\partial C(\tau_0, \tau)}{\partial \tau} = -\sum_{i=1}^{n} \theta_i$, the following is achieved:

$$\frac{\partial C_2(\tau_0, \tau)}{\partial \tau_0} = \frac{\partial g(\tau_0)}{\partial \tau_0} + pE_\theta \left[\frac{\partial C(\tau_0, \tau)}{\partial \tau_0} \right] = 0 \tag{5-38}$$

Compute the second derivative in Equation (5-37).

$$\frac{\partial^2 C_2(\tau_0, \tau)}{\partial \tau_0^2} = \frac{\partial^2 g(\tau_0)}{\partial \tau_0^2} + pE_\theta \left[\frac{\partial^2 C(\tau_0, \tau)}{\partial \tau_0^2} + \frac{\partial^2 C(\tau_0, \tau)}{\partial \tau_0 \partial \tau} \frac{\partial \tau}{\partial \tau_0} \right] \tag{5-39}$$

According to Hypothesis 3, as Equation (5-39) > 0, the optimal preventive measure τ_0 taken by the whole enterprise in the first stage must satisfy $\frac{\partial g(\tau_0)}{\partial \tau_0} + pE_\theta \left[\frac{\partial C(\tau_0, \tau)}{\partial \tau_0} \right] = 0.$

The optimal model when the scattered supply chains have the aid t_i

According to the preceding discussion, distributors in the scattered supply chains provide aid t_i for suppliers with disruptive events and achieve coordination in the second stage. Thus, the following conclusions can be drawn.

In the context where distributors provide aid t_i for suppliers, the conditions under which the scattered supply chains achieve coordination in the overall supply chain in the second stage after disruptive events are as follows:

$$\sum_{i=1}^{n} \frac{\partial t_i}{\partial \tau} = -\sum_{i=1}^{n} \theta_i$$

As the scattered supply chains in which distributors provide suppliers aid t_i in the first stage achieve coordination, the aid provided by distributors must satisfy the following conclusions.

In the context in which distributors provide aid for suppliers, the conditions that the scattered supply chains achieve coordination in the first stage are as follows:

$$\frac{\partial t_i}{\partial \tau_0} = 0$$

It proves that the target function τ_0 of the decision for suppliers in the first stage is as follows:

$$\min_{\tau_0} C_2(\tau_0, \tau) = g(\tau_0) + pE_\theta \left[C(\tau_0, \tau) - \sum_{i=1}^{n} t_i \right] \tag{5-40}$$

Compute the first and second derivatives in Equation (5-40), letting the first derivative be 0, and apply the following:

$$\frac{\partial C(\tau_0, \tau)}{\partial \tau} = \sum_{i=1}^{n} \frac{\partial t_i}{\partial \tau}$$

The following can be achieved:

$$\frac{\partial C_s(\tau_0, \tau)}{\partial \tau_0} = \frac{\partial g(\tau_0)}{\partial \tau_0} + pE_\theta \left[\frac{\partial C(\tau_0, \tau)}{\partial \tau_0} + \frac{\partial C(\tau_0, \tau)}{\partial \tau} \frac{\partial \tau}{\partial \tau_0} - \sum_{i=1}^{n} \frac{\partial t_i}{\partial \tau_0} - \sum_{i=1}^{n} \frac{\partial t_i}{\partial \tau} \frac{\partial \tau}{\partial \tau_0} \right]$$

$$= \frac{\partial g(\tau_0)}{\partial \tau_0} + pE_\theta \left[\frac{\partial C(\tau_0, \tau)}{\partial \tau_0} - \sum_{i=1}^{n} \frac{\partial t_i}{\partial \tau_0} \right] = 0 \tag{5-41}$$

$$\frac{\partial^2 C(\tau_0, \tau)}{\partial \tau_0^2} = \frac{\partial^2 g(\tau_0)}{\partial \tau_0^2} + pE_\theta \left[\frac{\partial^2 C(\tau_0, \tau)}{\partial \tau_0^2} + \frac{\partial^2 C(\tau_0, \tau)}{\partial \tau \partial \tau_0} \frac{\partial \tau}{\partial \tau_0} - \sum_{i=1}^{n} \frac{\partial^2 t_i}{\partial \tau_0^2} \right.$$

$$\left. - \sum_{i=1}^{n} \frac{\partial^2 t_i}{\partial \tau \partial \tau_0} \frac{\partial \tau}{\partial \tau_0} \right]$$

Comparing Equations (5-38) and (5-41), the following can be achieved. As $\sum_{i=1}^{n} \frac{\partial t_i}{\partial \tau_0} = 0$, the preventive measures in the scattered supply chains in the first stage are the same as those in the centralized supply chains. In other words, the scattered supply chains achieve coordination in the first stage. In practice, $\frac{\partial t_i}{\partial \tau_0} > 0$ is generally false. If $\frac{\partial t_i}{\partial \tau_0} > 0$, then it suggests that the more the preventive measures taken by suppliers in the first stage, the more is the aid the distributors provide in the second stage, which is not rational. The reason is that if the preventive measures by suppliers are in place, then even as the aid by distributors is small, the recovery time can still satisfy the demand of distributors.

Therefore, in general, here is $\dfrac{\partial t_i}{\partial \tau_0} \leq 0$, along with $\displaystyle\sum_{i=1}^{n} \dfrac{\partial t_i}{\partial \tau_0} = 0$, and $\dfrac{\partial t_i}{\partial \tau_0} = 0$ can be achieved.

It can be established from the preceding discussions that the aids that satisfy the following conclusions can achieve the two-stage coordination in supply chains:

As the aid provided by distributors to suppliers satisfies $\displaystyle\sum_{i=1}^{n} \dfrac{\partial t_i}{\partial \tau} = -\sum_{i=1}^{n} \theta_i$ and $\dfrac{\partial t_i}{\partial \tau_0} = 0$, the scattered supply chains can achieve two-stage coordination.

In the preceding discussions, according to the principles of equity and the cost of income distribution, the following conclusions can be drawn:

$$t_i = (A - \tau \sum_{i=1}^{n} \theta_i) \times \frac{\theta_i}{\sum_{i=1}^{n} \theta_i} \tag{5-42}$$

It is clear that the preceding equation satisfies the conditions $\displaystyle\sum_{i=1}^{n} \dfrac{\partial t_i}{\partial \tau} = -\sum_{i=1}^{n} \theta_i$ and $\dfrac{\partial t_i}{\partial \tau_0} = 0$, and thus the aid distribution methods expressed in the preceding equation can be seen as the coordination method in the two-stage supply chain. In practice, the methods of allocating the quantity of aid among many distributors are numerous, and Equation (5-42) is only one of them.

The coordinated method of supply chains based on penalty

The hypothesis and basic backdrop of models

Here, the focus is on supply chains in which the disruptive events are coordinated by means of suppliers paying the penalty to distributors. Relevant hypotheses and parameters may refer to the illustrations discussed earlier, where t_i represents the amount of penalty that suppliers pay distributors i $(i = 1, 2, \cdots, n)$. Some relevant hypotheses are similar to the discussions in the preceding text, but it is necessary to illustrate another hypothesis.

Hypothesis 7: $\dfrac{\partial^2 C(\tau_0, \tau)}{\partial \tau^2} + \displaystyle\sum_{i=1}^{n} \dfrac{\partial^2 t_i}{\partial \tau^2} \geq 0$. This hypothesis shows that the total cost function C_s of suppliers can still satisfy the convex function after penalty t_i.

The relevant research on centralized supply chains are the same as the discussions in the preceding text, and here directly consider the issue of coordination of scattered supply chains in which there is penalty t_i.

The optimal model when the scattered supply chains have penalty t$_i$

According to the preceding analysis, as the supply chain achieves coordination in the second stage, the following conclusions can be drawn. In the context where suppliers pay penalty t_i to distributors, the decision of the supply chain must satisfy certain conditions to achieve overall coordination after disruptive events occurred in the second stage.

$$\sum_{i=1}^{n}\frac{\partial t_i}{\partial \tau} = \sum_{i=1}^{n}\theta_i$$

As the supply chain achieves coordination in the first stage, the penalty paid by suppliers must satisfy the condition that, as suppliers pay the distributors penalty t_i, the conditions in the first stage that supply chains separately decide are as follows:

$$\frac{\partial t_i}{\partial \tau_0} = 0$$

It proves that the target function of τ_0 of suppliers in the first stage is as follows:

$$\min_{\tau_0} C_s(\tau_0, \tau) = g(\tau_0) + pE_\theta \left[C(\tau_0, \tau) + \sum_{i=1}^{n} t_i \right] \tag{5-43}$$

Compute the first and second derivative in Equation (5-43), letting the first derivative be 0, as:

$$\frac{\partial C(\tau)}{\partial \tau} = -\sum_{i=1}^{n}\frac{\partial t_i}{\partial \tau}$$

$$\frac{\partial C_s(\tau_0, \tau)}{\partial \tau_0} = \frac{\partial g(\tau_0)}{\partial \tau_0} + pE_\theta \left[\frac{\partial C(\tau_0, \tau)}{\partial \tau_0} + \frac{\partial C(\tau_0, \tau)}{\partial \tau}\frac{\partial \tau}{\partial \tau_0} + \sum_{i=1}^{n}\frac{\partial t_i}{\partial \tau_0} + \sum_{i=1}^{n}\frac{\partial t_i}{\partial \tau}\frac{\partial \tau}{\partial \tau_0} \right]$$

$$= \frac{\partial g(\tau_0)}{\partial \tau_0} + pE_\theta \left[\frac{\partial C(\tau_0, \tau)}{\partial \tau_0} + \sum_{i=1}^{n}\frac{\partial t_i}{\partial \tau_0} \right] = 0 \tag{5-44}$$

$$\frac{\partial^2 C(\tau_0, \tau)}{\partial \tau_0^2} = \frac{\partial^2 g(\tau_0)}{\partial \tau_0^2} + pE_\theta \left[\frac{\partial^2 C(\tau_0, \tau)}{\partial \tau_0^2} + \frac{\partial^2 C(\tau_0, \tau)}{\partial \tau \partial \tau_0}\frac{\partial \tau}{\partial \tau_0} + \sum_{i=1}^{n}\frac{\partial^2 t_i}{\partial \tau_0^2} \right.$$

$$\left. + \sum_{i=1}^{n}\frac{\partial^2 t_i}{\partial \tau \partial \tau_0}\frac{\partial \tau}{\partial \tau_0} \right]$$

Comparing Equations (5-38) and (5-44), the following can be inferred. As $\sum_{i=1}^{n}\frac{\partial t_i}{\partial \tau_0} = 0$, the decisions τ_{dc0} on preventive measures of the scattered supply chain in the first stage are the same as those of τ_{c0} in the centralized supply chain.

In other words, scattered supply chains can achieve coordination in the first stage. Similar to the case in which distributors provide aid, in practice, $\dfrac{\partial t_i}{\partial \tau_0} > 0$ is generally false. The reason is that, if $\dfrac{\partial t_i}{\partial \tau_0} > 0$, then it means that the more the preventive measures taken by suppliers in the first stage, the more is the penalty that suppliers must pay in the second stage, which is inconsistent with facts. The reason is that if preventive measures τ_0 are in place, then the recovery time of suppliers will drop, and thus the penalty paid will decrease. Therefore, in general, here is $\dfrac{\partial t_i}{\partial \tau_0} \leq 0$, along with $\dfrac{\partial t_i}{\partial \tau_0} = 0$, and the following can be achieved.

Based on the preceding conclusions, the quantum of aid that satisfies the following conclusions may achieve the two-stage coordination in supply chains.

As the penalty t_i paid by suppliers for distributors satisfies $\displaystyle\sum_{i=1}^{n} \dfrac{\partial t_i}{\partial \tau} = \sum_{i=1}^{n} \theta_i$ and $\dfrac{\partial t_i}{\partial \tau_0} = 0$, the scattered supply chain can achieve two-stage coordination.

Likewise, according to the backorder cost $\theta_i \tau$ produced within the recovery time of suppliers by distributors, the total penalty paid $T = \displaystyle\sum_{i=1}^{n} t_i = \beta + \tau \sum_{i=1}^{n} \theta_i$ by suppliers will be allocated. The basis of allocation is that the penalty paid by suppliers for a distributor and the backorder of distributors are in positive proportion.

$$t_i = \frac{T}{\tau \sum_{i=1}^{n} \theta_i} \tau \theta_i = \frac{\beta + \tau \sum_{i=1}^{n} \theta_i}{\sum_{i=1}^{n} \theta_i} \theta_i \qquad (5\text{-}45)$$

Evidently, the preceding equation satisfies the conditions $\displaystyle\sum_{i=1}^{n} \dfrac{\partial t_i}{\partial \tau} = \sum_{i=1}^{n} \theta_i$ and $\dfrac{\partial t_i}{\partial \tau_0} = 0$. Therefore, the penalty allocation method in this equation can be seen as the method of two-stage coordination in supply chains.

The coordinated model of two-stage supply chains with many suppliers and one distributor

The focus here is the supply chain with many suppliers and one distributor, where a supplier has been affected by disruptive events and has failed to effect supplies to distributors. If there are n suppliers in the supply chain, disruptive events are likely to occur in the second stage. Again, if disruptive events occur for supplier 1, the specific form of mechanism will be examined for the supply chain to achieve coordination (Sheng, 2008). Here, the effects that disruptive events have on supplier 1 and supplier $n-1$ are similar to the preceding discussions.

Likewise, the centralized supply chain will be considered first.

The optimal model of the centralized supply chains

Consider n suppliers and downstream distributors as a whole enterprise, and compute the optimal preventive measure τ_0 in the first stage and the optimal recovery time τ in the second stage of the whole enterprise. Above all, consider the decision procedure (decision variable is τ) in the second stage. The computation process and relevant conclusion of this model have already been introduced in the previous sections. Here, only the conclusions are discussed.

Considering n suppliers and downstream distributors as a whole enterprise, the optimal recovery time τ of the enterprise satisfies the following:

$$\frac{\partial C(\tau_0, \tau)}{\partial \tau} = -\theta + \Delta\theta + \psi$$

ψ indicates the extra profits gained within the unit recovery time for other $n-1$ suppliers, which are related to $\Delta\theta$. Apparently, if $\Delta\theta$ becomes larger, then other $n-1$ suppliers will provide more of extra products. The value of distributors is greater, and thus ψ is supposed to be bigger. Here, consider decision τ_0 in the first stage of the whole enterprise, and the backorder cost θ in the second stage has not been realized. However, the enterprise knows the probability density distribution $f(\theta)$ of θ. In addition, the whole enterprise in the first stage is aware of probability p of disruptive events in the second stage, and thus the target function of the whole enterprise in the first stage is as follows:

$$\min_{\tau_0} C_2(\tau_0, \tau) = g(\tau_0) + pE_\theta \left[C(\tau_0, \tau) + \left(\theta - \Delta\theta(\theta)\right)\tau - \psi(\theta)\tau \right] \qquad (5\text{-}46)$$

Where $E_\theta \left[C(\tau_0, \tau) + \left(\theta - \Delta\theta(\theta)\right)\tau - \psi(\theta)\tau \right]$ illustrates the expected cost to be incurred by the whole enterprise in the second stage after disruptive events happen, if disruptive events occur in the second stage. It is important to note that when expected cost is computed, the expected value of the random variable θ is computed. The reason is that parameters $\Delta\theta$ and ψ are supposed to be the function of θ. In this case, the optimal value should satisfy the following conclusions.

Considering the suppliers and downstream distributors as a whole enterprise, the optimal preventive measure τ_0 in the first stage should satisfy

$$\frac{\partial g(\tau_0)}{\partial \tau_0} + pE_\theta \left[\frac{\partial C(\tau_0, \tau)}{\partial \tau_0} \right] = 0.$$

This proves that computing the first derivative of Equation (5-46), letting the first derivative be 0:

$$\frac{\partial C_2(\tau_0, \tau)}{\partial \tau_0} = \frac{\partial g(\tau_0)}{\partial \tau_0} + pE_\theta \left\{ \left[\frac{\partial C(\tau_0, \tau)}{\partial \tau_0} + \frac{\partial C(\tau_0, \tau)}{\partial \tau} \frac{\partial \tau}{\partial \tau_0} \right] + \left[\theta - \Delta\theta(\theta) - \psi(\theta) \frac{\partial \tau}{\partial \tau_0} \right] \right\}$$

As $\dfrac{\partial C(\tau_0,\tau)}{\partial \tau} = -[\theta - \Delta\theta(\theta) - \psi(\theta)]$, the following is derived:

$$\frac{\partial C_2(\tau_0,\tau)}{\partial \tau_0} = \frac{\partial g(\tau_0)}{\partial \tau_0} + pE_\theta \left[\frac{\partial C(\tau_0,\tau)}{\partial \tau_0}\right] = 0 \tag{5-47}$$

Compute the second derivative in Equation (5-46).

$$\frac{\partial^2 C_2(\tau_0,\tau)}{\partial \tau_0^2} = \frac{\partial^2 g(\tau_0)}{\partial \tau_0^2} + pE_\theta \left[\frac{\partial^2 C(\tau_0,\tau)}{\partial \tau_0^2} + \frac{\partial^2 C(\tau_0,\tau)}{\partial \tau_0 \partial \tau} \frac{\partial \tau}{\partial \tau_0}\right] \tag{5-48}$$

According to Hypothesis 3 and Equation (5-48) > 0, the optimal preventive measure τ_0 in the first stage of the whole enterprise should satisfy $\dfrac{\partial g(\tau_0)}{\partial \tau_0} + pE_\theta \left[\dfrac{\partial C(\tau_0,\tau)}{\partial \tau_0}\right] = 0$.

The study of the scattered supply chain when downstream distributors can provide aid

According to the preceding analyses, in the context of n suppliers, when the supply chains achieve coordination in the second stage, the aid provided by distributors is supposed to satisfy the following conclusions.

In the scattered supply chain, if there is aid t provided by downstream distributors for the upstream suppliers, then the aid allows the scattered supply chain to achieve coordination, that is, to achieve the whole optimization. Here, the assistance satisfies the following:

$$\frac{\partial t}{\partial \tau} = -\theta + \Delta\theta + \psi$$

As the scattered supply chain achieves coordination in the first stage, the aid provided by distributors is supposed to satisfy the following conditions.

In the context where distributors provide aid t for suppliers, the conditions under which the scattered decisions of supply chain achieve coordination in the first stage are as follows:

$$\frac{\partial t}{\partial \tau_0} = 0$$

This proves that the target function of decision τ_0 for suppliers in the first stage is as follows:

$$\min_{\tau_0} C_s(\tau_0,\tau) = g(\tau_0) + pE_\theta[C(\tau_0,\tau) - t] \tag{5-49}$$

Compute the first and second derivatives of Equation (5-49), letting the first derivative be 0, and in the Equation $\dfrac{\partial C(\tau_0,\tau)}{\partial \tau} = \dfrac{\partial t}{\partial \tau}$, the following is achieved:

$$\frac{\partial C_s(\tau_0,\tau)}{\partial \tau_0} = \frac{\partial g(\tau_0)}{\partial \tau_0} + pE_\theta \left[\frac{\partial C(\tau_0,\tau)}{\partial \tau_0} + \frac{\partial C(\tau_0,\tau)}{\partial \tau} \frac{\partial \tau}{\partial \tau_0} - \frac{\partial t}{\partial \tau_0} - \frac{\partial t}{\partial \tau} \frac{\partial \tau}{\partial \tau_0} \right]$$

$$= \frac{\partial g(\tau_0)}{\partial \tau_0} + pE_\theta \left[\frac{\partial C(\tau_0,\tau)}{\partial \tau_0} - \frac{\partial t}{\partial \tau_0} \right] = 0 \qquad (5\text{-}50)$$

$$\frac{\partial^2 C(\tau_0,\tau)}{\partial \tau_0^2} = \frac{\partial^2 g(\tau_0)}{\partial \tau_0^2} + pE_\theta \left[\frac{\partial^2 C(\tau_0,\tau)}{\partial \tau_0^2} + \frac{\partial^2 C(\tau_0,\tau)}{\partial \tau \partial \tau_0} \frac{\partial \tau}{\partial \tau_0} - \frac{\partial^2 t}{\partial \tau_0^2} - \frac{\partial^2 t}{\partial \tau \partial \tau_0} \frac{\partial \tau}{\partial \tau_0} \right]$$

From Hypothesis 3, $\dfrac{\partial^2 C(\tau_0,\tau)}{\partial \tau_0^2} \geq 0$ can be known. Compare Equations (5-47) and (5-50), as decisions on the preventive measures in the first stage in the scattered supply chain are the same as those in the centralized supply chain.

Synthesize all the preceding conclusions, and the following can be known.

As aid t provided by distributors for suppliers satisfies $\dfrac{dt}{d\tau} = -\theta + \Delta\theta + \psi$ and $\dfrac{\partial t}{\partial \tau_0} = 0$, the scattered supply chain can achieve two-stage coordination.

Consider the following equation:

$$t = A + (-\theta + \Delta\theta + \psi)\tau$$

Where the size of A is determined by the negotiation and bargaining capacity of the suppliers and distributors. If the bargaining capacity of distributors is strong, then A should be less. Apparently, $t = A + (-\theta + \Delta\theta + \psi)\tau$ satisfies the conditions $\dfrac{dt}{d\tau} = -\theta + \Delta\theta + \psi$ and $\dfrac{\partial t}{\partial \tau_0} = 0$, and thus the supply chain can achieve coordination in two stages.

The study of the scattered supply chains when suppliers with emergency will pay the penalty

According to the preceding analyses, in the context of many suppliers, penalty that enables the supply chain to achieve coordination in the second stage should satisfy the following conditions.

In the scattered supply chain, if the upstream suppliers pay penalty t for the downstream suppliers, then the penalty t enables the scattered supply chain in the second stage to achieve coordination, that is, to achieve the whole optimization. Here, the penalty satisfies the following conditions:

$$\frac{\partial t}{\partial \tau} = \theta - \Delta\theta - \psi$$

As the scattered supply chain achieves coordination in the first stage, the penalty that suppliers pay for the distributors should satisfy the following conditions.

Here, the analytical methods are similar to the preceding sections, and thus the relevant conditions are discussed.

In the context where the upstream suppliers pay the penalty for the downstream distributors, the conditions under which decisions of the supply chain achieve coordination in the first stage are as follows:

$$\frac{\partial t}{\partial \tau_0} = 0$$

Therefore, as the penalty that upstream suppliers pay for the downstream distributors satisfies $\frac{\partial t}{\partial \tau} = \theta - \Delta\theta - \psi$ and $\frac{\partial t}{\partial \tau_0} = 0$, the scattered supply chain may achieve coordination in two stages.

Examples are provided to illustrate the specific forms of penalty that satisfies $\frac{\partial t}{\partial \tau} = \theta - \Delta\theta - \psi$ and $\frac{\partial t}{\partial \tau} = \theta - \Delta\theta - \psi$. Consider the equation:

$$t = A + (\theta - \Delta\theta - \psi)\tau$$

where the size of A depends on the bargaining capacity and negotiation of suppliers and distributors. Obviously, if the bargaining capacity of distributors is strong, then A will be greater.

Analysis of examples

To illustrate the specific application methods of the mathematical models, here are three analyses of examples (Sheng, 2008). First of all, the content of these three analyses of examples is discussed.

(1) The first analysis of examples is mainly concerned with the determination of the probability of disruptive events occurrence and supply chain coordination models in the context of risk-neutral suppliers and a distributor. In the coordination process of supply chains, the method by which distributors provide aid for suppliers is adopted. In terms of penalty paid by suppliers, the case is actually similar to that where distributors provide aid and thus the examples are not repeated.

(2) The second analysis of examples shows the coordinated models of supply chains in two stages composed of risk-averse suppliers and a distributor. According to the preceding conclusions, the coordinated method adopted is that suppliers pay the penalty for distributors.

(3) The third analysis of example illustrates the two-stage coordinated models of supply chain in the context of many suppliers and a distributor on the basis of aid. The decisions of distributors are discussed mainly on the basis of the flexible productivity provided by suppliers who have not been affected by disruptive events and the effects of disruptive events on distributors.

Analysis of example 1—the coordinated model of two-stage supply chains with risk-neutral

If a supply chain consists of a supplier and a distributor, suppliers are likely to suffer from disruptive events. For instance, the construction standards for factories by suppliers can resist the effects of a 12-grade typhoon. At the beginning of this year (i.e., the first stage), suppliers did not know whether a 12-grade typhoon would occur in the second stage. However, it is possible to predict that the probability of a 12-grade typhoon in this district is small. Once it occurs, it will seriously affect the production of suppliers. For instance, the roofs of factories would be destroyed; power would be cut off; and the factories and equipment would be damaged by water, and thus they would become unusable. In order to reduce the loss caused by disruptive events for suppliers, once disruptive events occur (i.e., more-than-12-grade typhoons), suppliers would resume production soon. Suppliers should take some preventive measures τ_0 at the beginning of the year (e.g., the materials for preventing typhoon and flood from affecting factories). If the suppliers have already known the degrees of the effects of the most 'unfavorable' events that occurred per year in the past decade at the beginning of the year (e.g., the relatively strong winds, including more-than-12-grade typhoon). Here, in the context where distributors provide aid t or do not provide aid t, compute the overall cost of the supply chain and the overall cost expectation, the optimal recovery time τ of suppliers, and the optimal preventive measure τ_0 of suppliers in the first stage. Suppose that the relevant data and parameters can be obtained (see Table 5.1):

Other parameters are as follows (i.e., parameters that satisfy relevant hypotheses):

In $C(\tau_0, \tau) = 5 + 10\tau_0^2 - 10\tau_0 + 10\tau^2 - 10\tau + 20\tau_0\tau$, θ is subject to $[0,10]$ and distributes evenly and $g(\tau_0, \tau) = 10\tau_0^2$, $t = 4 - \theta\tau$.

(1) Compute the probability of a more-than-12-grade typhoon (i.e., disruptive events) occurring within the year.

First, according to $-\ln\left(-\ln\dfrac{i}{n+1}\right) = \alpha(x_i - \mu)$, estimate the size of α and μ.

Here, $n = 10$. Let $-\alpha\mu = \beta$, and it is estimated that the model can transfer to $-\ln\left(-\ln\dfrac{i}{n+1}\right) = \theta x_i + \beta$. The data in Table 5.1 can be ranked in terms of their sizes, as shown in Table 5.2.

Apply the least-square estimation and achieve $\alpha = 1.93$ and $\beta = 1.44$. Substitute it into Equation (5-4).

Table 5.1 The maximum wind power parameters annually in the past decade

Year	1	2	3	4	5	6	7	8	9	10
Maximum wind power occurred within the year (r)	10.1	9.0	10.5	9.6	7.6	12.4	13.1	9.1	9.7	11.0

Table 5.2 Parameters after ranking

Maximum Wind Power Occurred within the Year (r)	7.6	9.0	9.1	9.6	9.7	10.1	10.5	11.0	12.4	13.1
$x = \ln r$		2.03	2.19	2.21	2.26	2.27	2.31	2.35	2.40	2.52	2.57
$y = -\ln\left(-\ln\dfrac{i}{n+1}\right)$		−0.87	−0.53	−0.26	−0.01	0.24	0.50	0.79	1.14	1.61	2.35

$$p = 1 - G(\ln 12) = 1 - \exp\left\{-\exp\left[-\alpha\left(\ln 12 - \mu\right)\right]\right\} = 0.16$$

(2) Consider the total cost in the context where there is aid and there is no aid.

Here, on the basis of the conditions available, it is possible to compute the total cost of supply chains before and after coordination of suppliers in the context where distributors have different backorder costs. The total cost contains the preventive measure cost $g(\tau_0)$ in the first stage among suppliers and the recovery cost $C(\tau_0, \tau)$ in the second stage and the backorder cost $\theta\tau$ of distributors. The results of computation can be summarized in Table 5.3.

The following conclusions can be drawn from the preceding data:

- If the backorder cost θ of distributors caused by disruptive events is small, then the total cost of supply chain is low when there is no t. The reason is that, if there is no t, the preventive measures by suppliers in the first stage will be small, and thus the overall preventive measures in the supply chain in the first stage will be small, even though the recovery time τ is long for suppliers in the second stage. Nevertheless, since θ is small, the increase of the total cost of supply chain is not obvious in the second stage. Therefore, when θ is small, the total cost of supply chain is low as there is no t.

Table 5.3 The total cost data of supply chains before and after coordination

Backorder cost (10,000 RMB/day)	0	1	2	3	4	5	6	7	8	9	10
The total cost data of supply chains before coordination (10,000 RMB/day)	2.5	3.0	3.5	4.0	4.5	5.0	5.5	6.0	6.5	7.0	7.5
The total cost data of supply chains after coordination (10,000 RMB/day)	2.725	3.125	3.475	3.775	4.025	4.225	4.375	4.475	4.545	4.595	4.635

- As θ is comparatively larger, the total cost of supply chain will be higher if there is no t. The reason is that if there is no aid t, the recovery time τ for suppliers in the second stage will increase. Since θ is comparatively greater, the cost in the second stage will rise with the longer recovery time. Thus, if the cost $g(\tau_0)$ of preventive measures is relatively low in the first stage, the sum of the cost in the first and second stages will increase. As a result, as θ is greater, the total cost of supply chain will increase if there is no t.
- Comparing the circumstances where there is t and there is no t, the total cost expected amounts to 1.6. This shows that, through aid, the supply chain can achieve coordination, and the total cost expected can be reduced.

(3) Consider the optimal recovery time and preventive measures by suppliers when there is aid and when there is no aid.
   - As there is aid, it is likely to compute the optimal recovery time $\tau = 0.46 - 0.042\theta$ in the second stage; if there is no aid, $\tau = 0.48$, and it can thus be seen that, if there is no aid, the suppliers will not consider the backorder cost of distributors. However, as there is t, the optimal time τ will increase as θ reduces. The reason is that if the recovery time increases, then the aid can be obtained by suppliers. Therefore, the suppliers can be motivated to recover production as soon as possible.
   - The preventive measures τ_0 adopted by suppliers in the first stage are 0.1 and 0.02 when there is and there is no aid, respectively. This shows that aid can be regarded as a coordinated measure that will motivate suppliers to take preventive and preparatory measures before the disruptive events occur. Thus, suppliers will not rush to take emergency measures, and then disruptive events occur.

Example 2—the coordinated model of two-stage supply chains with risk-averse

If a supply chain consists of risk-averse suppliers and a distributor, the disruptive events occur to suppliers in the second stage. Consider the preventive measures in advance and the decisions on recovery process after the events when suppliers pay and do not pay the penalty for distributors. Here are some relevant parameters in the hypothesis.

The recovery cost of suppliers is $C(\tau_0, \tau) = \tau^2 - 10\tau + \tau_0^2 - 10\tau_0 + 30$, and θ is subject to the even distribution in $[0,10]$: $g(\tau_0) = 10\tau_0^2$. The probability of disruptive events is $p = 0.2$, and the coefficient of risk aversion is $A = 0.5$.

(1) The step illustrates the computation process in the decision of suppliers in the second stage. After the disruptive events, the steps for computing the decision in the recovery process in the second stage for suppliers are as follows:

- Consider the decisions by suppliers when there is no penalty t.

Let $\dfrac{\partial C(\tau_0,\tau)}{\partial \tau} = 0$, and the following can be achieved:

$$\tau = 5$$

- Consider the decisions by suppliers when there is penalty t.

From $\dfrac{\partial C(\tau_0,\tau)}{\partial \tau} = -\dfrac{\partial t}{\partial \tau} = -\theta$, the following can be achieved:

$$\tau = 5 - \frac{1}{2}\theta$$

It can be seen from the computing results in this step that, as suppliers pay the penalty, the time required for recovery process in the second stage will reduce. Also, the reduced recovery time and the backorder of distributors are directly proportional. The results are relatively straightforward. If the backorder of distributors is huge, then the amount of penalty paid by suppliers will increase. Thus, suppliers are driven to recover supply as soon as possible.

(2) The step illustrates the computation process of supplier decision in the first stage. As $p = 0.2$ and $A = 0.5$, the computation steps of preventive measures by suppliers before disruptive events in the first stage are as follows:
  - Considering the decision by suppliers when there is no penalty t, substitute $\tau = 5$ into the equation.

$$\frac{\partial g(\tau_0)}{\partial \tau_0} + \left\{ p + 2A(p - p^2)E_\theta[C(\tau_0,\tau)+t] \right\} \times E_\theta\left[\frac{\partial C(\tau_0,\tau)}{\partial \tau_0} + \frac{\partial t}{\partial \tau_0} \right] = 0,$$

letting the parameter be $t = 0$ in the equation, and then the equation can be computed. Thus, the preventive measures adopted by suppliers in advance can be achieved: $\tau_0 = 0.27$.
  - Consider the decision by suppliers when there is penalty t, and substitute $\tau = 5 - \dfrac{1}{2}\theta$ into the equation.

$$\frac{\partial g(\tau_0)}{\partial \tau_0} + \left\{ p + 2A(p - p^2)E_\theta[C(\tau_0,\tau)+t] \right\} \times E_\theta\left[\frac{\partial C(\tau_0,\tau)}{\partial \tau_0} + \frac{\partial t}{\partial \tau_0} \right] = 0$$

Compute the solution of the equation, and the preventive measures by suppliers in advance can be achieved: $\tau_0 = 0.930$.

It can be seen from the results of this step that, when the suppliers pay the penalty, the preventive measures by the suppliers in the first stage will increase. It is conducive to the overall supply chain. The reason is that more preventive measures in advance can avoid and reduce the unfavorable effects on the overall supply chain.

(3) Consider the penalty paid by suppliers to achieve supply chain coordination, when there is penalty t. Based on the results mentioned earlier, the penalty

that enables the two stages of the overall supply chain to achieve the state of coordination is supposed to satisfy $t = \theta\tau$. In other words, after the disruptive events, as the afterward solutions, the distributors must pay the suppliers penalty $t = \theta\tau$. Substitute $\tau = 5 - \dfrac{1}{2}\theta$, and the following can be achieved:

$t = 5\theta - \dfrac{1}{2}\theta^2$, where $\theta \in [0,10]$. In this case, the scattered supply chain can achieve the overall coordination.

It can be seen from the preceding analysis that, as there is no penalty t, the decision by suppliers will be based on the maximum self-interest. The loss of distributors will not be considered in the decision. In other words, the decision by suppliers has nothing to do with θ. As there is the penalty, after the disruptive events occur to the suppliers, the optimal recovery time needed is the decreasing function of the backordering cost of distributors. In addition, the optimal recovery time here is less than that where there is no penalty. When there is penalty, more preventive measures will be taken by suppliers in the first stage. If disruptive events occur in the second stage, then suppliers will shorten the recovery time to reduce the penalty that they pay.

(4) In terms of probability in the case of different levels of risk aversion and disruptive events, the suppliers will analyze the optimal decisions of preventive measures in advance in the first stage, and compute in different cases where there is penalty or there is no penalty. Thus, the following conclusions are drawn.

As the coefficients of suppliers with risk aversion increase, the preventive measures by suppliers in advance in the first stage will rise. The reason is that the growth of risk-averse coefficient shows that suppliers will be conservative regarding the effects of disruptive events. Therefore, they would rather invest capital to reinforce the preventive measures in advance. Once the disruptive events occur, it is easier to deal with them to reduce their effects.

As the probability of disruptive events increases, suppliers will take more preventive measures in advance in the first stage. If they think that it is likely that disruptive events will occur, it is necessary to invest in preventive measures in the first stage. Here, suppliers should make sufficient preparation to prevent the circumstances where they are unprepared when disruptive events occur.

Example 3—the two-stage coordinated model based on many suppliers

If the scattered supply chain consists of three suppliers (suppliers 1, 2, and 3) and a distributor, supplier 1 will consider the specific forms of supporting mechanism at the beginning of the second stage when disruptive events occur.

Based on the preceding explanation, $\overline{\Delta\theta}$ is supposed to be related with the unused surplus productivity of the other two suppliers. That is to say, before the disruptive events occur, the actual utilized productivity of suppliers 2 and 3 are linked with their maximum productivity. Therefore, after the disruptive events occur, $\Delta\theta$ is supposed to be definite. If the disruptive events happen, suppliers 2 and 3 will consider the actual operation of distributors and their own surplus capacity and determine $\overline{\Delta\theta} = 6$. If distributors and supplier 1 bargain with one another, the basic expression of assistance provided by distributors is $t = 2 + (-\theta + \Delta\theta + \psi)\tau$. Thus, different circumstances are taken into account.

(1) If disruptive events happen to supplier 1, the following can be achieved: $\theta = 9$. Thus, as $\overline{\Delta\theta} < \theta$, here suppliers 2 and 3 should utilize all their surplus capacity and $\Delta\theta = \overline{\Delta\theta} = 6$. If $\Delta\theta = 6$, the extra profits obtained by suppliers 2 and 3 is 2, that is, $\psi = 2$. Thus, substitute each parameter into $t = 2 + (-\theta + \Delta\theta + \psi)\tau$, and here the assistance provided by distributors for supplier 1 is $t = 2 - \tau$.

(2) If disruptive events happen to supplier 1, the following can be achieved: $\theta = 4$. Thus, as $\overline{\Delta\theta} > \theta$, $\Delta\theta = \theta = 4$. Here, partial surplus capacity by suppliers 2 and 3 can satisfy the demand of distributors, and therefore the backorder cost will not be generated. In other words, it is not necessary to assist suppliers. As a result, the assistance provided by distributors for supplier 1 is supposed to be 0.

Conclusion

Here, the focus is on the method to determine the probability of supply chain disruptive events caused by natural disasters by means of the self-organized criticality and the extremum theory. When the system of disruptive events that occurred has self-organized criticality, such as the supply chain disruptive events caused by natural disasters, it is likely to determine the probability of the supply chain disruptive events that occurred.

Another point to note is the issue of preventive measures in advance and the recovery process afterward related to the three types of supply chains: the supply chain with one supplier and one distributor, the supply chain with one supplier and many distributors, and the supply chain with many suppliers and one distributor. In terms of the three types of supply chain structure, this study is concerned with when disruptive events happen and who fail to provide goods for downstream distributors, and it has also shown that distributors and suppliers will coordinate in order to prevent supply chain disruptive events in advance and recover afterwards. The coordinating methods include assistance and penalty.

In the two-stage coordinating model of supply chain with one supplier and one distributor, consider that disruptive events occur to risk-neutral or risk-averse suppliers. In terms of different risk preferences of these two suppliers, the circumstances of the centralized supply chain and the scattered supply chain are considered, and the relevant conclusions are drawn. For instance, if the probability of disruptive events increases for the centralized supply chain in the second stage, then the scattered supply chain will take more preventive measures in advance. Compared with the risk-neutral centralized supply chain, the centralized supply chain with risk aversion will take more preventive measures in the first stage. If suppliers with risk aversion adopt the mechanism where distributors provide assistance for suppliers, then supply chain cannot achieve coordination. The reason is that the preventive measures taken by suppliers in the first stage are less than those in the centralized supply chain. Here, the conditions and the mathematical expressions of the coordinating mechanism regarding the two-stage coordinating model of assistance and penalty measures of the supply chain with one supplier and one distributor can be achieved.

In terms of the supply chain with one supplier and many distributors, the study has considered the centralized and scattered supply chain, and discussed the coordinating method of supply chains on the basis of assistance and penalty. The coordinating process includes the preventive measures in advance and the recovery process afterward in the supply chain. After obtaining the total amount of assistance and penalty, the principle of distributing the assistance and penalty among many distributors has been proposed.

In terms of the supply chain consisting of many suppliers and a distributor, on the basis of coordination mechanism between aid and penalty, the conditions that must be satisfied are provided in relation to the preventive measures in advance and the coordination measures of recovery after disruptive events in supply chains.

6 Supply chain disruption risk management models with manufacturers as the core

Introduction

The complexity of supply chains mainly embodies the definite chaos, parallel interactions, and bullwhip effects. The definite chaos is generated by the fixed norms, excluding opportunity factors. In theory, it is predictable. However, the system is non-linear, non-repeatable, and sensitive to the initial conditions, which makes predictions difficult. Serial interactions happen in different stages of supply chains and are vertical, whereas parallel interactions refer to the interplay of different channels in the same stage, which is horizontal. If suppliers fail to provide goods for customers because of disruptive events or insufficient productivity, then the clients replan to order from other suppliers. Thus, the suppliers in the same stage have fluctuations in supply and demand due to their performance and reputation. The bullwhip effect refers to the enlargement and distortion as the demand changes transmit among supply chain members. These factors result in the complexity of supply chains and increase disruption risk.

The uncertainty of supply chain interior is also a potential factor that gives rise to disruption risk. Supply chain constitutes a network structure with vertical hierarchy and horizontal channels. It has a large number of members, and each member is driven and manipulated by "rationality," with the purpose of pursuing the maximal self-interest. However, they fail to coordinate and collaborate from the perspective of the overall supply chain. Numerous members constitute expansive geographical distribution of supply chain constituents, which helps extension of the network and increases the uncertainty and chance of disruption risk.

If suppliers, manufacturers, and retailers constitute a simplified three-stage supply chain system, this implies three nodes and two connecting chains. The manufacturers are located in the core position in the supply chain, whose upstream suppliers are in charge of providing raw materials and components. The downstream enterprises contact retailers and are in charge of selling products. The manufacturers are situated in the middle, between suppliers and retailers, and are in charge of purchasing raw materials and products, besides production and delivery.

Supply chain disruption risk may originate from outside the supply chain system, that is, because of extrinsic variables. These extrinsic variables are integrated with nodes and chains of the supply chain system, which might create the disruption of nodes and chains. The disruption of nodes may include supplier disruption, manufacturer disruption, and retailer disruption, and the disruption of chains may entail the disruption of supplier–manufacturer chain and the disruption of manufacturer–retailer chain. All these disruptions can result in disruption risk to manufacturers. Based on this, the supply chain disruption risk faced by manufacturers may consist of supply disruption risk, interior disruption risk, and demand disruption risk.

Supply chain disruption risk is caused by supplier node disruption and supplier–manufacturer chain disruption. The internal factors entail machine faults, workers' strikes, and financial problems, while external factors include natural disasters, terrorist attacks, and government policies. Disruptions of supplier–manufacturer chain are mainly caused by two factors: one is the abrupt external factors, and the other is the poor coordination between manufacturers and suppliers.

Demand disruption risk is caused by disruption of retailer nodes and the manufacturer–retailer chain. The disruption of retailer nodes is similar to the disruption of supplier nodes, including external and internal factors. The internal factors are mainly concerned with operations-related accidents, which result in considerable changes in demand from retailers; the external factors are mainly concerned with changes of demand of the ultimate consumers, which leads to substantial changes of demand that manufacturers expect from retailers. The internal disruption risk may originate from operations-related accidents at the manufacturers' end, and external factors derive from natural disasters, terrorist attacks, and political turmoil.

A point to note here is the issue of coordination among supply chain enterprises when disruption risk occurs to the three-stage supply chain system consisting of a supplier, a manufacturer, and a retailer. It includes coordination of demand disruption risk and supply disruption risk, coordination between manufacturers and retailers, and coordination between manufacturers and suppliers in each type of disruption risk.

Supply chain coordination under the risk of demand disruption

Manufacturers and retailers with demand disruption risk

In terms of the issue of supply chain coordination with demand disruption, Qi *et al.* (2004) introduced the notion of management of emergencies. On the basis of the supply chain model with one supplier and one retailer, the hypothesized demand in the model is the linear function of the price, and unit production cost is fixed. When the demand is definite, the use of overall discount contract may coordinate supply chains. As the demand gets disrupted, the partial cost is introduced into the target function, and the original quantity discount contract changes, to achieve the coordination of supply chains.

Here, based on Qi *et al.* (2004), the coordinating issue between manufacturers and retailers is further analyzed. The hypothesized demand is the linear function of price, that is, $Q = \bar{D} - kp$ (where $\bar{D}$ refers to market scale and k refers to the sensitivity coefficient of demand against price). What is different is that the fixed production cost of manufacturers and the fixed sales cost of retailers are considered in the model. In addition, in Qi *et al.*'s (2004) model, the optimal output decision of supply chains changes when demand disruption occurs, and thus it is necessary to adjust the contract between manufacturers and retailers. In other words, their model is concerned with the issue of how to adjust the contract when disruption occurs. To some extent, the adjustment of contract takes the effects of disruption into account, which is the partial cost of manufacturers. However, active measures by manufacturers related to disruption are not considered.

If this supply chain system has only one type of product, it needs one kind of raw material. Suppliers provide raw materials for manufacturers at unit price of $\dfrac{m}{t}$, and manufacturers provide products for retailers at unit price of w. The retailers sell the products to the ultimate consumers at retail price of p. Here, t refers to the demand coefficient of the unit product to raw materials, that is, one unit product needs t units of raw materials. Production cost of unit raw material is c_s; the production cost of unit product by manufacturers is m; fixed production cost is c_m; purchase cost of unit product of retailers is w; and fixed sales cost is c_r. Furthermore, it is hypothesized that suppliers, manufacturers, and retailers are risk-neutral.

Here, in addition to the effects of demand disruption, the active measures by manufacturers to deal with demand disruption are also considered. For instance, demand disruption is dealt with by affecting consumer demand. The active measures to deal with demand disruption entail a certain cost, and here this type of cost is regarded as the cost of dealing with demand disruption, marked as R_d. When disruption risk happens, the partial cost and the cost of dealing with disruption are considered in the target function. Also, when the issues related to coordinating between manufacturers and retailers are analyzed, the price of the unit raw materials $\dfrac{m}{t}$ is considered as given. Thus, the unit production cost of manufacturers m is also viewed as given (see the master degree thesis entitled 'Supply Chain Disruption Risks Management from the Perspective of Manufacturer' (Meng, 2009)).

Coordination between manufacturers and retailers without demand disruption risk

Without demand disruption risk, if manufacturers and retailers decide to cooperate, then the collaborated decision profits are marked as f^{mr}.

$$f^{mr} = Q(p-m) - c_m - c_r = Q\left(\frac{\bar{D}-Q}{k} - m\right) - c_m - c_r$$

Compute the first derivative from f^{mr}, letting the first derivative be 0, and the following can be obtained:

$$f^{mr\prime} = \frac{\bar{D}}{k} - \frac{2}{k}Q - m = 0$$

Thus, the following is obtained:

$$\bar{Q} = \frac{\bar{D} - mk}{2}$$

$$\bar{p} = \frac{\bar{D} - \bar{Q}}{k} = \frac{\bar{D} + mk}{2k}$$

$$\bar{f}^{mr} = \bar{Q}(\bar{p} - m) - c_m - c_r = \frac{(\bar{D} - mk)^2}{4k} - c_m - c_r$$

Where $\bar{Q}, \bar{p}, \bar{f}^{mr}$ indicate the production, retail price, and profits of collaborated decisions, respectively, when the profits of collaborated decisions are maximal.

When manufacturers and retailers take decisions individually, the optimal order of retailers is not necessarily $\bar{Q}$. As such, manufacturers and retailers fail to achieve the maximal overall profits. In order to achieve the overall maximal profits, manufacturers must design a type of wholesale contract. In this contract, the optimal order of retailers is $\bar{Q}$. In other words, this type of contract helps retailers achieve the maximal profits, and at the same time the overall profits of manufacturers and retailers can be maximized.

In order to design such a contract, profits of retailers are analyzed first, letting their profits be f^r:

$$f^r = Q(p - m) - c_r = Q\left(\frac{\bar{D} - Q}{k} - w\right) - c_r$$

Compute the first derivative of f^r, letting the first derivative be 0:

$$f^{r\prime} = \frac{\bar{D}}{k} - \frac{2}{k}Q - w = 0$$

The following is obtained: $Q = \dfrac{\bar{D} - wk}{k}$

In the normal context of $w > m$, $\dfrac{\bar{D} - wk}{2} < \dfrac{\bar{D} - mk}{2}$. That is to say, if the manufacturers simply set up the wholesale price as w, then the optimal order of the retailers is less than the optimal output where the overall profits of manufacturers and retailers can be maximized. In order to push retailers to order $\dfrac{\bar{D} - mk}{2}$, a complete quantity discount contract $AQDP(w_1, w_2, \bar{Q})$ is designed. In other words, when the order is no less than $\bar{Q}$, the wholesale price w_2 is adopted. Otherwise, w_1 is adopted, where $w_1 \succ w_2$. Below are the solutions of w_1 and w_2.

In order to avoid the order of retailers being lower, that is, $Q = \dfrac{\bar{D} - wk}{k}$, it is supposed that:

$$f^r = \frac{\bar{D} - w_1 k}{2}\left(\bar{D} - \frac{\bar{D} - \dfrac{\bar{D} - w_1 k}{2}}{k} - w_1 \right) - c_r < (1 - \eta)\bar{f}^{mr}$$

Where n is the profit-sharing that the manufacturers hope to obtain, as $0 \prec \eta \prec 1$. It can be computed from the preceding equation that:

$$w_1 > \frac{\bar{D}}{k} - \frac{1}{k}\sqrt{(1 - \eta)\left[(\bar{D} - mk)^2 - 4k\left(c_m - \frac{\eta}{1-\eta}c_r\right)\right]}$$

In order to motivate the retailers to order $\bar{Q} = \dfrac{\bar{D} - mk}{2}$, it is supposed that:

$$f^r = \frac{\bar{D} - mk}{2}\left(\bar{D} - \frac{\bar{D} - \dfrac{\bar{D} - mk}{2}}{k} - w_2 \right) - c_r = (1 - \eta)\bar{f}^{mr}$$

The following can be obtained:

$$w_2 = \eta\frac{\bar{D}}{2k} + (2 - \eta)\frac{m}{2} + 2(1 - \eta)\frac{1}{\bar{D} - mk}\left(c_m - \frac{\eta}{1-\eta}c_r\right)$$

In summary, the maximum total profits of manufacturers and retailers without demand disruption are when profit-sharing of manufacturers is η, and the manufacturers adopt the contract $AQDP(w_1, w_2, \bar{Q})$, where:

$$w_1 > \frac{\bar{D}}{k} - \frac{1}{k}\sqrt{(1 - \eta)\left[(\bar{D} - mk)^2 - 4k\left(c_m - \frac{\eta}{1-\eta}c_r\right)\right]}$$

$$w_2 = \eta\frac{\bar{D}}{2k} + (2 - \eta)\frac{m}{2} + 2(1 - \eta)\frac{1}{\bar{D} - mk}\left(c_m - \frac{\eta}{1-\eta}c_r\right)$$

$$0 < \eta < 1$$

Coordination between manufacturers and retailers with demand disruption risk

When the demand disruption risk emerges, $\bar{D}$ becomes $\bar{D}+\Delta D$. Here, the optimal output $\bar{Q}$ changes to $\bar{Q}+\Delta D$ accordingly. In this context, the partial cost is incurred. For instance, when the optimal output increases, more time is needed. At the same time, the cost to deal with the demand disruption risk is generated. These two types of cost add to the target function, and thus the target function f^{mr} changes into:

$$f^{mr} = Q\left(\frac{\bar{D}+\Delta D-Q}{k} - m\right) - c_m - c_r - \lambda_1(Q-\bar{Q})^+ - \lambda_2(\bar{Q}-Q)^+ - R_d$$

Where λ_1 refers to the unit partial cost as the optimal output increases; λ_2 refers to the unit partial cost as the optimal output drops; and $(X)^+ = \max\{X,0\}, R_d$ refers to the cost of dealing with demand disruption risk.

As the optimal output increases in the new target function, the new target function can be rewritten as:

$$f^{mr} = Q\left(\frac{\bar{D}+\Delta D-Q}{k} - m\right) - c_m - c_r - \lambda_1(Q-\bar{Q}) - R_d, (Q > \bar{Q})$$

Compute the first derivative from the preceding equation, and let the first derivative be 0.

$$f^{mr\prime} = \frac{\bar{D}+\Delta D}{k} - \frac{2}{k}Q - m - \lambda_1 = 0$$

Then: $Q = \dfrac{\bar{D}-mk}{2} + \dfrac{\Delta D - \lambda_1 k}{2} = \bar{Q} + \dfrac{\Delta D - \lambda_1 k}{2}$

As $0 < \Delta D < \lambda_1 k$, f^{mr} has the maximum value at $\bar{Q}$, that is, here the optimal output is still $\bar{Q}$.

As $\Delta D \geq \lambda_1 k$, f^{mr} has the maximal value at $Q = \dfrac{\bar{D}-mk}{2} + \dfrac{\Delta D - \lambda_1 k}{2} = \bar{Q} + \dfrac{\Delta D - \lambda_1 k}{2}$, that is, the optimal output is now $\bar{Q} + \dfrac{\Delta D - \lambda_1 k}{2}$.

As the optimal output decreases in the new target function, the new target function can be rewritten as:

$$f^{mr} = Q\left(\frac{\bar{D}+\Delta D-Q}{k} - m\right) - c_m - c_r - \lambda_2(\bar{Q}-Q) - R_d, (Q < \bar{Q})$$

Compute the first derivative from the preceding equation, and let the first derivative be 0.

$$f^{mr\prime} = \frac{\bar{D}+\Delta D}{k} - \frac{2}{k}Q - m + \lambda_2 = 0$$

Then: $Q = \dfrac{\bar{D}-mk}{2} + \dfrac{\Delta D + \lambda_2 k}{2} = \bar{Q} + \dfrac{\Delta D + \lambda_2 k}{2}$

As $-\lambda_2 k < \Delta D < 0$, f^{mr} has the maximal value at $\bar{Q}$, that is, the optimal output is still $\bar{Q}$.

As $\Delta D < -\lambda_2 k$, f^{mr} has the maximal value at $Q = \dfrac{\bar{D}-mk}{2} + \dfrac{\Delta D + \lambda_2 k}{2} = \bar{Q} + \dfrac{\Delta D + \lambda_2 k}{2}$, that is, the optimal output is now $\bar{Q} + \dfrac{\Delta D + \lambda_2 k}{2}$.

Based on the preceding analysis, the issue of coordinating between manufacturers and retailers will be discussed in the following four different circumstances.

(1) Scenario one: $0 < \Delta D < \lambda_1 k$

Here, f^{mr} has the maximal value at $\bar{Q}$, that is:

$$Q^*_{case1} = \bar{Q} = \frac{\bar{D}-mk}{2}$$

$$P^*_{case1} = \frac{\bar{D}+\Delta D - Q^*_{case1}}{k} = \frac{\bar{D}+mk+2\Delta D}{2k}$$

$$f^{mr}_{case1} = Q^*_{case1}\left(P^*_{case1} - m\right) - c_m - c_r - R_d$$

$$= \frac{\bar{D}-mk}{2}\frac{\bar{D}-mk+2\Delta D}{2k} - c_m - c_r - R_d$$

As the demand disruption risk happens, profits of retailers are as follows:

$$f^r = Q\left(\frac{\bar{D}+\Delta D - Q}{k} - w\right) - c_r$$

Compute the first derivative from the preceding equation, letting the first derivative be 0:

$$f^{r'} = \frac{\bar{D}+\Delta D}{k} - \frac{2}{k}Q - w = 0$$

The following can be achieved: $Q = \dfrac{\bar{D}+\Delta D - wk}{k}$

That is to say, given the definite wholesale price w, the optimal order of retailers is $Q = \dfrac{\bar{D}+\Delta D - wk}{k}$.

The following is the analysis of how to coordinate the profits between manufacturers and retailers.

If $\dfrac{\bar{D}+\Delta D - wk}{k} \le \bar{Q}$, the manufacturers adopt $AQDP\left(w_1, w_2, \bar{Q}\right)$ for coordination, and the following is the computation of w_1 and w_2.

In order to avoid the orders of retailers from being $\dfrac{\bar{D}+\Delta D-wk}{k}$, it is supposed to be:

$$f^r = \frac{\bar{D}+\Delta D-w_1 k}{2}\left(\bar{D}+\Delta D-\frac{\bar{D}+\Delta D-\frac{\bar{D}+\Delta D-w_1 k}{2}}{k}-w_1\right)$$

$$-c_r \prec (1-\eta)f^*_{case1}$$

The following can be achieved:

$$w_1 > \frac{\bar{D}+\Delta D}{k}$$

$$-\frac{1}{k}\sqrt{(1-\eta)\left[(\bar{D}-mk)\left((\bar{D}-mk)+2\Delta D\right)-4k\left(c_m+R_d-\frac{\eta}{1-\eta}c_r\right)\right]}$$

In order to motivate the retailers to order $\bar{Q}$, it is supposed to be:

$$f^r = \frac{\bar{D}-mk}{2}\left(\bar{D}-\frac{\bar{D}-\frac{\bar{D}-mk}{2}}{k}-w_2\right)-c_r = (1-\eta)f^*_{case1}$$

The following can be achieved:

$$w_2 = \eta\frac{\bar{D}+2\Delta D}{2k}+(2-\eta)\frac{m}{2}+(1-\eta)\frac{2}{\bar{D}-mk}\left(c_m+R_d-\frac{\eta}{1-\eta}c_r\right)$$

Given $\dfrac{\bar{D}+\Delta D-wk}{2} > \bar{Q}$, $AQDP(w_1,w_2,\bar{Q})$ has failed to coordinate the profits between manufacturers and retailers, and now another contract is necessary. Linear pricing with productivity limits is $CLPP(w_2,\bar{Q})$, that is, the single wholesale price w_2 that retailers settle. However, the maximal order from retailers cannot exceed $\bar{Q}$, and the solution of w_2 is the same as given in the preceding text.

In summary, in the context of $0 < \Delta D < \lambda_1 k$, given $\dfrac{\bar{D}+\Delta D-wk}{k} \leq \bar{Q}$, the manufacturers adopt $AQDP(w_1,w_2,\bar{Q})$ to coordinate the profits with retailers.

Given $\dfrac{\bar{D}+\Delta D-wk}{2} > \bar{Q}$, the manufacturers adopt $CLPP(w_2,\bar{Q})$ to coordinate the profits with retailers, where:

$$w_1 > \frac{\bar{D} + \Delta D}{k}$$

$$-\frac{1}{k}\sqrt{(1-\eta)\left[(\bar{D}-mk)\left((\bar{D}-mk)+2\Delta D\right)-4k\left(c_m+R_d-\frac{\eta}{1-\eta}c_r\right)\right]}$$

$$w_2 = \eta\frac{\bar{D} + 2\Delta D}{2k} + (2-\eta)\frac{m}{2} + (1-\eta)\frac{2}{\bar{D}-mk}\left(c_m+R_d-\frac{\eta}{1-\eta}c_r\right)$$

$$0 < \eta < 1$$

In the following analysis, computation of w_1 and w_2 is similar to the preceding case, and thus it is not discussed in detail.

(2) Scenario two: $\Delta D \geq \lambda_1 k$

Here, f^{mr} has the maximal value at $Q = \dfrac{\bar{D}-mk}{2} + \dfrac{\Delta D - \lambda_1 k}{2} = \bar{Q} + \dfrac{\Delta D - \lambda_1 k}{2}$, that is:

$$Q_{case2}^* = \frac{\bar{D}-mk}{2} + \frac{\Delta D - \lambda_1 k}{2}$$

$$P_{case2}^* = \frac{\bar{D} + \Delta D - Q_{case2}^*}{k} = \frac{\bar{D}+mk+\Delta D + \lambda_1 k}{2k}$$

$$f_{case2}^{mr} = Q_{case2}^*\left(P_{case2}^* - m\right) - c_m - c_r - \lambda_1\left(Q_{case2}^* - \bar{Q}\right) - R_d$$

$$= \frac{\bar{D}-mk+\Delta D - \lambda_1 k}{2}\frac{\bar{D}-mk+\Delta D+\lambda_1 k}{2k} - c_m - c_r$$

$$- \lambda_1\frac{\Delta D - \lambda_1 k}{2} - R_d$$

It is clear from the analysis of scenario one that, with demand disruption risk, given the definite wholesale price w, the optimal order of retailers is $Q = \dfrac{\bar{D} + \Delta D - wk}{2}$.

Given $Q = \dfrac{\bar{D} + \Delta D - wk}{2} \leq Q_{case2}^*$, the manufacturers should adopt $AQDP\left(w_1, w_2, Q_{case2}^*\right)$ to coordinate the profits, where:

$$w_1 > \frac{\bar{D} + \Delta D}{k}$$

$$-\frac{1}{k}\sqrt{(1-\eta)\left[\begin{array}{c}\left(\bar{D}-mk+\Delta D-\lambda_1 k\right)\left(\bar{D}-mk+\Delta D+\lambda_1 k\right) \\ -4k\left(c_m+\lambda_1\dfrac{\Delta D - \lambda_1 k}{2} + R_d - \dfrac{\eta}{1-\eta}c_r\right)\end{array}\right]}$$

$$w_2 = \eta \frac{\bar{D} + 2\Delta D}{2k} + (2 - \eta)\frac{m}{2} + \eta\frac{\lambda_1}{2}$$

$$+ (1 - \eta)\frac{2}{\bar{D} - mk + \Delta D - \lambda_1 k}\left[c_m + \lambda_1 \frac{\Delta D - \lambda_1 k}{2} + R_d - \frac{\eta}{1 - \eta}c_r \right]$$

Given $Q = \dfrac{\bar{D} + \Delta D - wk}{2} \succ Q^*_{case2}$, the adoption of $AQDP\left(w_1, w_2, Q^*_{case2}\right)$ fails to achieve the coordination with retailers, and it is necessary to adopt $CLPP\left(w_2, Q^*_{case2}\right)$, where w_2 is the same as given earlier.

In summary, in the context of $\Delta D \geq \lambda_1 k$:

Given $Q = \dfrac{\bar{D} + \Delta D - wk}{2} \leq Q^*_{case2}$, the manufacturers should adopt $AQDP\left(w_1, w_2, Q^*_{case2}\right)$ to coordinate profits with retailers.

Given $Q = \dfrac{\bar{D} + \Delta D - wk}{2} > Q^*_{case2}$, the manufacturers should adopt $CLPP\left(w_2, Q^*_{case2}\right)$ to coordinate with retailers, where:

$$w_1 > \frac{\bar{D} + \Delta D}{k}$$

$$-\frac{1}{k}\sqrt{(1 - \eta)\left[\begin{array}{c} \left(\bar{D} - mk + \Delta D - \lambda_1 k\right)\left(\bar{D} - mk + \Delta D + \lambda_1 k\right) \\ - 4k\left(c_m + \lambda_1 \dfrac{\Delta D - \lambda_1 k}{2} + R_d - \dfrac{\eta}{1 - \eta}c_r \right) \end{array} \right]}$$

$$w_2 = \eta \frac{\bar{D} + 2\Delta D}{2k} + (2 - \eta)\frac{m}{2} + \eta\frac{\lambda_1}{2}$$

$$+ (1 - \eta)\frac{2}{\bar{D} - mk + \Delta D - \lambda_1 k}\left[c_m + \lambda_1 \frac{\Delta D - \lambda_1 k}{2} + R_d - \frac{\eta}{1 - \eta}c_r \right]$$

$$0 < \eta < 1$$

(3) Scenario three: $-\lambda_2 k < \Delta D < 0$
Here, f^{mr} has the maximum value at $\bar{Q}$, that is:

$$Q^*_{case3} = \bar{Q} = \frac{\bar{D} - mk}{2}$$

$$P^*_{case3} = \frac{\bar{D} + \Delta D - Q^*_{case3}}{k} = \frac{\bar{D} + mk + 2\Delta D}{2k}$$

$$f_{case3}^{mr} = Q_{case3}^*\left(p_{case3}^* - m\right) - c_m - c_r - R_d$$

$$= \frac{\bar{D} - mk}{2}\frac{\bar{D} + mk + 2\Delta D}{2k} - c_m - c_r - R_d$$

As $\Delta D < 0$, f_{case3}^{mr} is likely to be less than 0, and $f_{case3}^{mr} > 0$ and $f_{case3}^{mr} \leq 0$ are discussed separately.

As $f_{case3}^{mr} > 0$:

As discussed in the preceding text, with demand disruption risk, given the definite wholesale price w, the optimal order of retailers is $Q = \dfrac{\bar{D} + \Delta D - wk}{2}$.

As $\Delta D < 0$ and $w > m$, $\dfrac{\bar{D} + \Delta D - wk}{2} \leq \bar{Q}$. Here, the manufacturers should adopt $AQDP\left(w_1, w_2, \bar{Q}\right)$ to coordinate the profits with retailers, where:

$$w_1 > \frac{\bar{D} + \Delta D}{k}$$

$$-\frac{1}{k}\sqrt{(1-\eta)\left[(\bar{D} - mk)(\bar{D} - mk + 2\Delta D) - 4k\left(c_m + R_d - \frac{\eta}{1-\eta}c_r\right)\right]}$$

$$w_2 = \eta\frac{\bar{D} + 2\Delta D}{2k} + (2-\eta)\frac{m}{2} + (1-\eta)\frac{2}{\bar{D} - mk}\left(c_m + R_d - \frac{\eta}{1-\eta}c_r\right)$$

If the profits of the retailers are less than c_r, the retailers will not place an order. Thus, the manufacturers will dispose all products of unit $\bar{Q}$ in the market, and the loss is $\lambda_2\bar{Q}$. In order to motivate retailers to order, it is important to ensure that the profits of retailers are no less than c_r, that is, $-\eta f_{case3}^{mr} \leq \lambda_2\bar{Q}$. To achieve this, the profits of the manufacturers have to be negative. However, as long as the loss is no more than $\lambda_2\bar{Q}$, that is, $-\eta f_{case3}^{mr} \leq \lambda_2\bar{Q}$, the goods can be sold to retailers. In this case, assuming that the profit-sharing of the manufacturers is η, the conditions that must be satisfied are $\eta \succ 1$. The following is the analysis of how to coordinate with retailers.

Given $\dfrac{\bar{D} + \Delta D - wk}{2} \leq \bar{Q}$, the manufacturers should adopt $AQDP\left(w_1, w_2, \bar{Q}\right)$ to coordinate the profits with retailers, where:

$$w_1 > \frac{\bar{D} + \Delta D}{k}$$

$$-\frac{1}{k}\sqrt{(1-\eta)\left[(\bar{D} - mk)(\bar{D} - mk + 2\Delta D) - 4k\left(c_m + R_d - \frac{\eta}{1-\eta}c_r\right)\right]}$$

$$w_2 = \eta \frac{\bar{D} + 2\Delta D}{2k} + (2-\eta)\frac{m}{2} + (1-\eta)\frac{2}{\bar{D} - mk}\left(c_m + R_d - \frac{\eta}{1-\eta}c_r\right)$$

Given $\dfrac{\bar{D} + \Delta D - wk}{2} > \bar{Q}$, the manufacturers should adopt $CLPP\left(w_2, \bar{Q}\right)$ for coordination, where w_2 is the same as given earlier.

In summary, in the context of $-\lambda_2 k < \Delta D < 0$, as $f_{case3}^{mr} > 0$, the manufacturers should adopt $AQDP\left(w_1, w_2, \bar{Q}\right)$ to coordinate the profits with retailers, where:

$$w_1 > \frac{\bar{D} + \Delta D}{k}$$

$$-\frac{1}{k}\sqrt{(1-\eta)\left[(\bar{D}-mk)(\bar{D}-mk+2\Delta D) - 4k\left(c_m + R_d - \frac{\eta}{1-\eta}c_r\right)\right]}$$

$$w_2 = \eta \frac{\bar{D} + 2\Delta D}{2k} + (2-\eta)\frac{m}{2} + (1-\eta)\frac{2}{\bar{D} - mk}\left(c_m + R_d - \frac{\eta}{1-\eta}c_r\right)$$

$$0 < \eta < 1$$

As $f_{case3}^{mr} \le 0$, if $(1-\eta)f_{case3}^{mr} \ge c_r, -\eta f_{case3}^{mr} \le \lambda_2 \bar{Q}$ satisfy the conditions:

Given $\dfrac{\bar{D} + \Delta D - wk}{2} \le \bar{Q},$ the manufacturers should adopt $AQDP\left(\mathrm{w}_1, \mathrm{w}_2, \bar{Q}\right)$ for coordination.

Given $\dfrac{\bar{D} + \Delta D - wk}{2} > \bar{Q}$, the manufacturers should adopt $CLPP\left(w_2, \bar{Q}\right)$ for coordination, where:

$$w_1 > \frac{\bar{D} + \Delta D}{k}$$

$$-\frac{1}{k}\sqrt{(1-\eta)\left[(\bar{D}-mk)(\bar{D}-mk+2\Delta D) - 4k\left(c_m + R_d - \frac{\eta}{1-\eta}c_r\right)\right]}$$

$$w_2 = \eta \frac{\bar{D} + 2\Delta D}{2k} + (2-\eta)\frac{m}{2} + (1-\eta)\frac{2}{\bar{D} - mk}\left(c_m + R_d - \frac{\eta}{1-\eta}c_r\right)$$

$$\eta > 1$$

When $(1-\eta)f_{case3}^{mr} \ge c_r$ and $-\eta f_{case3}^{mr} \le \lambda_2 \bar{Q}$ are not satisfied, the manufacturers will dispose all products in the secondary market, and the loss is $\lambda_2 \bar{Q}$.

(4) Scenario four: $\Delta D < -\lambda_2 k$

Here, f^{mr} has the maximum value at $Q = \dfrac{\bar{D}-mk}{2} + \dfrac{\Delta D + \lambda_2 k}{2} = \bar{Q} + \dfrac{\Delta D + \lambda_2 k}{2}$, that is:

$$Q^*_{case4} = \frac{\bar{D}-mk}{2} + \frac{\Delta D + \lambda_2 k}{2}$$

$$P^*_{case4} = \frac{\bar{D}+\Delta D - Q^*_{case4}}{k} = \frac{\bar{D}+mk+\Delta D - \lambda_2 k}{2k}$$

$$f^{mr}_{case4} = Q^*_{case4}\left(P^*_{case4}-m\right) - c_m - c_r - \lambda_2\left(\bar{Q}-Q^*_{case4}\right) - R_d$$

$$= \frac{\bar{D}-mk+\Delta D+\lambda_2 k}{2}\frac{\bar{D}-mk+\Delta D-\lambda_2 k}{2k} - c_m - c_r$$

$$- \lambda_2\frac{\Delta D+\lambda_2 k}{2} - R_d$$

Similar to scenario three, as $\Delta D \prec 0$, f^{mr}_{case4} is likely to be less than 0. Therefore, consider $f^{mr}_{case4} > 0$ and $f^{mr}_{case4} \leq 0$.

As $f^{mr}_{case4} \succ 0$:

As $w > m$, the optimal order $Q = \dfrac{\bar{D}+\Delta D - wk}{2}$ of retailers with the definite w is less than Q^*_{case4}, and the manufacturers may adopt $AQDP\left(w_1, w_2, Q^*_{case4}\right)$ to coordinate the profits with retailers, where:

$$w_1 > \frac{\bar{D}+\Delta D}{k}$$

$$-\frac{1}{k}\sqrt{(1-\eta)\left[\frac{\left(\bar{D}-mk+\Delta D+\lambda_2 k\right)\left(\bar{D}-mk+\Delta D-\lambda_2 k\right)}{-4k\left(c_m - \lambda_2\frac{\Delta D+\lambda_2 k}{2} + R_d - \frac{\eta}{1-\eta}c_r\right)}\right]}$$

$$w_2 = \eta\frac{\bar{D}+2\Delta D}{2k} + (2-\eta)\frac{m}{2} - \eta\frac{\lambda_2}{2}$$

$$+ (1-\eta)\frac{2}{\bar{D}-mk\Delta D+\lambda_2 k}\left(c_m - \lambda_2\frac{\Delta D+\lambda_2 k}{2} + R_d - \frac{\eta}{1-\eta}c_r\right)$$

$$0 < \eta < 1$$

As $f^{mr}_{case4} \leq 0$, if retailers place an order, the conditions of $(1-\eta)f^{mr}_{case4} \geq c_r$ should be satisfied. At the same time, in order to make manufacturers sell goods to retailers, the conditions of $-\eta f_{case4}^{mr} \leq \lambda_2 \bar{Q}$ should be satisfied. If these two conditions are satisfied, the manufacturers should coordinate the profits with retailers on the basis of the following methods:

Given $Q = \dfrac{\bar{D} + \Delta D - wk}{2} \leq Q_{case4}^{*}$, the manufacturers should adopt $AQDP\left(w_1, w_2, Q_{case4}^{*}\right)$ to coordinate the profits, where:

$$w_1 > \frac{\bar{D} + \Delta D}{k}$$

$$-\frac{1}{k}\sqrt{(1-\eta)\left[\begin{array}{c}\left(\bar{D} - mk + \Delta D + \lambda_2 k\right)\left(\bar{D} - mk + \Delta D - \lambda_2 k\right) \\ -4k\left(c_m - \lambda_2 \dfrac{\Delta D + \lambda_2 k}{2} + R_d - \dfrac{\eta}{1-\eta}c_r\right)\end{array}\right]}$$

$$w_2 = \eta \frac{\bar{D} + 2\Delta D}{2k} + (2-\eta)\frac{m}{2} - \eta\frac{\lambda_2}{2}$$

$$+ (1-\eta)\frac{2}{\bar{D} - mk\Delta D + \lambda_2 k}\left(c_m - \lambda_2 \frac{\Delta D + \lambda_2 k}{2} + R_d - \frac{\eta}{1-\eta}c_r\right)$$

$$\eta > 1$$

Given $Q = \dfrac{\bar{D} + \Delta D - wk}{2} \succ Q_{case4}^{*}$, it is necessary to adopt $CLPP\left(w_2, Q_{case4}^{*}\right)$ to coordinate the profits among retailers, where w_2 is the same as given earlier.

In summary, in the context of $\Delta D < -\lambda_2 k$, as $f_{case4}^{mr} > 0$, the manufacturers adopt $AQDP\left(w_1, w_2, Q_{case4}^{*}\right)$ to coordinate the profits with retailers, where:

$$w_1 > \frac{\bar{D} + \Delta D}{k}$$

$$-\frac{1}{k}\sqrt{(1-\eta)\left[\begin{array}{c}\left(\bar{D} - mk + \Delta D + \lambda_2 k\right)\left(\bar{D} - mk + \Delta D - \lambda_2 k\right) \\ -4k\left(c_m - \lambda_2 \dfrac{\Delta D + \lambda_2 k}{2} + R_d - \dfrac{\eta}{1-\eta}c_r\right)\end{array}\right]}$$

$$w_2 = \eta \frac{\bar{D} + 2\Delta D}{2k} + (2-\eta)\frac{m}{2} - \eta\frac{\lambda_2}{2}$$

$$+ (1-\eta)\frac{2}{\bar{D} - mk\Delta D + \lambda_2 k}\left(c_m - \lambda_2 \frac{\Delta D + \lambda_2 k}{2} + R_d - \frac{\eta}{1-\eta}c_r\right)$$

$$0 < \eta < 1$$

As $f_{case4}^{mr} \leq 0$, at $(1-\eta) f_{case4}^{mr} \geq c_r$, $-\eta f_{case4}^{mr} \leq \lambda_2 \bar{Q}$ satisfies the conditions:

Given $\quad Q = \dfrac{\bar{D} + \Delta D - wk}{2} \leq Q_{case4}^{*}$, the manufacturers adopt $AQDP\left(w_1, w_2, Q_{case4}^{*}\right)$ to coordinate.

Given $\quad Q = \dfrac{\bar{D} + \Delta D - wk}{2} > Q_{case4}^{*}$, the manufacturers adopt $CLPP\left(w_2, Q_{case4}^{*}\right)$ to coordinate, where:

$$w_1 > \frac{\bar{D} + \Delta D}{k}$$

$$-\frac{1}{k}\sqrt{(1-\eta)\left[\begin{array}{c} \left(\bar{D} - mk + \Delta D + \lambda_2 k\right)\left(\bar{D} - mk + \Delta D - \lambda_2 k\right) \\ -4k\left(c_m - \lambda_2 \dfrac{\Delta D + \lambda_2 k}{2} + R_d - \dfrac{\eta}{1-\eta} c_r\right) \end{array}\right]}$$

$$w_2 = \eta \frac{\bar{D} + 2\Delta D}{2k} + (2-\eta)\frac{m}{2} - \eta \frac{\lambda_2}{2}$$

$$+ (1-\eta)\frac{2}{\bar{D} - mk + \Delta D + \lambda_2 k}\left(c_m - \lambda_2 \frac{\Delta D + \lambda_2 k}{2} + R_d - \frac{\eta}{1-\eta} c_r\right)$$

$$\eta > 1$$

These conditions cannot be satisfied in the context of $(1-\eta) f_{case4}^{mr} \geq c_r$ and $-\eta f_{case4}^{mr} \leq \lambda_2 \bar{Q}$; the manufacturers will dispose all the products in the secondary market and suffer loss $\lambda_2 Q_{case4}^{*}$.

Manufacturers and suppliers with demand disruption risk

Demand for raw materials is decided on the basis of optimal output. However, considering the maximal profits of suppliers in relation to raw materials, the optimal supply of suppliers and the demand of manufacturers are not necessarily equal. Here, the issue of coordinating profits between manufacturers and suppliers emerges.

In order to find the appropriate coordinating solutions, the profits of suppliers are analyzed first. If suppliers determine the supply price for raw materials according to the demand of raw materials by manufacturers, the supply price is the linear function of demand: $m = m_0 - k_s Q$.

Here, in order to be closely linked with the issue of coordinating manufacturers and retailers, consider the supply and its price of suppliers from the perspective of production of manufacturers. In other words, Q in the equation refers to the production of manufacturers, rather than the supply of raw materials related to suppliers. m refers to the supply price determined by suppliers on the basis of materials needed by manufacturers in unit product rather than the unit price of raw materials. In the preceding analysis, the demand coefficient of the unit product against raw materials is defined as t. In other words, the unit product needs t units of raw materials. Therefore, the supply of suppliers is tQ, and the unit price of raw materials is $\dfrac{m}{t}$. Both m_0 and k_s are constants, which refer to the sensitivity coefficient of the price determined by suppliers against the demand of manufacturers, letting the profits of suppliers be f^s.

$$f^s = Q(m - tc_s) = Q(m_0 - k_s Q - tc_s)$$

Compute the first derivative from the preceding equation, letting the first derivative be 0.

$$f^{s'} = m_0 - 2k_s Q - tc_s = 0$$

The following can be achieved:

$$\bar{Q}^s = \frac{m_0 - tc_s}{2k_s}$$

$$\bar{m} = m_0 - k_s \bar{Q}^s = \frac{m_0 + tc_s}{2}$$

$$\bar{f}^s = \bar{Q}^s (\bar{m} - tc_s) = \frac{(m_0 - tc_s)^2}{4k_s}$$

That is to say, if the suppliers consider their own maximum profits, then the optimal supply can support manufactures to produce the unit $\bar{Q}^s$.

Coordination between manufacturers and suppliers without demand disruption risk

It is clear from the preceding analysis that, without demand disruption risk, the optimal output of manufacturers is $\bar{Q} = \dfrac{\bar{D} - mk}{2}$. Substitute $m = m_0 - k_s Q$, and the following can be obtained:

$$\bar{Q} = \frac{\bar{D} - mk}{2} = \frac{\bar{D} - (m_0 - k_s \bar{Q}) k}{2}$$

The following is achieved: $\bar{Q} = \dfrac{\bar{D} - m_0 k}{2 - kk_s}$

Given $\bar{Q}^s \neq \bar{Q}$, if suppliers are required to supply raw materials for $\bar{Q}$ units of the product, suppliers will not achieve the maximal profits. Here, suppliers are not willing to provide raw materials for $\bar{Q}$ units of the product. In order to manufacture $\bar{Q}$ units of products, the manufacturer must find a coordinating scheme to motivate suppliers to provide the raw materials for $\bar{Q}$ units of products. The subsidy program can help achieve this end. That is to say, manufacturers provide subsidy I for suppliers to push suppliers to provide raw materials. In this program, the key is to determine how much the subsidy I is.

As the suppliers need the raw materials to manufacture $\bar{Q}$ units of the product, the profits are as follows:

$$f^s\left(\bar{Q}\right) = \bar{Q}\left(m_0 - k_s\bar{Q} - tc_s\right) = \frac{\bar{D} - m_0 k}{2 - kk_s}\left(m_0 - k_s\frac{\bar{D} - m_0 k}{2 - kk_s} - tc_s\right)$$

$$= \frac{\bar{D} - m_0 k}{2 - kk_s}\left(\frac{2m_0 - k_s\bar{D}}{2 - kk_s} - tc_s\right)$$

Then subsidy I is supposed to be:

$$I_{\bar{Q}} = \bar{f}^s - f^s\left(\bar{Q}\right) = \frac{\left(m_0 - tc_s\right)^2}{4k_s} - \frac{\bar{D} - m_0 k}{2 - kk_s}\left(\frac{2m_0 - k_s\bar{D}}{2 - kk_s} - tc_s\right)$$

In the subsidy scheme mentioned in the preceding text, suppliers provide raw materials to manufacture $\bar{Q}$ units of the product.

Coordination between manufacturers and suppliers with demand disruption risk

When the coordination between manufacturers and retailers with demand disruption risk is analyzed, four aspects are discussed in greater detail. In scenarios one and three, the optimal output of manufacturers is still $\bar{Q}$; the optimal output in scenario two is Q^*_{case2}; and the optimal output in scenario four is Q^*_{case4}. If the optimal output of manufacturers is still $\bar{Q}$, then, in order to let suppliers provide raw materials, subsidy for suppliers and subsidy without demand disruption risk analyzed in the preceding text are the same. However, when the optimal outputs of manufacturers are Q^*_{case2} or Q^*_{case4}, the corresponding subsidy will change too.

(1) scenario one—the optimal output of the manufacturer is $Q^*_{case2} = \dfrac{\bar{D} - mk}{2} + \dfrac{\Delta D - \lambda_1 k}{2}$

Substituting $m = m_0 - k_s Q$ into Q^*_{case2}:

$$Q^*_{case2} = \frac{\bar{D} - \left(m_0 - k_s Q^*_{case2}\right)k}{2} + \frac{\Delta D - \lambda_1 k}{2}$$

The following is achieved: $Q^*_{case2} = \dfrac{\bar{D} + \Delta D - (m_0 + \lambda_1)k}{2 - kk_s}$

Here, if suppliers need raw materials for Q^*_{case4} units of the product, profits of suppliers are as follows:

$$f^s\left(Q^*_{case2}\right) = Q^*_{case2}\left(m_0 - k_s Q^*_{case2} - tc_s\right)$$

$$= \frac{\bar{D} + \Delta D - (m_0 + \lambda_1)k}{2 - kk_s}\left(m_0 - k_s \frac{\bar{D} + \Delta D - (m_0 + \lambda_1)k}{2 - kk_s} - tc_s\right)$$

$$= \frac{\bar{D} + \Delta D - (m_0 + \lambda_1)k}{2 - kk_s}\left(\frac{2m_0 - k_s\left(\bar{D} + \Delta D\right) + \lambda_1 kk_s}{2 - kk_s} - tc_s\right)$$

Here, to coordinate the profits among suppliers, that is, to provide raw materials for suppliers to manufacture Q^*_{case4} units of products, manufacturers should offer subsidy for suppliers as follows:

$$I_{Q^*_{case2}} = \bar{f}^s - f^s\left(Q^*_{case2}\right)$$

$$= \frac{\left(m_0 - tc_s\right)^2}{4k_s} - \frac{\bar{D} + \Delta D - (m_0 + \lambda_1)k}{2 - kk_s}$$

$$\times \left(\frac{2m_0 - k_s\left(\bar{D} + \Delta D\right) + \lambda_1 kk_s}{2 - kk_s} - tc_s\right)$$

(2) scenario two—the optimal output of manufacturers is $Q^*_{case4} = \dfrac{\bar{D} - mk}{2} + \dfrac{\Delta D + \lambda_1 k}{2}$

Substituting $m = m_0 - k_s Q$ into Q^*_{case4}

$$Q^*_{case4} = \frac{\bar{D} - \left(m_0 - k_s Q^*_{case4}\right)k}{2} + \frac{\Delta D + \lambda_2 k}{2}$$

The following is achieved:

$$Q^*_{case4} = \frac{\bar{D} + \Delta D - (m_0 - \lambda_2)k}{2 - kk_s}$$

Here, if suppliers need raw materials to manufacture Q^*_{case4} units of the product, the profits of suppliers are as follows:

$$f^s\left(Q^*_{case4}\right)=Q^*_{case4}\left(m_0-k_sQ^*_{case4}-tc_s\right)$$

$$=\frac{\bar{D}+\Delta D-\left(m_0-\lambda_2\right)k}{2-kk_s}\left(m_0-k_s\frac{\bar{D}+\Delta D-\left(m_0-\lambda_2\right)k}{2-kk_s}-tc_s\right)$$

$$=\frac{\bar{D}+\Delta D-\left(m_0-\lambda_2\right)k}{2-kk_s}\left(\frac{2m_0-k_s\left(\bar{D}+\Delta D\right)-\lambda_2kk_s}{2-kk_s}-tc_s\right)$$

Here, to coordinate the profits among suppliers, that is, to provide raw materials for suppliers to manufacture Q^*_{case4} units of the product, manufacturers should offer the following subsidy for suppliers:

$$I_{Q^*_{case2}}=\bar{f}^s-f^s\left(Q^*_{case4}\right)$$

$$=\frac{\left(m_0-tc_s\right)^2}{4k_s}-\frac{\bar{D}+\Delta D-\left(m_0-\lambda_2\right)k}{2-kk_s}$$

$$\times\left(\frac{2m_0-k_s\left(\bar{D}+\Delta D\right)-\lambda_2kk_s}{2-kk_s}-tc_s\right)$$

Supply chain coordination under the risk of supply disruption

Coordination between manufacturers and suppliers with supply disruption risk

Sheng (2008) analyzed how manufacturers and retailers coordinate in supply disruption risk on the basis of the two-stage supply chain model of manufacturers, and how retailers make the optimal preventive decisions for addressing disruption risk and achieve the overall maximal profits between manufacturers and retailers. The analysis shows that the manufacturers pay a certain amount of penalty for retailers to achieve the preceding goal. The optimal penalty that manufacturers should pay is the product of the backorder cost of retailers and the time needed for recovery of supply chains.

Here, in terms of the issue of coordinating between manufacturers and suppliers with supply disruption risk, it is important to discuss how to coordinate suppliers and manufacturers to use penalty contract to achieve supply chain coordination. What is different is that here it is hypothesized that suppliers and manufacturers are risk-neutral, and thus when the optimal preventive measures are pursued, the model of mean value and variance is no longer used. However, the model of minimal expected cost is deployed (Meng, 2009). Here, the focus of discussion is how to take advantage of penalty contract to achieve coordination between manufacturers and suppliers.

Considering supply disruption risk, if suppliers adopt proper preventive and emergency measures, the effects of supply disruption on manufacturers can be reduced. Preventive and emergency measures entail some cost. From the perspective of suppliers, investment in preventive and emergency measures is not consistent with the optimal overall profits between manufacturers and retailers. In this case, manufacturers may collect the penalty from suppliers to help suppliers achieve the maximal self-interest. At the same time, the overall profits of manufacturers and suppliers will be maximal.

In the penalty scheme, the following variables are considered:

T_0—the preventive measures adopted by suppliers before the supply disruption risk is generated, to prevent the supply disruption and reduce the loss caused by supply disruption

T—the time spent by suppliers after the supply disruption risk emerges, till recovery to normal

$C(T_0)$—the cost of suppliers when the preventive measure is T_0

$C(T_0, T)$—the cost incurred by the supplier to recover the production after supply disruption risk occurred

C_b—the backorder cost by manufacturers in the unit time within the time needed by suppliers to recover the production to normal

τ—the penalty paid by the manufacturers when suppliers fail to provide raw materials for manufacturers

p—the probability of disruption risk by suppliers

The centralized decision analysis by manufacturers and suppliers

If the manufacturers and suppliers form a whole enterprise, then they decide together. In this case, the optimal preventive and emergency measures are analyzed.

First, analyze the optimal emergency measures. In other words, compute the optimal time T when suppliers spend on recovering to the normal conditions after supply chain disruptive events occurred. Thus, it is important to consider the cost caused by supply chain disruption risk, letting the cost be C_1^{sm}.

$$C_1^{sm} = C(T_0, T) + C_b T$$

Compute the partial derivative of T from the preceding equation, letting the partial derivative be 0.

$$\frac{\partial C_1^{sm}}{\partial T} = \frac{\partial C(T_0, T)}{\partial T} + C_b = 0$$

The following can be achieved:

$$\frac{\partial C(T_0,T)}{\partial T} = -C_b \tag{6-1}$$

That is to say, the optimal T is supposed to satisfy the requirement of Equation (6-1).

Then, the optimal preventive measures are analyzed, that is, the optimal solution T_0 can be computed. Thus, it is necessary to consider prevention of supply disruption risk and the expected cost for preventing supply disruption risk, letting the expected cost be C_2^{sm}.

$$C_2^{sm} = C(T_0) + p[C(T_0,T) + C_b T]$$

Compute the partial derivative of T_0 from the preceding equation, letting the partial derivative be 0.

$$\frac{\partial C_2^{sm}}{\partial T_0} = \frac{\partial C(T_0)}{\partial T_0} + p\left[\frac{\partial C(T_0,T)}{\partial T_0} + \frac{\partial C(T_0,T)}{\partial T}\frac{\partial T}{\partial T_0} + C_b\frac{\partial T}{\partial T_0}\right] = 0$$

Substitute Equation (6-1), and the following can be achieved:

$$\frac{\partial C_2^{sm}}{\partial T_0} = \frac{\partial C(T_0)}{\partial T_0} + p\frac{\partial C(T_0,T)}{\partial T_0} = 0 \tag{6-2}$$

That is to say, the optimal T_0 should satisfy the requirement of Equation (6-2).

Coordination of manufacturers and suppliers with supply disruption risk

When suppliers and manufacturers decide things separately, the optimal T and T_0 determined from the suppliers' maximal self-interest are inconsistent with the requirements of Equations (6-1) and (6-2). In order to make the optimal decision that satisfy the requirements of Equations (6-1) and (6-2), it is necessary for the manufacturers to collect penalty τ from suppliers. Next, the conditions of the optimal penalty τ should be satisfied. Thus, it is necessary to consider from the perspective of the maximal profits of suppliers.

The cost brought by supply disruption risk to suppliers is analyzed first, letting the cost be C_1^s.

$$C_1^s = C(T_0,T) + \tau$$

First, analyze the cost brought by suppliers after the supply chain disruptive events occur, letting the cost be C_1^s.

Compute the partial derivative of T from the preceding equation, letting the partial derivative be 0.

$$\frac{\partial C_1^s}{\partial T} = \frac{\partial C(T_0,T)}{\partial T} + \frac{\partial \tau}{\partial T} = 0$$

The following can be achieved:

$$\frac{\partial C(T_0,T)}{\partial T} = -\frac{\partial \tau}{\partial T} \tag{6-3}$$

That is to say, after the supply chain disruptive events, when suppliers achieve their minimum cost, the optimal T is supposed to satisfy the requirement of Equation (6-3).

In order to achieve coordination between manufacturers and suppliers, that is, while the manufacturers achieve the minimal cost, the minimal overall profits of manufacturers and suppliers are achieved. Here the optimal T must still satisfy the requirement of Equation (6-1). Therefore, the conditions that the optimal T_0 must satisfy when manufacturers and suppliers coordinate are achieved.

$$\left\{ \begin{aligned} \frac{\partial C(T_0,T)}{\partial T} &= -C_b \\ \frac{\partial C(T_0,T)}{\partial T} &= -\frac{\partial \tau}{\partial T} \end{aligned} \right.$$

The following can be achieved.

$$\frac{\partial \tau}{\partial T} = C_b \tag{6-4}$$

Then, the preventive measures by suppliers before supply disruption risk and the expected cost of emergency measures when supply disruption occurs are analyzed, letting the cost be C_2^s:

$$C_2^s = C(T_0) + p\left[C(T_0,T) + \tau\right]$$

Compute the partial derivative of T_0 from the preceding equation, letting the partial derivative be 0.

$$\frac{\partial C_2^s}{\partial T_0} = \frac{\partial C(T_0)}{\partial T_0} + p\left[\frac{\partial C(T_0,T)}{\partial T_0} + \frac{\partial C(T_0,T)}{\partial T}\frac{\partial T}{\partial T_0} + \frac{\partial \tau}{\partial T_0} + \frac{\partial \tau}{\partial T}\frac{\partial T}{\partial T_0}\right] = 0$$

Substitute Equations (6-1) and (6-3), and then the following can be achieved:

$$\frac{\partial C_2^s}{\partial T_0} = \frac{\partial C(T_0)}{\partial T_0} + p\left[\frac{\partial C(T_0,T)}{\partial T_0} + \frac{\partial \tau}{\partial T_0}\right] = 0 \qquad (6\text{-}5)$$

In other words, before supply disruption happens, the optimal T_0 should satisfy the requirement of Equation (6-5), so that suppliers achieve the minimal expected cost.

In order to achieve coordination between manufacturers and suppliers, here the optimal T_0 must still satisfy the requirement of Equation (6-2). Therefore, the conditions, which the optimal T_0 must satisfy when manufacturers and suppliers coordinate, are achieved.

$$\left|\begin{array}{l} \dfrac{\partial C(T_0)}{\partial T_0} + p\dfrac{\partial C(T_0,T)}{\partial T_0} = 0 \\[4mm] \dfrac{\partial C(T_0)}{\partial T_0} + p\left[\dfrac{\partial C(T_0,T)}{\partial T_0} + \dfrac{\partial \tau}{\partial T_0}\right] = 0 \end{array}\right.$$

The following can be achieved:

$$\frac{\partial \tau}{\partial T_0} = 0 \qquad (6\text{-}6)$$

The conditions that the optimal penalty should satisfy are achieved according to Equations (6-4) and (6-6).

$$\left|\begin{array}{l} \dfrac{\partial \tau}{\partial T} = C_b \\[4mm] \dfrac{\partial \tau}{\partial T_0} = 0 \end{array}\right.$$

It can be known according to the conditions that the optimal penalty T should satisfy:

$$\tau = C_b T$$

That is to say, with supply disruption risk, in order to achieve coordination between manufacturers and suppliers, the manufacturers should collect the penalty from suppliers. The optimal penalty is the product of the time when suppliers recover the normal supply and the backorder cost within the unit time after supply disruptions occurs. In other words, it is the backorder cost caused by supply disruption risk.

Coordination between manufacturers and retailers without and with supply disruption risk

Coordination between manufacturers and retailers without supply disruption risk

When facing the issue of coordinating between manufacturers and suppliers with demand disruption risk, knowing that there is no disruption risk, the manufacturers and retailers decide the profits together (Meng, 2009).

$$f^{mr} = Q(p-m) - c_m - c_r = Q\left(\frac{\bar{D}-Q}{k} - m\right) - c_m - c_r$$

The following is achieved:

$$\bar{Q} = \frac{\bar{D}-mk}{2}$$

$$\bar{p} = \frac{\bar{D}-\bar{Q}}{k} = \frac{\bar{D}+mk}{2k}$$

$$\bar{f}^{mr} = \bar{Q}(\bar{p}-m) - c_m - c_r = \frac{(\bar{D}-mk)^2}{4k} - c_m - c_r$$

Without disruption risk, the manufacturers and retailers may adopt the contract $AQDP(w_1, w_2, \bar{Q})$ to coordinate, where:

$$w_1 > \frac{\bar{D}}{k} - \frac{1}{k}\sqrt{(1-\eta)\left[(\bar{D}-mk)^2 - 4k\left(c_m - \frac{\eta}{1-\eta}c_r\right)\right]}$$

$$w_2 = \eta\frac{\bar{D}}{2k} + (2-\eta)\frac{m}{2} + 2(1-\eta)\frac{1}{\bar{D}-mk}\left(c_m - \frac{\eta}{1-\eta}c_r\right)$$

$$0 < \eta < 1$$

Coordination between manufacturers and retailers with supply disruption risk

When supply disruption occurs, prices of raw materials change, compared with the normal circumstances. If the price of raw materials changes from m to $m + \Delta m$, in this case, the decision on the optimal output of manufacturers will change accordingly, assuming that Q changes to $Q + \Delta Q$. With the preceding changes brought by supply disruption, the manufacturers will assume partial cost and cost

R_s of dealing with supply disruption. Therefore, the profit function of collaborative decision of manufacturers and suppliers will change to:

$$f^{mr} = Q(p-m-\Delta m) - c_m - c_r - \lambda_1 (Q-\bar{Q})^+ - \lambda_2 (\bar{Q}-Q)^+ - R_s$$

Given $\Delta Q > 0$, f^{mr} may be rewritten as:

$$f^{mr} = Q(p-m-\Delta m) - c_m - c_r - \lambda_1 (Q-\bar{Q}) - R_s$$

$$= Q\left(\frac{\bar{D}-Q}{k} - m - \Delta m\right) - c_m - c_r - \lambda_1 (Q-\bar{Q}) - R_s, (Q \succ \bar{Q})$$

Compute the first derivative from the preceding equation, letting the first derivative be 0.

$$f^{mr'} = \frac{\bar{D}}{k} - \frac{2}{k}Q - m - \Delta m - \lambda_1 = 0$$

The following can be achieved:

$$Q = \frac{\bar{D}-mk}{2} - \frac{(\Delta m + \lambda_1)k}{2} = \bar{Q} - \frac{(\Delta m + \lambda_1)k}{2}$$

As $-\lambda_1 \leq \Delta m \prec 0$, $Q \leq \bar{Q}$, here f^{mr} has the maximal value at $\bar{Q}$.

As $\Delta m \prec -\lambda_1$, $Q > \bar{Q}$, here f^{mr} has the maximal value at $Q = \frac{\bar{D}-mk}{2} - \frac{(\Delta m + \lambda_1)k}{2}$.

Given $\Delta Q < 0$, f^{mr} can be rewritten as:

$$f^{mr} = Q(p-m-\Delta m) - c_m - c_r - \lambda_2 (\bar{Q}-Q) - R_s$$

$$= Q\left(\frac{\bar{D}-Q}{k} - m - \Delta m\right) - c_m - c_r - \lambda_2 (\bar{Q}-Q) - R_s, (Q < \bar{Q})$$

Compute the first derivative from the preceding equation, letting it be 0.

$$f^{mr'} = \frac{\bar{D}}{k} - \frac{2}{k}Q - m - \Delta m + \lambda_2 = 0$$

The following can be achieved:

$$Q = \frac{\bar{D} - mk}{2} + \frac{(\lambda_2 - \Delta m)k}{2} = \bar{Q} + \frac{(\lambda_2 - \Delta m)k}{2}$$

As $0 < \Delta m \le \lambda_2$, $Q \ge \bar{Q}$, here f^{mr} has the maximal value at $\bar{Q}$.

As $\Delta m > \lambda_2$, $Q < \bar{Q}$, here f^{mr} has the maximal value at $Q = \frac{\bar{D} - mk}{2} + \frac{(\lambda_2 - \Delta m)k}{2}$.

Based on the preceding analysis, the coordination between manufacturers and retailers is discussed in greater detail, under four different scenarios.

(1) Scenario one: $-\lambda_1 \le \Delta m < 0$

Here, f^{mr} has the maximal value at $\bar{Q}$, that is:

$$Q^*_{case1} = \bar{Q} = \frac{\bar{D} - mk}{2}$$

$$p^*_{case1} = \bar{p} = \frac{\bar{D} + mk}{2k}$$

$$\begin{aligned} f^{mr}_{case1} &= \bar{Q}(\bar{p} - m - \Delta m) - c_m - c_r - R_s \\ &= \frac{\bar{D} - mk}{2}\left(\frac{\bar{D} - mk}{2k} - \Delta m\right) - c_m - c_r - R_s \end{aligned}$$

With supply disruption, profits of retailers are as follows:

$$f^r = Q(p - m) - c_r = Q\left(\frac{\bar{D} - Q}{k} - w\right) - c_r$$

Compute the first derivative f^r from the preceding equation, letting it be 0.

$$f^{r'} = \frac{\bar{D}}{k} - \frac{2}{k}Q - w = 0$$

The following can be achieved: $Q = \frac{\bar{D} - wk}{2}$

In the normal context of $w > m$, thus, $\frac{\bar{D} - wk}{2} < \frac{\bar{D} - mk}{2}$, and the manufacturers adopt $AQDP(w_1, w_2, \bar{Q})$ to coordinate with retailers. The following are the solutions of w_1 and w_2.

In order to avoid the retailers' ordering $Q = \dfrac{\bar{D} - wk}{2}$, it is as follows:

$$f^r = \frac{\bar{D} - w_1 k}{2}\left(\frac{\bar{D} - \dfrac{\bar{D} - w_1 k}{2}}{k} - w_1\right) - c_r \prec (1-\eta) f^{mr}_{case1}$$

That is: $\dfrac{(\bar{D} - wk)^2}{4k} - c_r < (1-\eta)\left[\dfrac{\bar{D} - mk}{2}\left(\dfrac{\bar{D} - mk}{2k} - \Delta m\right) - c_m - c_r - R_s\right]$

The following is achieved:

$$w_1 > \frac{\bar{D}}{k} - \frac{1}{k}\sqrt{(1-\eta)\left[\begin{array}{c}(\bar{D} - mk)^2 - 2k(\bar{D} - mk)\Delta m\\ -4k\left(c_m + R_s - \dfrac{\eta}{1-\eta}c_r\right)\end{array}\right]}$$

In order to motivate retailers to order $\bar{Q} = \dfrac{\bar{D} - mk}{2}$, it is as follows:

$$f^r = \frac{\bar{D} - mk}{2}\left(\frac{\bar{D} - \dfrac{\bar{D} - mk}{2}}{k} - w_2\right) - c_r = (1-\eta) f^{mr}_{case1}$$

That is: $\dfrac{\bar{D} - mk}{2}\left(\dfrac{\bar{D} + mk}{2k} - w_2\right) - c_r = (1-\eta)\left[\dfrac{\bar{D} - mk}{2}\left[\dfrac{\bar{D} - mk}{2k} - \Delta m\right] - \right.$

$\left. c_m - c_r - R_s\right]$

The following can be achieved:

$$w_2 = \eta\frac{\bar{D}}{2k} + (2-\eta)\frac{m}{2} + (1-\eta)\Delta m + (1-\eta)\frac{2}{\bar{D} - mk}\left(c_m + R_s - \frac{\eta}{1-\eta}c_r\right)$$

In the following analyses, the method of computing w_1 and w_2 is similar to the preceding case, and thus it is not restated here.

In summary, in the context of $-\lambda_1 \le \Delta m \prec 0$, the manufacturers adopt $AQDP(w_1, w_2, \bar{Q})$ to coordinate with retailers, where:

$$w_1 > \frac{\bar{D}}{k} - \frac{1}{k} \sqrt{(1-\eta) \left[\begin{array}{c} (\bar{D}-mk)^2 - 2k(\bar{D}-mk)\Delta m \\ -4k\left(c_m + R_s - \dfrac{\eta}{1-\eta}c_r\right) \end{array} \right]}$$

$$w_2 = \eta\frac{\bar{D}}{2k} + (2-\eta)\frac{m}{2} + (1-\eta)\Delta m + (1-\eta)\frac{2}{\bar{D}-mk}\left(c_m + R_s - \frac{\eta}{1-\eta}c_r\right)$$

$$0 < \eta < 1$$

(2) Scenario two: $\Delta m < -\lambda_1$

Here, f^{mr} has the maximal value at $Q = \dfrac{\bar{D}-mk}{2} - \dfrac{(\Delta m + \lambda_1)k}{2}$; that is:

$$Q_{case2}^* = \frac{\bar{D}-mk}{2} - \frac{(\Delta m + \lambda_1)k}{2}$$

$$P_{case2}^* = \frac{\bar{D} - Q_{case2}^*}{k} = \frac{\bar{D} + mk + (\Delta m + \lambda_1)k}{2k}$$

$$f_{case2}^{mr} = Q_{case2}^*\left(P_{case2}^* - m - \Delta m\right) - c_m - c_r - \lambda_1\left(Q_{case2}^* - \bar{Q}\right) - R_s$$

$$= \frac{\bar{D}-mk-(\Delta m + \lambda_1)k}{2}\frac{\bar{D}-mk-(\Delta m - \lambda_1)k}{2k} - c_m - c_r$$

$$+ \lambda_1\frac{(\Delta m + \lambda_1)k}{2} - R_s$$

It can be known from the preceding analysis that, given w, the optimal order of retailers is $Q = \dfrac{\bar{D}-wk}{2}$.

In the normal context of $w > m$, $\dfrac{\bar{D}-wk}{2} < \dfrac{\bar{D}-mk}{2} - \dfrac{(\Delta m + \lambda_1)k}{2}$, and the manufacturers adopt $AQDP\left(w_1, w_2, Q_{case2}^*\right)$ to coordinate with retailers, where:

$$w_1 > \frac{\bar{D}}{k} - \frac{1}{k}\sqrt{(1-\eta)\left[\begin{array}{c} (\bar{D}-mk-\Delta mk - \lambda_1 k)(\bar{D}-mk-\Delta mk + \lambda_1 k) \\ -4k\left(c_m - \lambda_1\dfrac{(\Delta m + \lambda_1)k}{2} + R_s - \dfrac{\eta}{1-\eta}c_r\right) \end{array} \right]}$$

$$w_2 = \eta \frac{\bar{D}}{2k} + (2-\eta)\frac{m+\Delta m}{2} + \eta \frac{\lambda_1}{2}$$

$$+ (1-\eta)\frac{2}{\bar{D} - mk - \Delta mk - \lambda_1 k}\left(c_m - \lambda_1 \frac{(\Delta m + \lambda_1)k}{2} + R_s - \frac{\eta}{1-\eta}c_r\right)$$

$$0 < \eta < 1$$

(3) Scenario three: $0 < \Delta m < \lambda_2$

Here, f^{mr} has the maximal value at $\bar{Q}$, that is:

$$Q^*_{case3} = \bar{Q} = \frac{\bar{D} - mk}{2}$$

$$P^*_{case3} = \bar{p} = \frac{\bar{D} + mk}{2k}$$

$$f^{mr}_{case3} = \bar{Q}(\bar{p} - m - \Delta m) - c_m - c_r - R_s$$

$$= \frac{\bar{D} - mk}{2}\left(\frac{\bar{D} - mk}{2k} - \Delta m\right) - c_m - c_r - R_s$$

It can be known from the preceding analysis that, given w, the optimal order of retailers is $Q = \frac{\bar{D} - wk}{2}$.

As $\Delta m > 0$, f^{mr}_{case3} is likely to be less than 0, and $f^{mr}_{case3} > 0$ and $f^{mr}_{case3} \le 0$ are discussed.

As $f^{mr}_{case3} > 0$:

In the normal context of $w > m$, thus, $\frac{\bar{D} - wk}{2} \le \frac{\bar{D} - mk}{2}$, and the manu-facturers should adopt $QDP(w_1, w_2, \bar{Q})$ to coordinate the profits with manu-facturers, where:

$$w_1 > \frac{\bar{D}}{k} - \frac{1}{k}\sqrt{(1-\eta)\left[\begin{array}{c}(\bar{D} - mk)^2 - 2k(\bar{D} - mk)\Delta m \\ -4k\left(c_m + R_s - \frac{\eta}{1-\eta}c_r\right)\end{array}\right]}$$

$$w_2 = \eta\frac{\bar{D}}{2k} + (2-\eta)\frac{m}{2} + (1-\eta)\Delta m + (1-\eta)\frac{2}{\bar{D} - mk}\left(c_m + R_s - \frac{\eta}{1-\eta}c_r\right)$$

$$0 < \eta < 1$$

If the profits of retailers are negative, then they will not place orders. Here, the manufacturers will dispose all products $\bar{Q}$ in the secondary market and assume the loss $\lambda_2 \bar{Q}$. The manufacturers will attempt to reduce the loss and make the retailers place an order. In order to make the retailers order, it is important to ensure that the profits of retailers will be no less than c_r, that is, $(1-\eta) f_{case3}^{mr} \geq c_r$. However, if the loss is more than $\lambda_2 \bar{Q}$ when the manufacturers provide goods for retailers, then manufacturers will not sell goods to retailers. However, they would dispose all products in the secondary market. Thus, in order to let manufacturers provide goods for retailers, it is necessary to ensure that the loss of manufacturers is no more than $\lambda_2 \bar{Q}$, that is, $-\eta f_{case3}^{mr} \leq \lambda_2 \bar{Q}$. When the preceding two conditions are satisfied:

Given $\dfrac{\bar{D}-wk}{2} \leq \dfrac{\bar{D}-mk}{2}$, here, the manufacturers adopt $AQDP(w_1, w_2, \bar{Q})$ and can coordinate with retailers, where:

$$w_1 > \frac{\bar{D}}{k} - \frac{1}{k}\sqrt{(1-\eta)\left[\begin{array}{c}(\bar{D}-mk)^2 - 2k(\bar{D}-mk)\Delta m \\ -4k\left(c_m + R_s - \dfrac{\eta}{1-\eta}c_r\right)\end{array}\right]}$$

$$w_2 = \eta\frac{\bar{D}}{2k} + (2-\eta)\frac{m}{2} + (1-\eta)\Delta m + (1-\eta)\frac{2}{\bar{D}-mk}\left(c_m + R_s - \frac{\eta}{1-\eta}c_r\right)$$

$$\eta > 1$$

Given $\dfrac{\bar{D}-wk}{2} > \dfrac{\bar{D}-mk}{2}$, the manufacturers adopt $CLPP(w_2, \bar{Q})$ and coordinate with retailers, where w_2 is the same as given earlier.

In summary, in the context of $0 < \Delta m < \lambda_2$, as $f_{case3}^{mr} > 0$, the manufacturers adopt $AQDP(w_1, w_2, \bar{Q})$ and coordinate with retailers, where:

$$w_1 > \frac{\bar{D}}{k} - \frac{1}{k}\sqrt{(1-\eta)\left[\begin{array}{c}(\bar{D}-mk)^2 - 2k(\bar{D}-mk)\Delta m \\ -4k\left(c_m + R_s - \dfrac{\eta}{1-\eta}c_r\right)\end{array}\right]}$$

$$w_2 = \eta\frac{\bar{D}}{2k} + (2-\eta)\frac{m}{2} + (1-\eta)\Delta m + (1-\eta)\frac{2}{\bar{D}-mk}\left(c_m + R_s - \frac{\eta}{1-\eta}c_r\right)$$

$$0 < \eta < 1$$

As $f_{case3}^{mr} \leq 0$:

When the conditions are satisfied in the context of $(1-\eta)f_{case3}^{mr} \geq c_r$ and $-\eta f_{case3}^{mr} \leq \lambda_2 \bar{Q}$:

Given $\dfrac{\bar{D}-wk}{2} \leq \dfrac{\bar{D}-mk}{2}$, the manufacturers adopt $AQDP(w_1, w_2, \bar{Q})$ and coordinate with retailers

Given $\dfrac{\bar{D}-wk}{2} > \dfrac{\bar{D}-mk}{2}$, the manufacturers adopt $CLPP(w_2, \bar{Q})$ and coordinate with retailers, where:

$$w_1 > \frac{\bar{D}}{k} - \frac{1}{k}\sqrt{(1-\eta)\left[\frac{\left(\bar{D}-mk\right)^2 - 2k\left(\bar{D}-mk\right)\Delta m}{-4k\left(c_m + R_s - \frac{\eta}{1-\eta}c_r\right)}\right]}$$

$$w_2 = \eta \frac{\bar{D}}{2k} + (2-\eta)\frac{m}{2} + (1-\eta)\Delta m + (1-\eta)\frac{2}{\bar{D}-mk}\left(c_m + R_s - \frac{\eta}{1-\eta}c_r\right)$$

$$\eta > 1$$

When $(1-\eta)f_{case3}^{mr} \geq c_r$ and $-\eta f_{case3}^{mr} \leq \lambda_2 \bar{Q}$ are not satisfied, the manufacturers will dispose all products in the secondary market and suffer losses $\lambda_2 \bar{Q}$.

(4) Scenario four: $\Delta m > \lambda_2$

Here, f^{mr} has the maximal value at $Q = \dfrac{\bar{D}-mk}{2} + \dfrac{(\lambda_2 - \Delta m)k}{2}$, that is:

$$Q_{case4}^* = \frac{\bar{D}-mk}{2} + \frac{(\lambda_2 - \Delta m)k}{2}$$

$$P_{case4}^* = \frac{\bar{D}-Q_{case4}^*}{k} = \frac{\bar{D}+mk+(\Delta m - \lambda_2)k}{2k}$$

$$f_{case4}^{mr} = Q_{case4}^*\left(P_{case4}^* - m - \Delta m\right) - c_m - c_r - \lambda_2\left(\bar{Q} - Q_{case4}^*\right) - R_s$$

$$= \frac{\bar{D}-mk-(\Delta m - \lambda_2)k}{2}\frac{\bar{D}-mk-(\Delta m + \lambda_2)k}{2k} - c_m - c_r$$

$$+ \lambda_2\frac{(\lambda_2 - \Delta m)k}{2} - R_s$$

It can be established from the preceding that, given w, the optimal order of retailers is $Q = \dfrac{\bar{D} - wk}{2}$.

As $f_{case4}^{mr} > 0$:

Given $\dfrac{\bar{D} - wk}{2} \leq \dfrac{\bar{D} - mk}{2} - \dfrac{(\Delta m - \lambda_2)k}{2}$, the manufacturers adopt $AQDP\left(w_1, w_2, Q_{case4}^*\right)$ and coordinate with retailers, where:

$$w_1 > \frac{\bar{D}}{k} - \frac{1}{k}\sqrt{(1-\eta)\left[\begin{array}{c}(\bar{D} - mk - \Delta mk + \lambda_2 k)(\bar{D} - mk - \Delta mk - \lambda_2 k) \\ -4k\left(c_m - \lambda_2 \dfrac{(\lambda_2 - \Delta m)k}{2} + R_s - \dfrac{\eta}{1-\eta}c_r\right)\end{array}\right]}$$

$$w_2 = \eta\frac{\bar{D}}{2k} + (2-\eta)\frac{m+\Delta m}{2} - \eta\frac{\lambda_2}{2} + (1-\eta)\frac{2}{\bar{D} - mk - \Delta mk + \lambda_2 k}$$
$$\times\left(c_m - \lambda_2\frac{(\lambda_2 - \Delta m)k}{2} + R_s - \frac{\eta}{1-\eta}c_r\right)$$

$$0 < \eta < 1$$

Given $\dfrac{\bar{D} - wk}{2} > \dfrac{\bar{D} - mk}{2} - \dfrac{(\Delta m - \lambda_2)k}{2}$, the manufacturers adopt $CLPP\left(w_2, Q_{case4}^*\right)$ and coordinate with retailers, where w_2 is the same as given in the preceding text.

As $f_{case4}^{mr} \leq 0$, in order to let retailers order, it is necessary to ensure that the profits of retailers are no less than c_r, that is, $(1-\eta)f_{case3}^{mr} \geq c_r$. At the same time, in order to let the manufacturers provide goods, it is necessary to ensure that the loss of the manufacturers is no more than $\lambda_2\bar{Q}$, that is, $-\eta f_{case3}^{mr} \leq$. The preceding two conditions are satisfied.

Given $\dfrac{\bar{D} - wk}{2} \leq \dfrac{\bar{D} - mk}{2} - \dfrac{(\Delta m - \lambda_2)k}{2}$, the manufacturers adopt $AQDP\left(w_1, w_2, Q_{case4}^*\right)$ and coordinate with retailers, where:

$$w_1 > \frac{\bar{D}}{k} - \frac{1}{k}\sqrt{(1-\eta)\left[\begin{array}{c}(\bar{D} - mk - \Delta mk + \lambda_2 k)(\bar{D} - mk - \Delta mk - \lambda_2 k) \\ -4k\left(c_m - \lambda_2 \dfrac{(\lambda_2 - \Delta m)k}{2} + R_s - \dfrac{\eta}{1-\eta}c_r\right)\end{array}\right]}$$

$$w_2 = \eta \frac{\bar{D}}{2k} + (2-\eta)\frac{m+\Delta m}{2} - \eta\frac{\lambda_2}{2} + (1-\eta)\frac{2}{\bar{D}-mk-\Delta mk + \lambda_2 k}$$

$$\times \left[c_m - \lambda_2 \frac{(\lambda_2 - \Delta m)k}{2} + R_s - \frac{\eta}{1-\eta}c_r \right]$$

$$\eta > 1$$

Given $\dfrac{\bar{D}-wk}{2} > \dfrac{\bar{D}-mk}{2} - \dfrac{(\Delta m - \lambda_2)k}{2}$, the manufacturers adopt $CLPP\left(w_2, Q^*_{case4}\right)$ and coordinate with retailers, where w_2 is the same as the given in the preceding text.

In summary, in the context of $\Delta m > \lambda_2$, as $f^{mr}_{case4} > 0$, and given $\dfrac{\bar{D}-wk}{2} \leq \dfrac{\bar{D}-mk}{2} - \dfrac{(\Delta m - \lambda_2)k}{2}$, the manufacturers adopt $AQDP\left(w_1, w_2, Q^*_{case4}\right)$ and coordinate with retailers; given $\dfrac{\bar{D}-wk}{2} > \dfrac{\bar{D}-mk}{2} - \dfrac{(\Delta m - \lambda_2)k}{2}$, the manufacturers adopt $CLPP\left(w_2, Q^*_{case4}\right)$ and coordinate with retailers, where:

$$w_1 > \frac{\bar{D}}{k} - \frac{1}{k}\sqrt{(1-\eta)\left[\begin{array}{c}(\bar{D}-mk-\Delta mk + \lambda_2 k)(\bar{D}-mk-\Delta mk - \lambda_2 k)\\[2mm] -4k\left(c_m - \lambda_2 \frac{(\lambda_2 - \Delta m)k}{2} + R_s - \frac{\eta}{1-\eta}c_r\right)\end{array}\right]}$$

$$w_2 = \eta \frac{\bar{D}}{2k} + (2-\eta)\frac{m+\Delta m}{2} - \eta\frac{\lambda_2}{2} + (1-\eta)\frac{2}{\bar{D}-mk-\Delta mk + \lambda_2 k}$$

$$\left(c_m - \lambda_2 \frac{(\lambda_2 - \Delta m)k}{2} + R_s - \frac{\eta}{1-\eta}c_r\right)$$

$$0 < \eta < 1$$

As $f^{mr}_{case4} \leq 0$, when the conditions of $(1-\eta)f^{mr}_{case4} \geq c_r$ and $-\eta f^{mr}_{case4} \leq \lambda_2 \bar{Q}$ are satisfied, given $\dfrac{\bar{D}-wk}{2} \leq \dfrac{\bar{D}-mk}{2} - \dfrac{(\Delta m - \lambda_2)k}{2}$, the manufacturers adopt $AQDP\left(w_1, w_2, Q^*_{case4}\right)$ and coordinate with retailers; given $\dfrac{\bar{D}-wk}{2} > \dfrac{\bar{D}-mk}{2} - \dfrac{(\Delta m - \lambda_2)k}{2}$, the manufacturers adopt $CLPP\left(w_2, Q^*_{case4}\right)$ and coordinate with retailers, where:

$$w_1 > \frac{\bar{D}}{k} - \frac{1}{k}\sqrt{(1-\eta)\left[\begin{array}{c}(\bar{D}-mk-\Delta mk+\lambda_2 k)(\bar{D}-mk-\Delta mk-\lambda_2 k) \\ -4k\left(c_m-\lambda_2\frac{(\lambda_2-\Delta m)k}{2}+R_s-\frac{\eta}{1-\eta}c_r\right)\end{array}\right]}$$

$$w_2 = \eta\frac{\bar{D}}{2k} + (2-\eta)\frac{m+\Delta m}{2} - \eta\frac{\lambda_2}{2} + (1-\eta)\frac{2}{\bar{D}-mk-\Delta mk+\lambda_2 k}$$
$$\left(c_m-\lambda_2\frac{(\lambda_2-\Delta m)k}{2}+R_s-\frac{\eta}{1-\eta}c_r\right)$$

$$\eta > 1$$

When the conditions of $(1-\eta)f_{case4}^{mr} \ge c_r$ and $-\eta f_{case4}^{mr} \le \lambda_2 \bar{Q}$ are not satisfied, the manufacturers will dispose all products Q_{case4}^* in the secondary market and assume the loss $\lambda_2 Q_{case4}^*$.

Conclusion

The issue coordinating sudden demand disruption and supply disruption has been analyzed on the basis of the three-stage supply chain system of suppliers–manufacturers–retailers.

The coordination of manufacturers and suppliers with demand disruption is further investigated on the basis of the model of two-stage supply chain coordination. The partial cost is added into the target function, and, at the same time, the cost of dealing with demand disruption is also considered in the target function. In addition, the fixed cost of manufacturers and retailers is considered. The analysis shows that when the fixed cost and the cost of dealing with demand disruption are considered, the manufacturers take advantage of All Quantity Discount Pact (AQDP) or Constrained Linear Pricing Pact (CLPP) to coordinate with retailers, but the settlement of wholesale price in the contract changes. For coordinating manufacturers and suppliers with demand disruption, here the compensation program is designed. The manufacturers provide compensation for suppliers to motivate suppliers to provide raw materials for the optimal output. The amount of compensation is the gap of profits in relation to the supply of raw materials for optimal output and the profits of the optimal supply of suppliers. At the same time, the question, is how much will the manufacturers compensate the suppliers to achieve the optimal output in different contexts?

In the context of supply disruption risk, coordination of manufacturers and suppliers is further examined on the basis of penalty contract. Here, the penalty contract is used to coordinate the manufacturers and suppliers. What is different is that it is hypothesized that suppliers and manufacturers are risk-neutral. When the optimal program is analyzed, the model of the minimal expected cost is deployed rather than the model of average value and variance. However, the results are the same as in the previous studies. In other words, in order to achieve coordination between manufacturers and suppliers, the optimal penalty is the product of the backorder cost of manufacturers in unit time and the time needed for suppliers to restore normal supply. In terms of coordination between manufacturers and retailers with supply disruption, what is different from previous research is that part of the cost is added to the target function and the cost of dealing with supply disruption is also considered in the target function. It is also discussed how manufacturers coordinate with retailers through All Quantity Discount Pact (AQDP) and Constrained Linear Pricing Pact (CLPP).

7 Responding decision-making methods oriented to collaboration demands in disruption

Introduction

Supply chain is a functional network chain made up of suppliers, manufacturers, and distributors and many other bodies, which pursue different interests. It is important to adopt appropriate mechanisms and methods to reduce the conflicts among supply chain members and promote competitiveness of the supply chain as a whole and its profits. In the market, there are many uncertain factors that affect and disturb supply chains, to which it should respond swiftly and recover to the coordinating status.

Supply chain members pursue their own maximal self-interest, which may deviate from the overall target of the supply chain system. Therefore, it is necessary to coordinate the logistics, information flow, and capital flow among supply chain members to reduce the cost and increase profits and service levels. The nature of supply chain is such that it needs to effectively control the overall channel and links from raw materials to clients in order to increase customer satisficing and the core competitiveness of each member enterprise. The coordinating mechanism and strategies of supply chains are the bonds that link member enterprises and the interest of the entire supply chain.

Suppliers, manufacturers, distributors, retailers, and logistics providers coordinate among enterprises, which improves the agility of supply chains, and is the key to advance the supply chain operations flow. Insufficient coordination might bring some negative effects, such as higher inventory cost, longer delivery time, higher transportation cost, shortage or damage of goods, or lower customer service levels. This shows that the issue of supply chain coordination (SCC) is one of the key problems in managing supply chains, which is concerned with the operational efficiency of the supply chain system. The higher the supply chain coordination, the less are the barriers among member enterprises.

Recently, a number of events that can cause uncertainty have emerged worldwide, including natural disasters, terrorist attacks, epidemics, etc. In addition to these disastrous events, micro uncertain events with different degrees of seriousness are more common, such as demand information changes, supply disruption, and accidental damage of manufacturing equipment. Compared with single enterprises, a supply chain system has a complicated structure and the decision environment confronted is more dynamic and uncertain. Each link of purchase, production, distribution, and transportation is affected by uncertain events. In many cases, the disturbance caused by uncertain events makes the supply chain system non-static, and thus supply chain coordination is dynamic. These events exert some negative influence on enterprise operations.

In order to maintain supply chain coordination, when confronting uncertain events, certain procedures and methods are supposed to be followed, and a program for responding to uncertain events needs to be scientifically established. Uncertain events might bring new coordination requirements, and it is likely that the original coordination strategies get affected, which means that it is necessary to differentiate degrees of effects. As uncertain events have some influence on the original coordination strategies, if the effects are not obvious, then supply chain coordination strategies do not have to be adjusted. If the effects are relatively prominent and within a certain range, then supply chain coordination strategies have to be adjusted and revised. If the effects exceed a certain range, the original coordination strategies might need to be altered and cannot be applicable.

In the uncertain events confronted by supply chains, disruptive events are an important type, which has the features of disruption and cause the need for disruption coordination. It requires that the supply chain be able to respond within the given time constraints. In the model of supply chain management, when confronting disruptive events, it is necessary for enterprises to reinforce the coordination between upstream suppliers and downstream distributors. Therefore, here, the focus is on the response related to the disruption in the purchasing and distributing links.

Method of constraint satisficing optimization

Whether it is public events or enterprise operations that affect supply chain operations, including each link of purchase, production, distribution, and transportation, the disruption needs to be addressed in a coordinated manner. In an environment where disruption needs to be addressed, the target that the coordination aims to achieve and the constraints confronted are diverse. In the decision-making process, decision-makers' preferences play very important roles. Thus, it is better to adopt the method of constraint satisficing optimization (see the PhD dissertation entitled, 'Supply Chain Response Decision Method Based on Coordination System' (Zhao, 2007)).

The concept of constraint satisficing optimization

The method of constraint satisficing optimization (CSO) refers to the decision program that seeks to make decision-makers feel satisfied and maximize satisficing under some constraints.

- Constraints
  Disruptive events often need urgent coordination. On the one hand, the constraint is concerned with time, which requires that the decision be made within a certain time limit, and the time available for decision-makers to analyze and contemplate is limited. On the other hand, different from the case

where plans are made, within the limited time, it is often difficult to arrange people, finance, and machinery, and the usable resources are very limited.

- Satisficing optimization

 When facing the demand for disruption coordination, supply chains are subject to certain constraints. It is often necessary to realize a number of targets simultaneously. In the light of modern cybernetics, the constraints that decision-makers confront and the targets to be realized are interchangeable. It is very difficult to achieve optimality from these targets (constraints) and to obtain the optimal program to deal with problems. Decision-makers improve a target and have to concede in relation to another target to some extent. As a result, the ultimate decisions need to be satisfying, rather than being the optimal decisions. The decision-makers have to accept "satisfying" program, because they do not have other choices.

- Preferences and satisficing requirement

 In terms of different targets or constraints, different decision-makers have different preferences. On the other hand, in the case of one specific target, the target (function) has a certain value, and different decision-makers might aim at different degrees of satisficing. Thus, in the decisions, preference of the decision-maker is reflected. On the other hand, in terms of a certain target or constraint, decision-makers have a scale—the requirement of satisficing. It is acceptable if it is higher than this requirement of satisficing, but it is unacceptable if it is lower. In enterprises, this preference penetrates the decision-making process. However, the traditional optimization method does not support the display of decision-makers' preferences.

The process of constraint satisficing optimization

The basic forms of constraint satisficing optimization

The issue of constraint satisficing optimization is concerned with multiple targets and constraints. Its standard forms can be expressed as follows:

$$
\begin{aligned}
\max f_i(x) \quad & i \in [1,m] \\
\min g_j(x) \quad & j \in [1,n] \\
st. \ c(x) \leq 0
\end{aligned}
\tag{7-1}
$$

In the preceding equation, x is the decision vector; $f_i(x)$ is m targets that need to be maximized; $g_j(x)$ is n targets that need to be minimized; and $c(x) \leq 0$ is the constraint condition.

The solution process of the constraint satisficing optimization

The solution process of the constraint satisficing optimization can be disintegrated into identification of preference, solution of the model related to satisficing

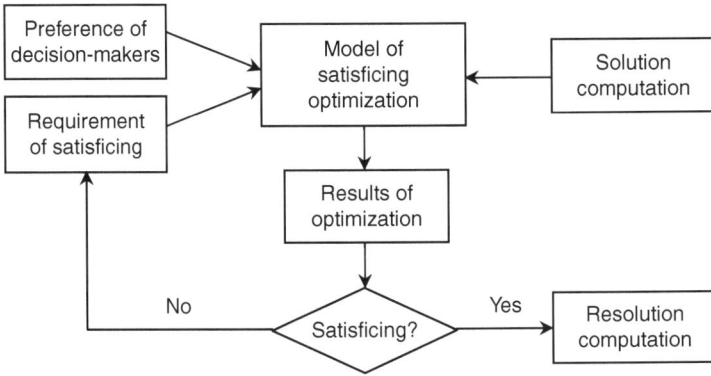

Figure 7.1 The process of resolution of the issue of constraint satisfaction optimization.

optimization, and the rule of preference adjustment by decision-makers, as illustrated in Figure 7.1.

(1) The identification of preference related to decision-makers

By means of each form of function, decision-makers may describe the degrees of satisficing at different levels in relation to the target function. In order to identify preferences of decision-makers, the minimization and maximization of each target under the constraints are determined first, and then, within the range of minimization and maximization, the display forms of satisficing are selected.

In terms of the target function $f_i(x)$ and $f_i(x)$, compute its minimization and maximization under the constraint of $c(x) \leq 0$, respectively, marked as $f_i^{\min}$, $f_i^{\max}$, $g_j^{\min}$, and $g_j^{\max}$.

When the expression forms of satisficing are described, two principles are to be followed.

- When the target function has $f_i^{\min}$ and $g_j^{\max}$, decision-makers' satisficing achieves the minimization, marked as $\mu_{\tilde{f}_i}(f_i) = \mu_{\tilde{g}_i}(g_j) = 0$. When the target function has $f_i^{\max}$ and $g_j^{\min}$, decision-makers' satisficing achieves the maximization, marked as $\mu_{\tilde{f}_i}(f_i) = \mu_{\tilde{g}_i}(g_j) = 1$.

- Decision-makers are rational. With respect to a target with forward direction, that is, decision-makers hope to develop toward the maximum target, the higher the target function, the higher is the decision-makers' satisficing. In other words, the satisficing toward forward direction by decision-makers is the single increasing function of the value of the target function. With respect to the target toward backward direction, that is, decision-makers hope to develop toward minimization, the less the value of target function, the higher is the satisficing of decision-makers. In other words, the satisficing toward backward direction by decision-makers is the single decreasing function of the value of the target function.

As a next step, the target function determined by decision-makers varies between minimization and maximization, and the forms of displaying satisficing are $\mu_{\tilde{f}_i}(f_i)$ and $\mu_{\tilde{g}_i}(g_j)$, and the corresponding satisficing requirements are $\bar{\mu}_{\tilde{f}_i}$ and $\bar{\mu}_{\tilde{g}_j}$, respectively. The forms can be continuous or discrete function.

(2) The model and solution of construction satisficing optimization

The satisficing function replaces the original target function, and the model of satisficing optimization is formulated as:

$$\max_i \mu_{\tilde{f}_i}(f_i) \quad i \in [1,m]$$

$$\max_{\tilde{g}_i} \mu_{\tilde{g}_i}(g_j) \quad j \in [1,n] \tag{7-2}$$

$$st. \ \mu_{\tilde{f}_i}(f_i) \geq \bar{\mu}_{\tilde{f}_i}$$

$$\mu_{\tilde{g}_j}(g_j) \geq \bar{\mu}_{\tilde{g}_j}$$

$$c(x) \leq 0$$

By means of the analytical hierarchy process, the decision-makers determine the weight of different targets and change the issue of optimizing multiple targets into that of a single target. Computation is by intellectual algorithms such as genetic algorithm and ant colony optimization, according to specific circumstances, and then the corresponding algorithm is designed.

(3) Adjust the preference parameter

To explore the problem further, the preference system of decision-makers might change dynamically. Integrating the results of solution, decision-makers might hope to adjust the forms of satisficing. In particular, when the solution does not produce satisfying results, decision-makers have to adjust the forms of satisficing. It is likely to refer to the Reference Direction Interactive Method (RDIM) to adjust the requirement of satisficing according to Mohan and Nguyen (1998). When it is necessary to adjust satisficing function, or the satisficing is not specified for reference, it may adjust the preference parameters by integrating the describing process of satisficing.

One emergency purchasing strategy in consumption supply chain system based on constraint satisficing

Disruptive events often change the market demand temporarily. To ensure market position and satisfy market demand, manufacturers undertake adaptive production and change their purchasing plans. This change needs coordination among many suppliers, and thus the issue of emergency manufacturing coordination with supply is generated. Liu et al. (2002) considered the constraint of time and demand and took the minimal number of supply points as the target, and proposed a mathematical model of multiple points collaboration and constructed a practical program.

In the environment of exigent production and supply, timely supply might increase the cost of suppliers. For instance, the change of the settled production plan to satisfy the exigent demand as priority, and tap the potential of production and other temporary measures, result in higher production cost. Because each supplier has different manufacturing techniques and management levels, their offers differ too. Therefore, the choice of supply points must take the purchase cost into account. In many cases, although purchase demand has the intensive features of time, it is often not very definite but fuzzy to some degree. To illustrate, time constraint can be expressed as requirements of materials for exigent production before a certain time, as soon as possible.

In terms of purchasing cost, fuzzy time requirement, and material demand, the issue of multiple points collaboration can be expanded into the issue of a multiple target decision. It is impractical to realize optimization with many targets, and decision-makers often have to weigh among targets. When each target is satisfied, the decision program of the overall maximal satisficing is pursued, that is, satisficing decision. Integrating preferences, decision-makers might revise the parameters of satisficing decisions according to the results of satisficing optimization and thus affect the satisficing strategies (Zhao, 2007).

The model of constraint satisficing optimization related to emergent purchase

In the study of two-stage supply chains with M suppliers and one manufacturer, these suppliers provide the same type of materials for manufacturers, and manufacturers make the finished products and then deliver them to clients. Some disruptive events lead to exigent demand of products, the demand is fuzzy on the basis of the objective conditions and expert knowledge, and it is required to offer sufficient goods at one time within a certain time limit as soon as possible. Through need analysis, the manufacturers determine that the demand for a certain material is a ladder-shaped fuzzy number $\tilde{D}$, and its membership function is $\mu_{\tilde{D}}(D(\phi))(D_L \leq D \leq D_U)$. Due to the constraints on the time limit, the manufacturers request that they should get the necessary materials before time T. The material quantity provided by each supplier is Q_i; the time when the materials should arrive at the manufacturers (supply time) is t_i; and material price is p_i $(i=1,2,\cdots,M)$. The hypotheses are as follows.

(1) Many suppliers involved in supply provide goods once and manufacture according to the order.

(2) In order to ensure that there is a practical program, given $\sum_{i=1}^{M} Q_i \geq D_L$, although $\sum_{i=1}^{M} Q_i$ is likely to be less than D_L, manufacturers may expand the range of suppliers to ensure that the hypothesis is correct.

The decision variables $\phi(s,q)$ are introduced; s in the variables refers to the combination of suppliers; and q refers to the combination of supply. The target of decisions is to seek the optimal strategy ϕ^*, to ensure that, within the allowed time limit, at reasonable price, manufacturers will obtain the appropriate amount of materials from proper suppliers, to satisfy the demand of emergency production, and guarantee that the system is stable maximally.

Target function

The strategy $\phi(s,q)$ entails $N(\phi)$ suppliers, whose supply time is t_r ($r=1$, 2, ..., $N(\phi)$). In one consumption exigent supply chain system, the exigent time $\phi(s,q)$ is defined as $T(\phi) = \max\{t_r\}$.

On the basis of time optimization, considering the economy of strategy at the same time, that is, under the constraint of time and supply, the cost sacrifice made should not be too much. In the strategy $\phi(s,q)$, if the unit material price charged by each supplier is p_r, and the order is q_r, then the total cost paid by manufacturers is $C(\phi) = \sum\limits_{r=1}^{N(\phi)} p_r q_r$. Here, the issue of the number of supply points is also considered and can be one of the targets that are to be realized. The number of exigent supply points is associated with the transaction costs of enterprises.

The total material purchased by manufacturers from suppliers $D(\phi) = \sum\limits_{r=1}^{N(\phi)} q_r$ should be appropriate, and the target requires that the membership function develop toward maximization. Insufficient purchase fails to satisfy emergency demand, and it is associated with the economic quantity of suppliers. Redundant purchase will cause overstock of materials and capital.

Constraint conditions

The preceding targets are achieved under certain constraints, and the major constraint is concerned with time and material demand. Time constraint refers to the constraint on the crash time of program $\phi(s,q)$, and this constraint can be expressed as $T(\phi) \leq T$. The constraint on material demand means that the total material purchased by each supplier should satisfy the fuzzy demand $\widetilde{D}$, and the constraint can be expressed as $D_L \leq \sum\limits_{r=1}^{N(\phi)} q_r \leq D_U$.

When a supplier group is selected, the maximal material quantity provided by suppliers is determined accordingly, marked as Q_r. The constraint can be expressed as $q_r \leq Q_r$. In addition, the number of supply points selected is less than that of the usable, that is, $N(\phi) \leq M$. To summarize, the issue of emergent manufacture and purchase in supply chains is that of optimization related to a set of multiple targets and constraints, and the model is as follows:

$$\min T(\phi)$$

$$\min\ C(\phi) = \sum_{r=1}^{N(\phi)} p_r q_r$$

$$\min\ N(\phi)$$

$$\max\ \mu_{\widetilde{D}}\big(D(\phi)\big)$$

$$st.\ T(\phi) \le T \tag{7-3}$$

$$D_L \le \sum_{r=1}^{N(\phi)} q_r \le D_U$$

$$q_r \le Q_r$$

$$N(\phi) \le M$$

In Equation (7-3), the constraint conditions constitute the constraint set Φ. min and max are not maximization and minimization in a traditional sense, but they indicate that decision-makers hope that the target develops toward minimization and maximization. This model shows that, with the demand for disruption, in one consumption supply chain system, manufacturers and suppliers coordinate in supply and purchase.

The decision methods of interactive satisficing

In Equation (7-3), there are a number of target functions, and these targets cannot always achieve optimization at the same time. As far as one target is concerned, its function value varies between complete dissatisfaction (in the constraint set Φ, the target with forward direction will take minimization, the target with backward direction will take maximization, and the satisficing is 0) and complete satisfaction (in the constraint set Φ, the target with forward direction will take maximization, the target with backward direction will take minimization, and the satisficing is 1). With different values of target functions, the decision-makers' satisficing changes accordingly, which can be expressed in the range [0,1]. In terms of the issue of multiple-points supply, the optimal purchase program is supposed to make the overall satisficing of decision-makers to achieve maximization, that is, the comprehensive satisficing of each target achieves maximization.

In the satisficing decisions, decision-makers show their preference in two aspects. One is the balance of each target by decision-makers; the other is the satisficing of different values for a certain target by decision-makers, and the satisficing requirement of specific targets. The former is reflected in the form of target weight and does not provide in-depth analysis. The reasons are as follows.

(1) There is much research on the methods of determining the weight when there is information about preference. A certain scale can be used to compare each target in a group of two, constituting the fuzzy judgment matrix, fuzzy complementary judgment, or mixed judgment matrix, and then arrange

the judgment matrix according to the sequence, to achieve the weight. The sequence theory of each judgment matrix is either mature or has already developed to some extent.

(2) In terms of decisions, the constraint set determines the selected range of practical strategies. The target function is a principle of program optimization. That is to say, weight cannot affect the practical solutions set. However, the satisficing function and requirement of each target by decision-makers affect the practical solutions set. From this perspective, the effects of satisficing decision parameters are more important.

(3) In terms of decision-makers, the understanding of the major difference among targets is stable. In terms of the use of various weighting methods, there is a slight difference in weight values obtained. From the overall perspective, the decision-makers' understanding of the significance of each target is often stable. When decisions are made, and which is more important—cost, time, or other targets? It can be decided by a qualitative analysis. After one optimization, it is not necessary to adjust the weight of each target. This is totally different from satisficing of different values for a specific target by decision-makers and the satisficing requirement of a specific target. After one optimization, decision-makers have a new understanding of each target on the basis of their knowledge and are likely to adjust the satisficing decision parameters. For instance, decision-makers might have higher satisficing in relation to target requirement of time and cost. However, after getting the resolutions, it is found that there is no practical solution, which means that the time requirement cannot be satisfied if decision-makers are satisfied with the cost and spending. Decision-makers have to loosen the satisficing requirement on the targets of cost or time, or change the satisficing function. They think that the satisficing requirements specified can also be achieved in a higher cost level or at a later time.

Therefore, each target weight is not analyzed here, and is taken as known information.

Constraint satisfying optimization model

The three target functions of time, cost, and number of suppliers constitute a single target-planning problem with Φ, respectively. It is important to solve these three single target planning problems, and the extremum is $T_{max}, T_{min}, C_{max}, C_{min}, N_{max}$ and N_{min}. On this basis, the decision-makers (i.e., manufacturers) specify the satisficing function $\mu_{\widetilde{T}}(T(\phi))$, $\mu_{\widetilde{C}}(C(\phi))$ and $\mu_{\widetilde{N}}(N(\phi))$ of the three targets $T(\phi), C(\phi)$, and $N(\phi)$, and they are the decreasing functions of $T(\phi), C(\phi)$, and $N(\phi)$. $\bar{\mu}_T, \bar{\mu}_C, \bar{\mu}_N$, and $\bar{\mu}_D$ refer to the satisficing levels of each target required. Equation (7-3) is changed into the constraint satisficing optimization model in Equation (7-4). In Equation (7-4), $\alpha_T, \alpha_C, \alpha_N$, and α_D are the weight of each target, and $\alpha_T + \alpha_C + \alpha_N + \alpha_D = 1$.

$$\max \mu = \alpha_T \mu_{\widetilde{T}}\left(T(\phi)\right) + \alpha_C \mu_{\widetilde{C}}\left(C(\phi)\right) + \alpha_N \mu_{\widetilde{N}}\left(N(\phi)\right) + \alpha_D \mu_{\widetilde{D}}\left(D(\phi)\right)$$

$$st. \qquad\qquad\qquad \mu_{\widetilde{T}}\left(T(\phi)\right) \geq \bar{\mu}_T$$

$$\mu_{\widetilde{C}}\left(C(\phi)\right) \geq \bar{\mu}_C \qquad\qquad\qquad (7\text{-}4)$$

$$\mu_{\widetilde{N}}\left(N(\phi)\right) \geq \bar{\mu}_N$$

$$\mu_{\widetilde{D}}\left(D(\phi)\right) \geq \bar{\mu}_D$$

$$q_r \leq Q_r$$

The model of ergodic search algorithms

In Equation (7-4), the time satisficing and satisficing of the number of supply points depend on the combination of suppliers chosen. On choosing a supplier combination, Equation (7-4) is degenerated into the planning issue of q_r.

$$\max \mu = \alpha_C \mu_{\widetilde{C}}\left(C(\phi)\right) + \alpha_D \mu_{\widetilde{D}}\left(D(\phi)\right)$$

$$st. \qquad \mu_{\widetilde{C}}\left(C(\phi)\right) \geq \bar{\mu}_C$$

$$\mu_{\widetilde{D}}\left(D(\phi)\right) \geq \bar{\mu}_D \qquad\qquad\qquad (7\text{-}5)$$

$$q_r \leq Q_r$$

In order to solve Equation (7-4), the following ergodic search algorithm is proposed.

Step 1: Initialize $k = 1$, $\mu_{\max} = 0$, $\mu_T = \mu_C = \mu_N = \mu_D = 0$

Step 2: In the kth supplier combination, judge whether the constraints $\mu_{\widetilde{T}}\left(T(\phi)\right) \geq \bar{\mu}_T$ and $\mu_{\widetilde{N}}\left(N(\phi)\right) \geq \bar{\mu}_N$ are accepted. If the constraint is satisfied, the planning Equation (7-5) is solved. If the corresponding target function value μ^* of the optimal solution q^* is more than $\mu_{\max}$, then let $\mu_{\max} = \mu^*$ and turn to step 3. If the constraint is not satisfied, or there is no solution for Equation (7-5) or $\mu^* \leq \mu_{\max}$, then turn to step 3 directly.

Step 3: $k = k+1$, given $k \leq \sum\limits_{i=1}^{M} C_M^i$, return to step 2, otherwise turn to step 4

Step 4: Output $\mu_T = \mu_{\widetilde{T}}\left(T(\phi^*)\right)$, $\mu_C = \mu_{\widetilde{C}}\left(C(\phi^*)\right)$, $\mu_N = \mu_{\widetilde{N}}\left(N(\phi^*)\right)$,

$\mu_D = \mu_{\widetilde{D}}\left(D(\phi)\right)$, k, q^*, $\mu_{\max}$, and complete.

The adjustment method of satisficing decision parameter

After one ergodic search algorithm, the first thing is to determine whether the optimization results are satisfactory. If further improvement is necessary, the satisficing optimization parameters can be adjusted. In Equation (7-4), the parameters determined by decision-makers entail the satisficing function and requirements, and decision-makers can select and adjust. If the satisficing function needs adjustment, including the parameters and types of functions adjusted, the following rules can be adopted. If the requirements of targets in terms of time, cost, and number of supply points are relaxed, then the function of the image in coordinate axis above the image of original function is adopted. If the requirements of targets on time, cost, and number of supply points are reinforced, then the function of the image in coordinate axis below the image of original function is adopted. In addition, the satisficing requirement of each target can also be adjusted directly.

When it is decided to adjust the satisficing requirement of each target, the reference membership adjustment method proposed by Mohan and Nguyen can be followed. First, specify the reference satisficing level μ_T^r, μ_C^r, μ_N^r and μ_D^r, and then determine the number of interpolating and extrapolating points as n_1 and n_2. According to Equation (7-6), compute interpolating and extrapolating points. Together with reference satisficing and $\{\mu_T, \mu_C, \mu_N, \mu_D\}$, repeat the ergodic search. Select the satisficing results, or choose one result as the starting point of re-adjustment.

$$
\left\{
\begin{aligned}
& \mu_T + \frac{k\left(\mu_T^r - \mu_T\right)}{(n_1 + 1)}, \mu_C + \frac{k\left(\mu_C^r - \mu_C\right)}{(n_1 + 1)}, \mu_N + \frac{k\left(\mu_N^r - \mu_N\right)}{(n_1 + 1)}, \\
& \mu_D + \frac{k\left(\mu_D^r - \mu_D\right)}{(n_1 + 1)}, \\
& k = 0, 1, \cdots, n_1 + n_2 + 1
\end{aligned}
\right\}
\tag{7-6}
$$

The emergency purchase strategy in continuous consumption supply chain system based on constraint satisficing

The description of the emergency purchase strategy in continuous consumption supply chain system

The study is concerned with the two-stage supply chain with M suppliers of raw materials and one manufacturer, where different suppliers of raw materials offer the same raw materials for manufacturers. Affected by some disruptive events, manufacturers need continuous emergency production and the consumption of raw materials is continuous. Here "continuity" compares with the circumstance where the production is stopped while waiting for the raw materials, but it is allowed to have the normal production break such as staff break and the adjustment and preparation for machines. Through need analysis and production techniques, the demand of raw materials is determined as fuzzy $\tilde{D}$, and the latest time for starting production is t_U. In order to obtain the supply from suppliers, the manufacturers adopt the compensation price that is higher than the normal transaction price (Zhao, 2007).

(1) Suppliers involved in providing raw materials manufacture according to the order and provide sufficient goods.
(2) The compensation price level only affects the quantity of materials that suppliers are willing to offer. No matter what the price levels are, the supply time (from the time when the manufacturers deliver the order to the time when the raw materials are received) of each supplier will not change.
(3) The consumption of raw materials is well-distributed, and the speed of consumption is v.

The manufacturers inquire about the price of raw materials from suppliers, which is confined by time and cost, and they get partial information. P_{sj} shows that suppliers $s(s = 1, 2, \cdots, M)$ can implement $j(j = 1, 2, \cdots, n)$ compensation price level. In the compensation price level P_{sj}, the quantity of raw materials that suppliers are willing to offer is Q_{sj}.

Decision target is to pursue the optimal coordinating strategy, which includes supplier combination, price combination, and purchase combination. In other words, issues of which suppliers, at what price, and how much raw material is purchased will be considered to enable manufacturers to produce in time, at a reasonable price to purchase appropriate amount of raw materials from suppliers to start production as soon as possible to continuously satisfy the demand of exigent supply. At the same time, the stability of the system is guaranteed maximally.

The model of constraint satisficing optimization

Target function

Urgency is the primary feature of the scenario, and thus the start of emergency production as soon as possible is the first target of the model of coordinating emergency manufacturing and purchase. Without considering constraints, construction includes the $i(i = 1, 2, \cdots, M)$ supplier combination, with a total of C_M^i. ϕ_{ik} refers to the k th combination $\left(k \le C_M^i\right)$; supply time of each supplier is $t_r\left(\phi_{ik}\right)(r = 1, 2, \cdots, i)$, without losing universality, given $t_1\left(\phi_{ik}\right) \le t_2\left(\phi_{ik}\right) \le \cdots \le t_i\left(\phi_{ik}\right)$. With respect to continuous consumption, the starting time of production related to the combination ϕ_{ik} is $T\left(\phi_{ik}\right) \in \left[t_1\left(\phi_{ik}\right), t_U\right], t_1\left(\phi_{ik}\right) \le t_U$.

Manufacturers consider the economics of the strategy, and it is required that the purchase price is minimal. With respect to the combination ϕ_{ik}, if the unit price paid is $p_r\left(\phi_{ik}\right)$ and the order is $q_r\left(\phi_{ik}\right)$, then the total cost paid is $C\left(\phi_{ik}\right) = \sum_{r=1}^{i} p_r\left(\phi_{ik}\right) q_r\left(\phi_{ik}\right)$.

Because the number of suppliers involved affects the stability of the emergency system, the number of suppliers in the combination ϕ_{ik} is marked as $N\left(\phi_{ik}\right)$.

Constraint condition and the model of emergency purchase coordination

In the model of emergency purchase coordination, the major constraints include time constraint, continuous condition constraint, raw material demand constraint, the constraint of suppliers' supply will, and suppliers' quantity constraint.

Time constraint refers to the constraint on the starting time of emergency production, which can be expressed as: $T\left(\phi_{ik}\right) \leq t_U$.

In order to satisfy the consumption continuity conditions, it is required that the next batch of raw materials arrives at the manufacturers no sooner than the inventory is used up. There is some constraint on the time between the time of starting production and the time of raw materials offered by each supplier. In terms of the relationship between t_U and $t_i\left(\phi_{ik}\right)$, two circumstances are analyzed.

(1) $t_U \geq t_i\left(\phi_{ik}\right)$. Given $T\left(\phi_{ik}\right) \in \left[t_d\left(\phi_{ik}\right), t_{d+1}\left(\phi_{ik}\right)\right]$ $(d \in Z^+$ and $d \leq i-1)$, with respect to $t_{g_0}\left(\phi_{ik}\right)\left(g_0 = d+1, d+2, \cdots, i\right)$, the constraint is

$$t_{g_0}\left(\phi_{ik}\right) \leq T\left(\phi_{ik}\right) + \dfrac{\sum\limits_{e=1}^{g_0-1} q_e\left(\phi_{ik}\right)}{v}.$$ Given $T\left(\phi_{ik}\right) = t_i\left(\phi_{ik}\right)$, the constraint does not exist.

(2) $t_U \geq t_i\left(\phi_{ik}\right)$. It is certain that the integer is $f \in [1, i-1]$, making $t_f\left(\phi_{ik}\right) \leq t_U < t_{f+1}\left(\phi_{ik}\right)$ acceptable. Given $T\left(\phi_{ik}\right) \in \left[t_d\left(\phi_{ik}\right), t_{d+1}\left(\phi_{ik}\right)\right]$ $(d \in Z^+$, $d \leq f-1)$, with respect to $t_{g_1}\left(\phi_{ik}\right)\left(g_1 = d+1, d+2, \cdots, i\right)$, the condition

$$t_{g_1}\left(\phi_{ik}\right) \leq T\left(\phi_{ik}\right) + \dfrac{\sum\limits_{e=1}^{g_1-1} q_e\left(\phi_{ik}\right)}{v}$$ must be satisfied. Given $t_f\left(\phi_{ik}\right) \leq T\left(\phi_{ik}\right) \leq t_U$,

the constraint is $t_{g_2}\left(\phi_{ik}\right) \leq T\left(\phi_{ik}\right) + \dfrac{\sum\limits_{e=1}^{g_2-1} q_e\left(\phi_{ik}\right)}{v}$ $\left(g_2 = f+1, f+2, \cdots, i\right)$.

In summary, in the premise of no misunderstanding, the continuous constraint can be simplified as: the constraint $t_g\left(\phi_{ik}\right) \leq T\left(\phi_{ik}\right) + \dfrac{\sum\limits_{e=1}^{g-1} q_e\left(\phi_{ik}\right)}{v}$,

$g = d(f)+1, d(f)+2, \cdots, i$ corresponds to $t_d\left(\phi_{ik}\right) \leq T\left(\phi_{ik}\right) \leq \min\left\{t_{d+1}\left(\phi_{ik}\right), t_U\right\}$.

The demand constraint of raw materials is the sum of the materials purchased by each supplier, which satisfies the fuzzy demand $\tilde{D}$, that is, $D\left(\phi_{ik}\right) = \sum\limits_{r=1}^{i} q_r\left(\phi_{ik}\right) = \tilde{D}$.

$P_r\left(\phi_{ik}\right) a$ and $Q_r\left(\phi_{ik}\right)$ indicate the compensation price adopted for supplier r and the supply set of supplier r, respectively, and the constraints are $p_r\left(\phi_{ik}\right) \in P_r\left(\phi_{ik}\right)$ and $q_r\left(\phi_{ik}\right) \leq_{p_r = P_r^h\left(\phi_{ik}\right)} Q_r^h\left(\phi_{ik}\right)\left(h = 1, 2, \cdots, n\right)$. The latter means that if $p_r\left(\phi_{ik}\right)$

takes the hth value in $P_r\left(\phi_{ik}\right)$, then $q_r\left(\phi_{ik}\right)$ has the limit in the hth value in $Q_r\left(\phi_{ik}\right)$. Furthermore, the number of suppliers involved in supply does not exceed the number of suppliers available, that is, $N\left(\phi_{ik}\right) \leq M$.

To summarize, the model of emergency manufacture and purchase coordination in supply chains can be found in Equation (7-7), which shows that the manufacturers and suppliers coordinate to purchase and supply in the continuous consumption supply chain system, confronting disrupted demand.

Satisficing optimization algorithm

The process of preference identification related to decision-makers and adjustment regulations of satisficing are similar to the preceding analysis, and thus the focus here is the analysis of satisficing optimization algorithm of emergency system of continuous consumption.

$$\min \ T\left(\phi_{ik}\right)$$

$$\min \ C\left(\phi_{ik}\right) = \sum_{r=1}^{i} P_r\left(\phi_{ik}\right) q_r\left(\phi_{ik}\right)$$

$$\min \ N\left(\phi_{ik}\right)$$

$$\text{st.} \quad T\left(\phi_{ik}\right) \leq t_U$$

$$t_g\left(\phi_{ik}\right) \leq T\left(\phi_{ik}\right) + \frac{\sum_{e=1}^{g-1} q_e\left(\phi_{ik}\right)}{v} \tag{7-7}$$

$$D\left(\phi_{ik}\right) = \sum_{r=1}^{i} q_r\left(\phi_{ik}\right) = \tilde{D}$$

$$P_r\left(\phi_{ik}\right) \in P_r\left(\phi_{ik}\right)$$

$$q_r\left(\phi_{ik}\right) \leq_{P_r = P_r^h\left(\phi_{ik}\right)} Q_r^h\left(\phi_{ik}\right)$$

$$N\left(\phi_{ik}\right) \leq M$$

The three targets of supplier number of decision-makers in relation to emergency production starting time, purchase cost, and participating supply and the satisficing function of raw materials demand constraint are marked as follows: $\mu_{\tilde{T}\left(\phi_{ik}\right)}T\left(\phi_{ik}\right)$, $\mu_{\tilde{C}\left(\phi_{ik}\right)}C\left(\phi_{ik}\right)$, $\mu_{\tilde{N}\left(\phi_{ik}\right)}N\left(\phi_{ik}\right)$, and $\mu_{\tilde{D}\left(\phi_{ik}\right)}D\left(\phi_{ik}\right)$. After the satisficing function is introduced, the model of emergency purchase coordination is changed into the model of constraint satisficing optimization.

$$\max \ \beta_1 \mu_{\tilde{T}\left(\phi_{ik}\right)}T\left(\phi_{ik}\right) + \beta_2 \mu_{\tilde{C}\left(\phi_{ik}\right)}C\left(\phi_{ik}\right)$$

$$\text{st.} \quad \mu_{\tilde{T}\left(\phi_{ik}\right)}T\left(\phi_{ik}\right) \geq \bar{\mu}_T$$

$$\mu_{\tilde{C}(\phi_{ik})} C(\phi_{ik}) \geq \bar{\mu}_C$$

$$\mu_{\tilde{D}(\phi_{ik})} D(\phi_{ik}) \geq \bar{\mu}_D \qquad\qquad (7\text{-}8)$$

$$t_g(\phi_{ik}) \leq T(\phi_{ik}) + \frac{\sum_{e=1}^{g-1} q_e(\phi_{ik})}{v} \qquad T(\phi_{ik}) \in \Omega$$

$$q_r(\phi_{ik}) \leq \sum_{P_r = P_r^h(\phi_{ik})} Q_r^h(\phi_{ik})$$

In the preceding equation, $\bar{\mu}_T$, $\bar{\mu}_C$, and $\bar{\mu}_D$ are the sets of satisficing requirements for three targets (constraints) of time, cost, and purchasing quantity set by decision-makers. α_1, α_2, and α_3 indicate the weight of the preceding three targets' distribution by decision-makers, and then, in the equation, $\beta_1 = \dfrac{\alpha_1}{(\alpha_1 + \alpha_2)}$ and $\beta_2 = \dfrac{\alpha_2}{(\alpha_1 + \alpha_2)}$.

In terms of the issue of purchase coordinating satisficing optimization in the continuous consumption emergency supply chain system, the following algorithms are proposed.

Step 1: Arrange suppliers according to the supplying time, and arrange the compensation price of each supplier in ascending order. Arrange the amount of raw materials that suppliers are willing to provide, and initialize $\mu_{max} = 0$.

Step 2: Select the supplier combination, compensation price combination, and time zones.

Step 3: Solve the problem of specific satisficing optimization in Equation (7-8), and compute the comprehensive satisficing by $\mu = \alpha_1 \mu_{\tilde{T}(\phi_{ik})} T(\phi_{ik}) + \alpha_2 \mu_{\tilde{C}(\phi_{ik})} C(\phi_{ik}) + \alpha_3 \mu_{\tilde{N}(\phi_{ik})} N(\phi_{ik})$. Given $\mu > \mu_{max}$, then let $\mu_{max} = \mu$, and record the optimal solution, and repeat step 2. If there is no solution for Equation (7-8) or $\mu < \mu_{max}$, repeat step 2 directly.

Step 4: Output the optimal solution. If the coordinating strategies are not unique, optimize according to a certain criterion such as time, cost, or other targets that decision-makers are concerned with, and complete.

The responding decisions of supply chain distribution confronting production disruption

Overall, with regard to the uncertain events in production system, previous studies have mainly been concerned with production recovery, and little research has focused on the effects of production disruption on distributors and retailers. In the complicated and changeable market competition scenario, a diversity of disruptive events can result in production disruptions in enterprises, and thus distributors and retailers can encounter stockout risk. Disruptive events exert profound impacts on manufacturing enterprises, which are forced to regulate their sales and plans of logistics. If distributors or retailers do not accept adjustment, from the legal perspective, they cannot get compensation such as liquidated damages, for the reason that these events are irresistible. As a result of this, they will bear higher stockout loss because they are not capable of satisfying the market demand. After both parties in the transaction agree with adjustment related to plans of sales and logistics, the most important problem is how they can make scientific amendments concerning the decisions of distribution and logistics. Even though the loss is unavoidable and the clients' demand cannot be completely met, the loss will be reduced to the minimum and the clients' demand will be maximally satisfied. Alternatively, the profit level of the supply chain after re-adjustment will be optimized, and the stockout cost will be minimized.

The description of the responding issue of supply chain distribution

This study is concerned with two-tier supply chain systems consisting of one manu-facturer and M retailers, and retailers encounter indefinite demand. Manufacturers produce and sell one product to retailers, and the unit production cost is C. Manufacturers receive orders from each retailer at 00:00, the transport time from manufacturers to each retailer and the related cost with retailers, such as the transport cost, are considered as known constants. The sales period of each retailer starts from day T_s, and stops at the end of day T_E. After manufacturers receive orders, the plan of production and logistics is made, and production is organized and started. Disruptive events such as the supply of raw materials and machine faults contribute to production disruptions from day T_I $(T_I \geq T_s)$ to day T_R. The assumptions are as follows.

(1) The productivity of manufacturers is a constant. Although manufacturers are likely to improve productivity after the production is recovered, it will not affect the property.
(2) Universality is not lost, if the supply of manufacturers for retailers should start from the production disruption. Before production is disrupted, the manufacturers will determine the sales program according to the circum-stance before disruptive events, and provide sufficient goods for retailers. After production disruption, these retailers will be excluded when responding decisions are made.

Sales and delivery time of retailers from manufacturers constitute the complete distribution strategy, which indicates when, to which retailer, and how manufactur-ers should distribute the materials. Ideal distributors are supposed to accomplish the following. First, the number of products should be reasonably distributed. Due to the production disruption, the number of products provided by manufacturers might not satisfy the demand of all orders. It is possible that the limited production tends to concentrate on a particular retailer, whose profits might increase. At the same time, the profits of other retailers will decrease. That particular retailer can reduce its stockout cost, whereas the stockout cost for other retailers will rise. As a conse-quence, there exists the issue of reasonable distribution. Second, the delivery time should be proper. Manufacturers might hope to delay the delivery, and thus the capacity of supply will rise. However, the transport and selling time make them unable to defer the supply.

The model of distributing decisions

Target function

The nature of supply chain management is such that the supply chain is viewed as a unity, and the competitive advantage of the overall supply chain is promoted for the overall optimization, in order to ensure the profit level of each member enterprise. From the perspective of the supply chain system, there are two targets: one is that the profit level develops toward maximization; and the other is that the shortage cost develops toward minimization (Zhao, 2007).

(1) The profits develop toward maximization. In other words, the gap *PF* between sales revenue and cost maximizes. Here, the concept of "supply sequencing" is introduced, referring to the time sequence when suppliers send products to each retailer. In terms of the supply chain consisting of M retailers, there are $M!$ types of supply sequencing. For instance, if $M = 3$, there are three retailers in the supply chain: R_1, R_2, R_3, then the number of supply sequencing types is $3! = 6$. Therefore, the set of supply sequencing is as follows.

$$\Phi = \left\{ R_1, R_2, R_3; \ R_1, R_3, R_2; \ R_2, R_1, R_3; R_2, R_3, R_1; \ R_3, R_1, R_2; \ R_3, R_2, R_1 \right\}$$

$R_{jk} \ (j = 1, 2, \cdots, M; k = 1, 2, \cdots, M!)$ is marked as retailer j of the supply sequencing k, and the related cost such as transportation cost is C_{jk}. In the market where R_{jk} is confronted, the selling price of products is P_{jk}, and q_{jk} is the number of products provided by manufacturers for R_{jk}. From the perspective of supply chain systems, as the transfer payment from manufacturers to retailers is not linked with decision-making, the first target of distribution decision-making model is as follows:

$$\max PF = \sum_{j=1}^{M} \left(P_{jk} - C - C_{jk} \right) q_{jk} \quad \left(\forall k \right) \tag{7-9}$$

(2) Stockout cost develops toward minimization. Stockout cost refers to the opportunity loss caused by unsatisfied market demand. Stockout means the current sales opportunity is lost, and it is likely that the profit opportunity will be lost as a result. Actually, stockout cost is opportunity cost. Although it is not the actual spending of the enterprises, it negatively influences corporate image and reputation. It is likely to result in diversion of purchasing behaviors of consumers. Therefore, from the long-term perspective, it affects the overall profits of the supply chain. Stockout cost reflects the degree of customer satisfaction to some extent. The higher the stockout cost is, the lower the degree of customer satisfaction. In the market competition driven by customer demand, the pursuit of minimizing stockout cost contributes to

improving the level of customer satisfaction. This embodies the concept of supply chain management that focuses on the creation of value for clients through the efforts by suppliers and retailers in the overall supply chain.

The market demand confronted by R_{jk} is D_{jk}, when retailers fail to satisfy the demand during the entire sales period, and the unit shortage cost generated is S_{jk}. The second target in the distributing decision model is that the shortage cost *SA* in supply chain system develops toward minimization, that is:

$$\text{min } SA = \sum_{j=1}^{M}\left(D_{jk} - q_{jk}\right)S_{jk} \quad \left(\forall k\right) \tag{7-10}$$

Some scholars integrate theses two targets and pursue the maximization of $\left(PF - SA\right)$. However, in the practice of enterprises, considering the importance of shortage, decision-makers not only attend to *PF*, but also pay attention to *SA*. Therefore, here, the profit level and shortage cost are two individual targets and are controlled separately.

Constraint condition

There are four types of constraints in the model: resource constraint, time constraint, rationality constraint, and other constraints.

(1) Resource constraint: Owing to production disruption, orders from retailers may not be completely satisfied. The time (supply time point) when manufacturers deliver goods to retailers R_{jk} is marked as t_{jk}; the time of each supply is marked as t_{jk}; the products provided will not exceed the inventory Q_s at the beginning; adding the production $v\left(T_I + \max\left\{t_{jk} - T_R, 0\right\}\right)$ during this period from 0 to t_{jk}, and then deducting the quantity $\sum_{d=1}^{j-1} q_{dk}$ that has been sold to the retailers at the previous supply time $\left(j-1\right)$, that is:

$$q_{jk} \leq Q_s + v\left(T_I + \max\left\{t_{jk} - T_R, 0\right\}\right) - \sum_{d=1}^{j-1} q_{dk} \tag{7-11}$$

In Equation (7-11), *v* is productivity. Here, hypothesis (1) is deployed, and in fact, if manufacturers' productivity after production recovery increases to a new constant, the expression of the second item on the right of the sign of inequality in Equation (7-11) will be affected, but the nature of the problem will not be influenced.

(2) Time constraint: in the context of production disruption, in order to increase the supply capacity, the manufacturers might hope to delay supply. However, owing to the sales period, supply time cannot be too late; otherwise, the sales period will be missed. There is a certain sequential dependence relationship

among the time points of supply. The transportation time from manufacturers to retailers R_{jk} is marked as TR_{jk}, and the time constraint is as follows:

$$t_{jk} \le T_E - TR_{jk} \tag{7-12}$$

$$t_{ik} \le t_{(i+1)k} \quad i=1,2,\cdots,M-1$$

(3) Rationality constraint: the inventory quantity provided by manufacturers to each supplier is no more than the order D_{jk}, that is:

$$0 \le q_{jk} \le D_{jk} \tag{7-13}$$

(4) Other constraints: According to hypothesis (2), the constraint is as follows:

$$t_{1k} \ge T_I \tag{7-14}$$

In addition, decision-makers might add other constraints on the basis of their own requirements. For instance, to some extent, it is required that the number of products offered to some districts will not be less than a certain limit. Equations (7-9) and (7-14) constitute the conditions of production disruption, and supply chains coordinate the decision problems of responses through adjusting distributing plans.

The decision-making process of constraint satisficing

The rationality analysis of applying satisficing decision methods

The satisficing decision techniques are introduced to solve this problem for two reasons:

(1) The distributing decision in the context of production disruption is a problem of multiple targets, and thus the solution of the problem is the satisficing solution by decision-makers for certain preferences, on the basis of satisfying decision-makers. There is a conflict between profit level and shortage cost, and therefore they cannot be optimized simultaneously. Decision-makers change their targets of profit level, and they might concede in the target of shortage cost to some degree. As a result, the ultimate decision will be a satisfying one, but not the optimal one.
(2) Distinct decision-makers have different preferences. In terms of the same profit levels or shortage cost levels, some decision-makers consider it acceptable, while others consider it unacceptable. In practice, this preference penetrates the decision process, but the traditional optimal method does not support the display of preferences of decision-makers.

In light of the method of the constraint satisficing decision, when the satisficing of decision-makers are described, the constraint set composed of constraint conditions in the model of distributing decision is marked as Θ, and maximization and minimization of profit level *PF* and shortage cost *SA* in the constraint set Θ are marked as PF_{max}, PF_{min}, and SA_{max}, SA_{min}. Next, the satisficing functions $\mu_{\widetilde{PF}}(PF)$, $\mu_{\widetilde{SA}}(SA)$ of each target within the range $[PF_{max}, PF_{min}]$, $[SA_{max}, SA_{min}]$ are specified. For instance, the lower and upper bound of the satisficing function changing parts related to the profit level or shortage cost are marked as PF_L, PF_U, SA_L, and SA_U , respectively, which display decision-makers' preferences and may adopt a ladder-shaped satisficing function:

$$\mu_{\widetilde{PF}}(PF) = \begin{cases} 0 & PF_{min} \leq PF < PF_L \\ \dfrac{PF - PF_L}{PF_U - PF_L} & PF_L \leq PF \leq PF_U \\ 1 & PF_U < PF \leq PF_{max} \end{cases}$$

$$\mu_{\widetilde{SA}}(SA) = \begin{cases} 1 & SA_{min} \leq SA < SA_L \\ \dfrac{SA_U - SA}{SA_U - SA_L} & SA_L \leq SA \leq SA_U \\ 0 & SA_U < SA \leq SA_{max} \end{cases}$$

Satisficing decision rules

In the condition of production disruption, many targets in the model of distributing decisions are connected, and for integrating different preferences of distinct decision-makers, three types of decision rules are proposed.

Rule 1: On the basis of what the decision-makers consider satisfactory profit and shortage cost level, the maximal satisficing of shortage cost is sought, as illustrated in Equation (7-15).

$$\max \mu_{\widetilde{SA}}(SA)$$
$$st. \quad \mu_{\widetilde{PF}}(PF) \geq \bar{\mu}_{PF} \qquad (7\text{-}15)$$
$$\mu_{\widetilde{SA}}(SA) \geq \bar{\mu}_{SA}$$

Rule 2: On the basis of profit and shortage cost considered acceptable by the decision-makers, the maximal satisficing of profit is as illustrated in Equation (7-16).

$$\max \mu_{\widetilde{PF}}(PF)$$
$$st. \quad \mu_{\widetilde{PF}}(PF) \geq \bar{\mu}_{PF} \qquad (7\text{-}16)$$
$$\mu_{\widetilde{SA}}(SA) \geq \bar{\mu}_{SA}$$

Rule 3: On the basis of profit and shortage cost considered acceptable by the decision-makers, a way of optimization is sought. For instance, the comprehensive satisficing level SS achieves the maximization, as illustrated in Equation (7-17).

$$\max SS = \alpha\mu_{\widetilde{PF}}(PF) + (1-\alpha)\mu_{\widetilde{SA}}(SA)$$

$$st. \quad \mu_{\widetilde{PF}}(PF) \geq \bar{\mu}_{PF} \tag{7-17}$$

$$\mu_{\widetilde{SA}}(SA) \geq \bar{\mu}_{SA}$$

Equations (7-15) and (7-17) omit the constraint set Q, $\bar{\mu}_{PF}$ and $\bar{\mu}_{SA}$ which indicate to the satisficing requirement by decision-makers in terms of the two targets: profit level and shortage cost. α represents the weight of the profit level target.

Constraint satisficing algorithm

Taking rule 3 as an illustration, design the constraint satisficing algorithm. Similar studies can be carried out in the corresponding algorithms of rules 1 and 2.

Step 1: Analyze the potential supply sequence, $M!$ types in total
Step 2: $k = 1$, $SS_{max} = 0$, $Mark = 0$
Step 3: Given $k > M!$, turn to step 7, otherwise turn to the next step
Step 4: Take k type of retailer replenishment sequence, and initialize the corresponding parameters
Step 5: In terms of the definite k, if the model of the constraint satisficing plan composed by Equation (7-17) and the constraint set Θ has the solution, and the optimality of the target function is $SS^* > SS_{max}$, then $k^* = k$, $q_j^* = q_{jk}$, $t_j^* = t_{jk}$, $Mark = 1$, and $SS_{max} = SS^*$. Turn to the next step; otherwise directly turn to the next step
Step 6: $k = k + 1$ and turn to step 3
Step 7: Output , k^*, q_j^*, t_j^*, SS_{max}, and $Mark$, and complete

Output $Mark = 0$, which shows that the algorithm has no solution, and this means that decision-makers have higher satisficing requirements for the two targets. It is necessary to relax the requirement, that is, reduce $\bar{\mu}_{PF}$ and $\bar{\mu}_{SA}$. Or, according to the rules discussed earlier, the expression forms of satisficing of decision-makers are adjusted.

Conclusion

Supply chains operate in complex and dynamic environments, and the factors that cause uncertainty are intrinsic as well as extrinsic. Thus, random variables are adopted to describe these uncertain factors. Supply chains deal with these uncertain factors from the overall supply chain perspective to establish the overall profits or cost model by means of relevant tools to solve problems. In the study, the trading parties can be viewed as individual decision-makers who consider their own targets and adopt gaming methods to seek the balanced solutions.

In the complicated economic environment, the satisficing decision is always consistent with the decision model of decision-makers. The findings in satisficing game and optimization lend more weight to the corresponding decisions of supply chain coordination. Some results have been achieved in relation to the identification of preferences of decision-makers, the mechanism of target constraint, and optimal algorithms.

Supply chain coordination has many targets and constraints, and the preference of decision-makers plays a very important role in it. Much of the information is often fuzzy, and decision-makers are required to make decisions that will make them feel satisfied. In the solving process, by satisficing function, the multiple target decision can be transferred into a single target decision, on which optimization is based.

By introducing the rule of preference adjustment by decision-makers, the method of constraint satisficing is improved and applied to the corresponding decision of supply chain coordination in the environment of disruption coordination demand. This method can reflect the preference of decision-makers and help dynamic adjustment until the decision-makers are satisfied with the results of their decisions.

Here, the issue of multiple coordinated supplies with production disruption in relation to one consumption system and continuous consumption system is considered. In the conditions of time constraint, product demand constraint, supplier number constraint involved in supplying, and continuous constraint in the continuous consumption system, optimize the time and cost for emergency purchase and the stable target.

Production might get disrupted over a certain period, which influences the supplying capacity of the manufacturers related to distributors. In order to ensure the reasonable supply sequence and supply after production disruption, the model of supply chain distributing decision is established for satisficing optimization, with the purpose of reducing the negative effects of production disruption on supply chain systems.

8 Conclusions and further research

Conclusions

In terms of supply chain node enterprises as the standards for classification, supply chain disruption risks can be categorized into six types: the supply risk, demand risk, and environment risk from the enterprise exterior, and control risk, process risk, and accidental event risk from the enterprise interior. In terms of the overall supply chain system, the supply chain disruption risk consists of extrinsic risk and intrinsic risk of supply chains and internal risk of enterprises.

The forms of supply chain disruption risk conduction include conduction in the form of bubble evaporation, element scarcity, structure collapse, tsunami and waves, chain reaction, and paths. The supply chain disruption risk conduction is random, abrupt, synchronic, non-linear, path-dependent, risk variable, and non-reversible. The conduction process of supply chain disruption risk covers key conducting elements such as risk origins, risk flow, risk carrier, risk conducting paths, risk threshold value, and risk subsystems.

Supply chain disruption risk conducting carriers can be grouped into two major types: macro-carriers and micro-carriers. Macro-carriers mainly refer to the environment risk, demand risk, and financial risk bearing and conducting supply chain exterior, including event carrier, market carrier, and exchange rate carrier, among others. Micro-carriers mainly refer to those bearing and conducting supply chain interior risk, including capital, cost, quality, technique, and information. If carriers are divided by existing forms, supply chain disruption risk conducting carriers include dominant and covert carriers. Supply chain disruption risk conducting carriers are random, existing, bearing, conducting, and path-dependent.

The key path of supply chain disruption risk conduction changes dynamically with time and can be disintegrated into three stages: preliminary risk conduction, secondary risk conduction, and continuous expansion. The model of supply chain disruption risk conduction path can be established, and the function of conduction among risk elements can be considered. Thus, the description of supply chain disruption risk conduction can approximate the reality, which helps find the most threatening risk elements and node enterprise in the supply chain network.

The fundamental elements of supply chain disruption risk conduction can be measured by risk flow, risk flow density, risk penetrating rate, risk absorption rate, risk feedback rate, and enterprise risk bearing capacity. The energy of supply chain disruption risk conduction can be measured by economic loss, product function loss, and enterprise reputation loss. In theory, the extent of effects of risk elements and the efficiency index of risk flow transfer can be measured, and the vector model of general energy related to supply chain disruption risk conduction can be achieved.

Supply chain disruptive events are abrupt, destructive, urgent, spreading, chained/extensive, complicated, and unpredictable. They show small probability but substantial effects. The loss evaluation of supply chain disruptive events does not have universal expressions, with continuity, after-effects, and information incompleteness.

The superposition method of loss evaluation related to supply chain disruptive events indicates that the loss to enterprises can be disintegrated into several stages. In each stage, three aspects are considered: supply chain structure, coping strategies, and supply chain disruptive events themselves, to seek time nodes when factors change. In every two time nodes (i.e., within the evaluation period), a single factor is analyzed; and the function expressions related to the changing trajectory of the performance level in the next stage can be further predicted which can be superposed on the basis of analysis in the previous evaluating stage. At the same time, the information is rolled and updated, and thus the predication can be revised. The loss evaluation of supply chain disruptive events can be divided into five stages: typology stage—short-term evaluation—rolling-updating—loss analysis—summary. The stage of information updating in the process of loss evaluation related to supply chain disruptive events can help adjust function expressions of performance tendency, and thus more accurate function expressions of operation status trajectory can be provided for enterprises.

In the absence of cooperation, quantity models determined by different parties individually have some negative effects. However, suppliers can build the quantity models of optimal production under the condition that purchasers have already made decisions. In the cooperative games, supply–demand parties can build optimal quantity models and the price discounts can help solve the problems of profit distribution, and thus the overall profits of supply chains can achieve optimality. In terms of the two extreme disruptions, caused by change in market information and diversity of consumer demand, it is likely that the inventory results from overproduction and the opportunity of profits will be lost due to insufficient production. In the context of demand disruption, suppliers and retailers achieve the maximal profits in supply chains through adjusting their own strategies.

In terms of supply chain disruptive events caused by natural disasters, the self-organized criticality and extremum value theory can be deployed to determine their probability.

In the two-stage coordinating models of supply chains composed of one supplier and one distributor, disruptive events can occur and the supplier can be either risk-neutral or risk-averse, which can be discussed in the context of the centralized and scattered supply chains. If the probability of disruptive events increases in the second stage of the centralized supply chains, then more preventive measures are adopted in advance. In terms of the centralized supply chains with risk neutrality, more preventive measures in the first stage are adopted in the centralized supply chains with risk aversion. If suppliers are risk-averse and take the mechanism where distributors provide assistance for suppliers, then supply chains do not achieve coordination. The reason is that the preventive measures by suppliers in the first stage are less than those in the case of the centralized supply chains. In the case of disruption, assistance or penalty measures can be taken to coordinate supply chains.

In supply chains with one supplier and many distributors, coordinating methods for disruption risk can be discussed on the basis of the centralized and scattered supply chain, assistance, and penalty measures, including preventive measures and recovery processes after the disruptive events. After obtaining the total amount of assistance or penalty, the amount of assistance or penalty can be distributed among a number of distributors to coordinate supply chains.

In supply chains with many suppliers and one distributor, on the basis of the coordinating mechanism of assistance and penalty, the conditions that the coordinating measures in relation to the preventive measures and coordinating measures of the recovery process after disruptive events in supply chains can also be achieved.

In three-stage supply chains made up of suppliers–manufacturers–retailers, in the coordinating model of manufacturers and retailers with demand disruption risk, the partial cost can be added to the target function, and the cost of dealing with demand disruption risk can also be added to the target function. In addition, the fixed cost of manufacturers and retailers can be taken into account. The analysis shows that, when fixed cost and the cost of dealing with demand disruption are considered, manufacturers take advantage of All Quantity Discount Pact (AQDP) or Constraint Linear Pricing Pact (CLPP) to coordinate with retailers. However, the settlement of wholesale price in the contract might vary. In terms of the coordinating issue of manufacturers and suppliers with demand disruption risk, a compensation program can be designed, and the manufacturers can provide raw materials needed for optimal production by offering compensation to motivate suppliers.

The penalty contract can be deployed to coordinate manufacturers and suppliers with supply disruption risk. If suppliers and manufacturers are risk-neutral, when the optimal penalty program is analyzed, the model of the minimal expected cost is deployed. In order to achieve coordination between manufacturers and suppliers, the optimal penalty amount is the product of the backorder cost related to manufacturers and the time needed for the suppliers to recover production to the normal. In terms of coordination between manufacturers and retailers with supply disruption risk, the partial cost and the cost of dealing with supply disruption can be added to the target function, under different circumstances of the issue of how suppliers coordiante with retailers through All Quantity Discount (AQDP) and Constraint Linear Pricing Pact (CLPP).

Supply chain coordination has many targets and constraints, where the decision-makers' preference plays a very crucial role. A lot of information is often fuzzy, and the decision-makers require that the decisions make them feel satisfied. In the solving process, the multiple target decisions are transformed into single target decisions through the satisficing function to optimize on this basis. The method of constraint satisficing can be improved by introducing the adjusting rules of decision-makers' preference and applied to the responding decisions of supply chain coordination in the environment of disruption.

In terms of one consumption system and continuous consumption system, the issue of multiple coordinating-supply should be considered in the case of supply chain disruption. In the condition of time constraint, product demand constraint, supplier quantity constraint involved in supply, and the continuous constraint in the continuous consumption system, optimize the time and cost of emergency purchase and stable target.

Production disruption may affect the supply capacity of manufacturers and distributors over a period of time. To ensure the rational supply sequence and quantity after production disruption, the supply chain distribution decision models can be established in the context of production disruption and then optimized, with the purpose of reducing the negative effects of production disruption on the supply chain system.

Further research

In terms of research on the origin, classification, and influence of supply chain disruption risks, future research may focus on whether the analysis and classification of source of current supply chain disruption risk are appropriate. On the basis of systematic typology, both enterprise internal resources (environment) and enterprise external resources (environment) are considered. The conduction speed and influence surface of supply chain disruption risks are concerned with time, the stages of supply chains, and the response of supply chain enterprises, because the effects of supply chain disruption risks are the function of supply chain enterprise resources transfer. In terms of different supply chain disruption risks, the effective description of their properties and characteristics are the foundation of solutions. With respect to the conduction mechanism of supply chain disruption risks, it is important to discuss whether it is possible to borrow the relatively mature research methods and tools in finance risk conduction to investigate and describe the supply chain disruption risk.

In terms of identification of supply chain disruption risk, future research may focus on identification, similarities, and differences in evaluating different types of supply chain disruption risks; the index and parameters when the model is established; identification, width, and depth of the assessed objects; identification and stage setting of the assessed results; and the validity in the empirical tests. It may be interesting to find out whether it is possible to build a model of identification and evaluation of co-adaptation on the basis of fine adjustment. Positive purchasing management is adopted to deal with supply chain disruption risk, which might increase contract risk. Here, the problem is the collaborative form of supply chain enterprise groups. There is high uncertainty in supply chain disruption risk, and the preventive measures in advance are the major solutions. However, the cost of enterprises increases, and it is possible to encounter flaws in the plan. Supply chain enterprises can set up workflows and contracts to deal with later events, and here the problem is how to achieve optimal efficiency and profits in relation to resource allocation.

In terms of inventory or manufacturing management strategies during supply disturbance caused by supply chain disruption, future research should focus on determination of the size of risk at different time nodes by continuous identification and assessment on the basis of identification and evaluation of supply chain disruption risk. Therefore, order, safe inventory opportunity, dynamic enlargement, or reduction of safe inventory can be determined to deal with the risk. Here, the risk is the function of ordering size and safe inventory, which requires description of the correlation between risk and ordering size and safe inventory, and thus the interaction between risk and finance is caused. Different supply chain disruption risks are set as ordinary or accidental, and it is necessary to determine the standards and parameters on the basis of the origins, properties, and characteristics of disruption risks, with the purpose of improving the time relationship between disruption risks and ordering size and safe inventory.

In terms of the coordinated method of managing supply chain disruptions, future research should center on the supplier list being pre-stored in the enterprise databank to deal with supply chain disruption risks, but the selection of suppliers is based on the premise of efficiency and profits. It is necessary to depict the relationships among supply chain disruption risks, capacity, and will of suppliers to help ensure that the priority sequence of dealing with risky suppliers is followed. When the manufacturers deal with supply chain disruption risk through changing output, how to determine the investment sensitivity coefficient and the index of its range of fluctuation is linked with the determination of the intensity of disruption risk and duration. Also, it is important to investigate how to coordinate the supply chain enterprises with different organizational structures in the context of supply chain disruptive risks.

In terms of recovery of supply chain disruptions, the future focus may be that, under the influence of single factor or multiple factors, how will the recovery capacity of supply chain enterprises be assessed? What objects should be considered in greater detail? How are standards and parameters established? In the process of recovering supply chain disruption, what is the control of the advanced coordinated workflow? What are the classification standards and specific objects? Is it possible to establish the crisis response mechanism in different degrees? How do we evaluate whether the enterprises have already recovered and achieved the status before disruption? What are the specific standards and parameters?

References

Abad, P. L. Determining Optimal Selling Price and Lot Size when the Supplier Offers All-Unit Quantity Discounts. *Decision Science*, 1988, 19(3): 622–634.

Abboud, N. E. A Discrete-time Markov Production-Inventory Model with Machine Breakdowns. *Computers and Industrial Engineering*, 2001, 39(1–2): 95–107.

Adhitya, A., Srinivasan, R., and Karimi, I. A. A Model-based Rescheduling Framework for Managing Abnormal Supply Chain Events. *Computers and Chemical Engineering*, 2007, 31(5): 496–518.

Anupindi, R. and Akella, R. Diversification under Supply Uncertainty. *Management Science*, 1993, 39(8): 944–963.

Cavinato, J. L. Supply Chain Logistics Risks: From the Back Room to the Board Room. *International Journal of Physical Distribution & Logistics Management*, 2004, 34(5): 388–396.

Chapman, P., Christopher, M., Juttner, U., Peck, H., and Wilding, R. Identifying and Managing Supply Chain Vulnerability. *Logistics and Transport Focus*, 2002, 4(4): 59–64.

Cheng, G. P. and Liu, Q. To Study on Changing for Transmitting Path of the Supply Chain Risk. *Value Engineering*, 2009, 28(4): 1–3.

Cheng, G. P. and Qiu, Y. G. Research on the Mode of the Supply Chain Risk Conduction. *Journal of Wuhan University of Technology (Social Sciences Edition)*, 2009, 22(2): 36–41.

Chen, J. H. and Xu, L. Q. Application of Elasticity Coefficient in a Study about Supply Chain Risk Conduction. *Journal of Anhui Agricultural Sciences*, 2007, 47(1): 313–314.

Choi, T. Y. and Krause, D. R. The Supply Base and Its Complexity: Implications for Transaction Costs, Risks, Responsiveness, and Innovation. *Journal of Operations Management*, 2006, 24(5): 637–652.

Chopra, S. and Sodhi, M. S. Managing Risk to Avoid Supply Chain Breakdown. *MIT Sloan Management Review*, 2004, 46(1): 53–61.

Christopher, M. *Logistics and Supply Chain Management: Strategies for Reducing Costs and Improving Service*. London: Pitman Publishing, 1992.

Christopher, M., McKinnon, A., Sharp, J., Wilding, R., Peck, H., Chapman, P., Jüttner, U., and Bolumole, V. Supply Chain Vulnerability, Report for Department of Transport, Local Government and the Regions, Cranfield University, Cranfield, 2002.

Cranfield Management School. Supply Chain Vulnerability. Cranfield University, 2002.

Ding, L. Thoughts on Supply Chain Event Prevention. *Northern Economy and Trade*, 2006, 26(5): 42–43.

Dong, J. Research on the Loss Assessment of Emergencies in Supply Chain. Shanghai Jiao Tong University, Master's degree thesis, 2011.

Elkins, D., Handfield, R. B., Blackhurst, J., and Craighead, C. W. 18 Ways to Guard Against Disruption. *Supply Chain Management*, 2005, 9(1): 46–53.

Ellis, S. C., Henry, R. M., and Shockley, J. Buyer Perceptions of Supply Disruption Risk: A Behavioral View and Empirical Assessment. *Journal of Operations Management*, 2010, 28(1): 34–46.

Gan, X., Sethi, S., and Yan, H. Channel Coordination with a Risk-Neutral Supplier and a Downside-Risk-Averse Retailer. *Production and Operations Management*, 2005, 14(1): 80–89.

Goh, M., Lim, J. Y. S., and Meng, F. W. A Stochastic Model for Risk Management in Global Supply Chain Networks. European *Journal of Operational Research*, 2007, 182(1): 164–173.

Haddon, W. On the Escape of Tigers: An Ecological Note. *Technological Review*, 1970, 72(7): 44–47.

Hallikas, J., Karvonen, I., Pulkkinen, U., Virolainen, V. M., and Tuominen, M. Risks Management Processes in Supplier Networks. *International Journal of Production Economics*, 2004, 90(1): 47–58.

Harland, C. M., Brenchley, R., and Walker, H. Risk in Supply Networks. *Journal of Purchasing and Supply Management*, 2003, 9(2): 51–62.

Hendricks, K. B. and Singhal, V. R. An Empirical Analysis of the Effect of Supply Chain Disruptions on Long-Run Stock Price Performance and Equity Risk of the Firm. *Production and Operations Management*, 2005, 14(1): 35–52.

Hendricks, K. B. and Singhal, V. R. The Effect of Supply Chain Glitches on Shareholder Wealth. *Journal of Operations Management*, 2003, 21(5): 501–523.

Jeuland, A. P. and Shugan, S. M. Managing Channel Profits. *Marketing Science*, 1983, 2(3): 239–272.

Jüttner, U. Supply Chain Risk Management: Understanding the Business Requirements from a Practitioner Perspective. *International Journal of Logistics Management*, 2005, 16(1): 120–141.

Khouja, M. The Single-period (news-vendor) Problem: Literature Review and Suggestions for Future Research. *Omega*, 1999, 27(5): 537–553.

Kleindorfer, P. R. and Saad, G. H. Managing Disruption Risks in Supply Chains. *Production and Operations Management*, 2005, 14(1): 53–68.

Knemeyer, A. M., Zinn, W., and Eroglu, C. Proactive Planning for Catastrophic Events in Supply Chains. *Journal of Operations Management*, 2009, 27(2): 141–153.

Kull, T. and Closs, D. The Risk of Second-Tier Supplier Failures in Serial Supply Chains: Implications for Order Policies and Distributor Autonomy. *European Journal of Operational Research*, 2008, 186(3): 1158–1174.

Kumara, A. and Wainer, J. Meta Workflows as a Control and Coordination Mechanism for Exception Handling in Workflow Systems. *Decision Support Systems*, 2005, 40(1): 89–105.

Lee, H. L., Padmanabhan, V., and Whang, S. The Bullwhip Effect in Supply Chain. *Sloan Management Review*, 1997, 38(2): 93–102.

Lee, H. and Rosenblatt, M. J. A Generalized Quantity Discount Pricing Model to Increase Supplier's Profits. *Management Science*, 1986, 32(9): 1177–1185.

Lei, Z. and Xu, J. P. A Discussion of Emergency Management of Supply Chain Events. *Project Management Technology*, 2004, 2(5): 26–29.

Li, C. and Zhang, J. The Construction of Supply Chain in the form of Lotus Rhizome Node. *Commercial Economy Studies*, 2003, 4(18): 18–19.

Liu, C. L., He, J. M., and Shi, J. J. A Study of Collaboration-supply in Supply Chain. *Journal of Management Sciences in China*, 2002, 5(2): 2.

Liu, J., Hao, X. Q., Min, L. M., and Li, A. G. The Application of Data Searching Technology in Emergency Management on the Basis of Fuzzy Algorithm. *Mining Safety & Environmental Protection*, 2007a, 36(2): 85–87.

Liu, R., Kumar, A., and Aalst, W. V. D. A Formal Modeling Approach for Supply Chain Event Management. *Decision Support Systems*, 2007b, 43(3): 761–778.

Li, Y. X. How VRP Management in Supply Chains Cope with Events. *China Economist*, 2006, 21(3): 156–157.

Li, Z. L., Xu, S. H., and Hayya, J. A Periodic-Review Inventory System with Supply Interruptions. *Probability in the Engineering and Informational Sciences*, 2004, 18(1): 33–53.

Maqbool, D. and Srikanth, K. N. Pricing Policies for Quantity Discounts. *Management Science*, 1987, 33(10): 1247–1252.

Meng, C. C. Supply Chain Disruption Risks Management from the Perspective of Manufacturers. China University of Petroleum, Master's degree thesis, 2009.

Meulbroek, L. The Promise and Challenge of Integrated Risk Management. *Risk Management and Insurance Review*, 2002, 5(4): 55–66.

Mohan, C. and Nguyen, H. T. Reference Direction Interactive Method for Solving Multiobjective Fuzzy Programming Problems. *European Journal of Operational Research*, 1998, 107(3): 599–613.

Moinzadeh, K. and Aggarwal, P. Analysis of a Production/Inventory System Subject to Random Disruptions. *Management Science*, 1997, 43(11): 1577–1588.

Nagurney, A., Cruz, J., Dong, J., and Zhang, D. Supply Chain Networks, Electronic Commerce and Supply Side and Demand Side Risk. *European Journal of Operational Research*, 2004, 64(1): 120–142.

Neiger, D., Rotaru, K., and Churilov, L. Supply Chain Risk Identification with Value-focused Process Engineering. *Journal of Operations Management*, 2009, 27(2): 154–168.

Oloruntoba, R. An Analysis of the Cyclone Larry Emergency Relief Chain: Some Key Success Factors. *International Journal of Production Economics*, 2010, 126(1): 85–101.

Parlar, M. Continuous-Review Inventory Problem with Random Supply Interruptions. *European Journal of Operations Research*, 1997, 99(2): 366–385.

Porter, M. E. *The Competitive Advantage: Creating and Sustaining Superior Performance*. New York: Free Press, 1985.

Qi, X., Bard, J. F., and Yu, G. Supply Chain Coordination with Demand Disruptions. *Omega*, 2004, 32(4): 301–312.

Qiu, Y. G. Research on the Supply Chain Risk Transmission and Control. Wuhan University of Technology, Ph.D. thesis, 2010.

Scheller-Wolf, A. and Tayur, S. Risk Sharing in Supply Chains Using Order Bands: Analytical Results and Managerial Insights. *International Journal of Production Economics*, 2009, 121(2): 715–727.

Schoenherra, T., Tummala, V. M. R., and Harrison, T. P. Assessing Supply Chain Risks with the Analytic Hierarchy Process: Providing Decision Support for the Offshoring Decision by a US Manufacturing Company. *Journal of Purchasing and Supply Management*, 2008, 14(2): 100–111.

Sheffi, Y. Supply Chain Disruption Management. Presentation at the CMI Supply Chains Under Stress Conference, Adastral Park, Ipswith, United Kingdom, 2003.

Sheffi, Y. Supply Chain Management under the Threat of International Terrorism. *The International Journal of Logistics Management*, 2001, 12(2): 1–11.

Sheffi, Y. and Rice, J. B. A Supply Chain View of the Resilient Enterprise. *MIT Sloan Management Review*, 2005, 47(1): 41–48.

Shen, Z. H. Supply Chain Model with Demand Disruptions. Hunan University, Master's degree thesis, 2007.

Sheng, F. Z. Research on Countermeasures of Supply Disruption. Shanghai Jiao Tong University, Ph.D. thesis, 2008.

Smeltzer, L. R. and Siferd, S. P. Proactive Supply Management: The Management of Risk. *International Journal of Purchasing and Materials Management*, 1998, 34(1): 38–45.

Svensson, G. A Conceptual Framework for the Analysis of Vulnerabilities in Supply Chains. *International Journal of Physical Distribution and Logistics Management*, 2000, 30(9): 731–749.

Tang, C. S. Perspectives in Supply Chain Risk Management. *International Journal of Production Economics*, 2006, 103(2): 451–488.

Tapiero, C. S. Consumers Risk and Quality Control in a Collaborative Supply Chain. *European Journal of Operational Research*, 2007, 182(2): 683–694.

Taskin, S. and Lodree, E. J., Jr. Inventory Decisions for Emergency Supplies Based on Hurricane Count Predictions. *International Journal of Production Economics*, 2010, 126(1): 66–75.

Trkman, P. and McCormack, K. Supply Chain Risk in Turbulent Environments: A Conceptual Model for Managing Supply Chain Network Risk. *International Journal of Production Economics*, 2009, 119(2): 247–258.

Tuncel, G. and Alpan, G. Risk Assessment and Management for Supply Chain Networks: A Case Study. *Computers in Industry*, 2010, 61(3): 250–259.

Wang, H. and Hu, J. S. Coordination Mechanism Analysis of Three-Level Supply Chain under Disruption. *Journal of Qingdao University (Natural Science Edition)*, 2006, 19(9): 71–76.

Wang, Y. and Chen, J. F. Supply Chain Event Management: From Technology to Methodology. *Forecasting*, 2004, 23(1): 62–65.

Wu, D. S., and Olson, D. L. Supply Chain Risk, Simulation, and Vendor Selection. *International Journal of Production Economics*, 2008, 114(2): 646–655.

Wu, T., Blackhurst, J., and Chidambaram, V. A Model for Inbound Supply Risk Analysis. *Computers in Industry*, 2006, 57(4): 350–365.

Xiao, T. J. and Yu, G. Supply Chain Disruption Management and Evolutionarily Stable Strategies of Retailers in the Quantity-setting Duopoly Situation with Homogeneous Goods. *European Journal of Operational Research*, 2006, 173(2): 648–668.

Xiao, T. J., Yu, G., Sheng, Z. H., and Xia, Y. S. Coordination of a Supply Chain with One Manufacturer and Two Retailers under Demand Promotion and Disruption Management Decisions. *Annals of Operations Research*, 2005, 135(1): 87–109.

Xia, Y., Yang, M., Golany, B., Gilbert, S., and Yu, G. Real Time Disruption Management in a Two-Stage Production and Inventory System. *IIE Transactions*, 2004, 36: 111–125.

Xu, M. H., Qi, X. T., Yu, G., Zhang, H. Q., and Gao, C. X. The Demand Disruption Management Problem for a Supply Chain System with Nonlinear Demand Functions. *Journal of Systems Science and Systems Engineering*, 2003, 12(1): 82–97.

Yates, J. F. and Stone, E. R. The Risk Construct, Risk-Taking Behavior. In *Risk Taking Behavior*. New York: John Wiley & Sons, 1992.

Yoo, T., Cho, H., and Yucesan, E. Hybrid Algorithm for Discrete Event Simulation Based Supply Chain Optimization. *Expert Systems with Applications*, 2010, 37(3): 2354–2361.

Yu, H. and Chen, J. Response to the Disruption of Supply Chain with Price-depended Demand. *Systems Engineering—Theory & Practice*, 2007, 27(3): 36–41.

Yu, H., Chen, J., and Yu, G. How to Coordinate Supply Chain under Disruption. *Systems Engineering—Theory & Practice*, 2005, 25(7): 9–16.

Yu, H., Chen, J., and Yu, G. Managing Wholesale Price Contract in the Supply Chain under Disruption. *Systems Engineering—Theory & Practice*, 2006, 26(8): 33–41.

Yu, H., Chen, J., and Yu, G. Supply Chain Coordination under Disruptions with Buy Back Contract. *Systems Engineering—Theory & Practice*, 2005, 25(8): 38–43.

Zeng, F. H. and Wang, H. L. Demand Disruption Management for Supply Chain System with Quantity Discount Contract. *Journal of Liaoning Technical University*, 2007, 20(6): 454–456.

Zhai, Y. K. Study on the Risk Conduction Knowledge-supported and Control in Co-enterprise Cooperative Innovation. *Scientific Management Research*, 2008, 28(1): 78–85.

Zhang, K. F., Han, Y. S., and Pan, X. W. Research on Supply Chain Exception Event Management System. *Computer Integrated Manufacturing Systems*, 2004, 10(11): 1402–1407.

Zhao, Z. G. Supply Chain Response Decision Method Based on Coordination System. Harbin Institute of Technology, Ph.D. dissertation, 2007.

Zhou, Y. J., Qiu, W. H., and Wang, Z. R. A Review on Supply Chain Risk Management. *Systems Engineering*, 2006, 24(3): 1–7.

Zhu, X. Q. On the Carriers of Conduction of SCR. *Journal of Yangtze University*, 2009, 32(1): 66–68.

Zhu, Z. H. and Li, Y. F. A Study of Typology, Classification, and Staging of Supply Chain Events. Jiang Lu, Reports on Academic Frontier in Logistics in China. Beijing: China's Materials Press, 2006, pp. 74–80.

Zsidisin, G. A. A Grounded Definition of Supply Risk. *Journal of Purchasing and Supply Management*, 2003, 9(5/6): 217–224.

Author index

Subject index